GW00670490

Ireland's Greatest Racehorses

Ireland's Greatest Racehorses

Brian O'Connor

To my darling Jessica

First published 2011 by
Aurum Press Limited
7 Greenland Street
London NW1 0ND
www.aurumpress.co.uk

A catalogue record for this book is available from the British Library.

ISBN 978 1 84513 669 7

10 9 8 7 6 5 4 3 2 1
2015 2014 2013 2012 2011

Typeset by SX Composing DTP, Rayleigh, Essex

Printed by MPG Books, Bodmin, Cornwall

Contents

Acknowledgements

Thanks to Niamh and Peter, Johnny and Jessica. Thanks also to the many various O'Connors who knowingly or unknowingly contributed. And to everyone at Aurum, especially Graham Coster and Barbara Phelan, Melissa Smith and Jake Hemingway.

Introduction

This book is as much about the people that shaped the lives of Ireland's greatest racehorses as it is about the animals. It can't be any other way, though there have been times in the winner's enclosure when pitching that timeless 'how do you feel?' query at a stamping, sweating thoroughbred would have yielded more revelatory results than the grudgingly incoherent replies of those closest to them. But that reality doesn't deflect from racing's fundamental reality, which is that ultimately everything in it revolves around these maddeningly mysterious, enthrallingly romantic and eternally fascinating creatures. The lines may belong to the men and women but the fundamental narrative is about the horses.

Of course, the vast majority of humanity somehow manages to rub along quite happily while possessing only the vaguest aware - ness of racing's existence. But there are also many millions whose obsession with the beast is as real to them as it is unfathomable to others. It doesn't matter if it is a hairy-arsed pony in a boggy field or a hugely valuable stallion in a paddock: people will invariably be drawn towards them, stopping the car if need be and simply peering over a gate at the figure that usually can be contrarily relied upon to gallop off in the opposite direction.

It's the same obsession that makes an engine, any engine, appear irresistible to those of a mechanical mindset. Or the way an angler can't spot water without watching out for a swirl and some bubbles. In sporting terms, there are New Zealanders who are drawn to a rugby ball like All-Black magnets, favela kids in Rio who can't see an empty can without flicking it into a Maracana fantasy and quietly elegant Sikh gentlemen for whom the thud of bat on ball is evocative of Sach Khand.

Ireland famously possesses a higher percentage than most nations of those of us who can look at a galloping racehorse and see beauty and grace, albeit with a bandy-legged little man perched on top. Indeed, along with black beer, sectarian violence and painfully mannered rock'n'roll stars, horses are probably what this wet rock on the edge of Europe is most famous for. There's something about half a tonne of equine grace in motion that grabs the public consciousness more than most anywhere else.

Maybe as a result, the danger of that affection veering towards anthropomorphism is less prevalent than it might be. Dewy-eyed sentimentality about animals is largely frowned upon in favour of a hard-nosed scepticism that nevertheless can't quite disguise the deep-seated respect for a good horse. The dozen listed here are among the best of the best.

Whether they are the absolute, certain twelve best, no questions asked, guvnor, is another matter. In a sport that surfs on a vast, pulsing wave of opinions and prejudices, the chances of such certitude are about the same as sitting down on Christmas Day and picking the following summer's Derby winner. And since waiting for that to happen could mean waiting a lifetime, there's no getting away from the arbitrariness involved in coming to a final selection.

It would be nice to outline certain criteria that boiled the list down but that would be to coat my own prejudices in dodgy jargon and a pseudo-scientific approach. Never forget that another of racing's glories is that no system ever devised has even come close to being right. Anything dependant on the fluctuating gastro-intestinal fortitude of a dumb animal is by definition immune to systematic analysis.

All of which ass-covering is not going to prevent some displeasure at the following list of horses. Certainly those anoraks whose job it is to boil down flesh-and-blood competition to cold figures are likely to scoff at a collection that doesn't include the likes of Sir Ivor, Cottage Rake or Captain Christy. But a handicap, no matter how eminent or logical the source, is just one person's opinion. Timeform, the venerable ratings organisation born out of Phil Bull's determined independence, is hugely respected world-wide and it is their rating of Arkle that has contributed to the great steeplechaser's almost mythical reputation. On the flat, however, the highest mark ever awarded by them to an Irish-trained runner is the 145 given to the now all-but-forgotten two-year old-champion Windy City.

The word 'great' can also be justifiably played around with. Vintage Crop, for instance, could hardly figure in terms of pure ability and yet the story of his Melbourne Cup success has an epic sweep that few others can match.

If the great horses that were bred in Ireland were to be included in a list such as this, then *War and Peace* would look like a workshy novella by comparison, so instead the focus is on those trained here. Racing has become a truly international sport, thriving in the age of digital information and inexpensive travel, to an extent unimaginable even a couple of decades ago. It means that Ireland's elite carry a resonance throughout the world, certainly at a scale unparalleled at the top level of any other major sport.

Some of the names here will be as familiar to race fans in Dunedin and Durban as they will in Dublin: others not so much. What they all possess, though, are stories layered with grandeur, tragedy, regret, but most of all beauty. Because what it all boils down to is that there are surely few things more elementally beautiful in this post-industrial, oh-so-digitally enhanced world of ours than the sight of a thoroughbred running for the sheer unadulterated joy of it.

Arkle

Certitude has become scarce in Ireland. Any naive faith there might have been in the country's political leadership has been destroyed by countless examples of self-serving ineptitude. They in turn have woven seamlessly into the busted flush of a preening business elite. Overshadowing it all is the moral vacuousness of a religious establishment desperately clinging to the last remnants of its relevance.

So in terms of certainties, there aren't plentiful options in the great big picture of what actually matters. However, among the trivialities some articles of faith do remain. And in the great triviality that is horse racing there is the calm nirvana that comes with knowing absolutely that Arkle is the greatest steeplechaser ever to have peered through a bridle. In a sport that for a lot of people remains more of a religion than anything any cleric might have to offer, that is a belief no scepticism can dilute.

The result is that this thin, floppy-eared animal who died in 1970 is now much more than he was even when romping to a Cheltenham Gold Cup hat-trick. Arkle today is an Irish folk-hero, a symbol, a totemic figure of excellence. The myth is now so overwhelming, it's impossible to reduce it back to the creature that munched hay and crapped in the corner. Six years after his death his skeleton was dug up and is now an exhibit at the Irish National Stud's Horse Museum in Co. Kildare, as distant a relic as any fossil to most of those walking past. For those who do remember him, time and nostalgia have cast a hue of invulnerability, the bare facts of which actually manage to stack up pretty well against the legend.

Arkle won twenty-two of his twenty-six starts over fences. The defeats are almost as creditable as the victories. One came when he slipped. Two were a result of conceding stones in weight and the other was due to damn near breaking his leg. Even with that he still almost won.

For a country short of many things in the 1960s, but perhaps principally self-confidence, the charismatic steeplechaser that carried the colours of a duchess became a source of huge national pride that such excellence could come from this comparatively insignificant, rain-soaked country. Maybe it was a pride of its time, impossible to replicate in the modern digital age, but real just the same. And if anything time has embellished it. Instant replays from any number of camera angles may be a technological marvel but they don't leave much room for imagination. And, as any Gypsy Rose Lee enthusiast will tell you, it's what you don't see that's sexiest.

All that remains of Arkle's races are a few grainy, black-and-white clips containing jockeys with woollen pullovers and racetracks that resemble point-to-points more than modern amphitheatres. For those weaned on iPhones and the minutiae of apps, it must look positively prehistoric, from a time when the exactitude of form lines and handicapping were certainly not as precise as they are now. And it's that imprecision that has encouraged recent attempts at revisionism.

Arkle's 1964 Cheltenham Gold Cup defeat of Mill House remains racing's quintessential 'mano-a-mano', head-to-head clash with a *frisson* of nationalist fervour added to an already boiling pot of expectation. However, it was his record in handicaps that catapulted Arkle to another level again for purists. Carrying twelve and a half stone and more – and conceding two stone plus to his rivals – became almost de rigueur. His superiority was so pronounced, the novel step of arranging handicaps with Arkle and without him was introduced. The result was that normal handicapping rules had to be thrown out.

At a time when official centralised figures had yet to be introduced in a manner recognisable to today's handicappers, it was Timeform, the Halifax-based firm started by the cantankerous visionary Phil Bull, that calculated Arkle's worth at 212. Flyingbolt, his contemporary at Tom Dreaper's yard, was rated just 2lb lower. Nothing else has ever even come close. Over the years the figure has become a benchmark, apparently statistical proof of Arkle – and by definition Flyingbolt's – freakishness. However, the increasing tendency among those who sweat up about such things is to sprinkle those figures with more than a little scepticism.

Handicapping by definition is opinionated, shaped by the prejudices and preferences of whoever is doing the totting up. It is also not unknown for certain periods in racing history to include ratings that overall are noticeably more generous than in others. The fact that the two highest steeplechase marks of the last six decades happen to coincide jars with some observers. There is even the rumour that Bull was so dismissive of jump racing that he used the winter sport as a chance to break in any new recruits to the organisation before promoting them to the real stuff on the flat. So that mythical Timeform figure has come under pressure.

Reassessing it though is not easy. The British Horseracing Authority's senior jumps handicapper Phil Smith tried to come up with a rating for Arkle based on modern techniques and had to give up.

'There was no central handicapping,' Smith said. 'There were lots of different people involved and they would say that Horse A should get so many pounds from Horse B one week, and then change their minds completely the next week, even when there hadn't been any racing in between.'

It's a different story now. A modern superstar like Kauto Star, a dual Gold Cup and four-time King George winner, has at his peak achieved an official rating of 190. That means in a theoretical handicap clash between Kauto Star and Arkle, the latter would have to concede over a stone and a half. To those who weren't around to see Arkle, it is all but impossible to imagine any steeplechaser could pull that off. It is possibly the greatest tribute to the horse known as 'Himself' that those who did witness him in his pomp still vehemently believe that he could.

Phil Smith's suspicion is that there must be a biological limit to the rating that any horse is capable of. No doubt that will provoke an argument as to what that limit might be, but only the perverse will argue with the assertion that, whatever the cut-off point is, Arkle is the figure teetering on the edge of it.

Bare figures alone though can never explain the pull that the Arkle legend still manages to exert. To the devout he couldn't and still can't do any wrong. The stories contain an almost evangelical zeal about the qualities this particular quadruped exhibited. His owner, Anne, Duchess of Westminster, widow of the second Duke Of Westminster, but born plain old Anne Sullivan in Co. Cork, was a formidable woman who normally didn't indulge in the sentimental when it came to her horses. Once, when quizzed about some people's habits of attributing human characteristics to animals, she sniffed with patrician disdain: 'Sounds a bit daft to me.' But Arkle, again, was different.

'When he was out in the field, and you shouted to him, he came galloping for his sugar. When I drove into the yard at Tom Dreaper's, he knew my voice. He'd go bang, bang, bang on the stable door. But I think he knew my car as well. He'd go thump, thump, thump – knowing there was a sugar lump,' the Duchess later remembered.

Such stories are plentiful, like when eight-year-old Valerie

Dreaper, the trainer's daughter, was bouncing a tennis ball outside Arkle's box and it flew over the stable's half-door. The little girl's searches in the straw around the big horse's feet failed to find it and she was leaving when she received a nudge in the back. There wedged between some sharp equine teeth was the ball presented back to her. Paddy Woods, Arkle's regular work rider, can remember one racegoer peering over a parade ring fence, studying form, when Himself, walking past, deftly grabbed the race card and made off with it.

If some of the stories lapse towards sentiment, it only reflects the depth of feeling that Arkle generated. Attempts to explain just why he was so good on the racetrack have ventured that it was because he genuinely liked people's company and tried extra hard to please them. It's a fanciful idea which doesn't reflect the reality that sporting greatness rarely comes so neatly packaged.

Flyingbolt, for one, was notoriously bad-tempered, just aching for the chance to kick the eye out of an unsuspecting victim. Nijinsky carried himself with a lofty disdain that suggested the efforts of those ordinary mortals scurrying around after him were only his due. Foinavon, the famous 100–1 winner of the 1967 Grand National, whose inability to run fast enough to keep up with the leaders ironically paid off so dramatically when everything else came to a halt at the fence now named after him, also used to carry the same famous yellow and black colours as Arkle. But he was sold off before his date with destiny due to a lack of urgency. Famously, after one heavy fall at Baldoyle, he lay prostrate on the ground. Jockey Pat Taaffe rushed to his side, fearing the worst, only to discover Foinavon picking grass, not even bothering to get up. 'If he'd been a man,' Taaffe said, 'he'd have spent his days, hands in pockets, whistling through his teeth, scuffling the dust.'

Arkle's nature was a lot more agreeable, so much so that he thrived on the attention people gave to him. Entering a parade ring, his habit was to stop, extend his neck and have a good look around, relishing the atmosphere. It gave the thousands who flocked to see him in the flesh an opportunity to witness rare sporting excellence. The impact was such that songs and poems were written about the charismatic Irish steeplechaser. At the peak of his fame, sackfuls of fan mail used to arrive at Tom Dreaper's yard in Kisallaghan in North Co. Dublin. Some were addressed simply, 'Arkle, Ireland'. None were returned to sender. Not surprisingly, Arkle's image even appeared on stamps in Ireland. Rather more surprising is that the West African republic of Togo paid him the same compliment on their two-franc stamp in 1985.

A 1966 editorial in the *Irish Times* tried to explain the Arkle phenomenon in unexpectedly florid style:

> The answer is the glamour of success and personality. He has again and again confirmed his supremacy over all rivals in Britain. Every time he appears on an English racecourse he raises the morale at home. He is so emphatically the best. And more than this: he looks the best. He even looks as if he knew he was best. Not with the swagger and air of self-glory which characterises, say, Mr Cassius Clay: but with the dignity, the look of supreme self-assurance, that marks President de Gaulle.

One can only imagine the Gaullist hauteur with which Le Grande Zohra would have greeted comparison with a horse but journalistic enthusiasm for Arkle never waned. In the weeks after the serious injury that ended his career, updates on Arkle's condition featured on both the front and back pages in Ireland and Britain. Some took the job of reporting the patient's health very seriously. One photographer approached the stable lad guarding the horse's privacy at Kempton's racecourse stables and whispered: 'Two hundred and fifty quid for a photo.' The retort was appropriately direct and included: 'Not for two million and fifty!'

What can be safely said is that if Arkle eventually grew into looking like the best, then it was a case of maturity, and maybe the eye seeing what it wanted to see. The young son of a bargain-basement stallion in Archive and the mare Bright Cherry was certainly no oil painting when he entered the world at Ballymacoll Stud on 19 April 1957. By the age of three, when he was sent to the Ballsbridge Sales in Dublin, he was a lanky, unfurnished horse that his breeder, Mary Baker, was delighted to get 1,250 guineas for. Tom Dreaper, one of the top jumps trainers in Ireland, had bid on behalf of the Duchess of Westminster.

The gangling recruit arrived in Dreaper's Greenogue yard a year later having been taken in the interim to the Duchess's property in Cheshire. He returned with a name. The Westminster properties included several thousand acres of Sutherland near Cape Wrath at the northwestern tip of Scotland. Arkle is a 787-metre mountain in a range that also includes Foinaven and Ben Stack (the equine version of which was a two-mile champion chaser contemporary of Arkle). It would become a name to conjure any number of emotions but when Arkle first stepped into Greenogue he didn't leave much of an impression.

'Unfurnished – and he moved bad,' was one verdict. 'Gangly,' was another. Pat Taaffe, who rode Arkle in all his races over fences, memorably opined: 'You could have driven a wheelbarrow through his hind legs!' In a stable that contained the dual two-mile champion Fortria as well as a number of other future Irish Grand National winners, the new youngster was very much an also-ran. And it remained that way for quite some time despite what hindsight might lead some to claim. Two starts in bumpers, the first at the then lowly and now defunct Mullingar, yielded a third and a fourth placing which allowed his amateur jockey, the future Bank Of Ireland chief executive Mark Hely-Hutchinson, to dine out for years on how he was the only jockey who couldn't manage to win on Arkle. Four starts over hurdles later that season yielded a pair of victories and the 1962–63 season opened with another pair of wins in handicap hurdles. It was then that Arkle encountered the crucial factor in his transformation into a steeplechase superstar.

Fences weren't new to him before that first public chase appearance at Cheltenham in November 1962. Youngsters at the Dreaper yard were lunged over open ditches before graduating to little bush fences and then promoted to proper fences. Crucially Dreaper believed in his horses being regularly popped over the obstacles because it kept their muscles trim and their eye in. Before the Honeybourne Chase, Arkle's eye was famously well in. Even in a yard that had moulded the career of a top chaser like the former Gold Cup hero Prince Regent, the youngster's fluency over fences was noticeable. In fact reports on the new recruit were so positive he started an 11–8 favourite in a field of twelve. Still a couple of months off his sixth birthday, Arkle barely came off the bridle to win by twenty lengths. Just over an hour later Fortria again won the Mackeson Gold Cup, but the prescient were enthusing about Dreaper's other winner that day.

A couple of months later and a pre-Cheltenham Festival warm-up at Leopardstown saw Arkle carry 12st 11lb, the largest weight he ever was to carry, in a conditions chase. Nevertheless he started a 1–2 favourite and won easily. That set him up for the Broadway Chase (now the RSA Chase) back at Cheltenham and his 4–9 odds were justified in style. Two days later another six-year-old managed to make an even greater splash. The giant Mill House, trained in Lambourn by Fulke Walwyn, destroyed Fortria by a dozen lengths in a manner that suggested he might be the best chaser seen in England since Golden Miller. If there was a new dawn of steeplechasing at Cheltenham 1963, most believed it centred on the enormous Mill House rather than the greyhound-like Arkle. The latter had two more runs as a novice, easily winning at both Fairyhouse and Punchestown. But already anticipation was growing about a possible Gold Cup clash between the brightest young stars in Britain and Ireland.

Arkle and Mill House are now as synonymous in sporting history as Ali and Frasier, Borg and McEnroe, Coe and Ovett. However, it was much more than an individual rivalry. During a comparatively uneventful period in Anglo–Irish history, age-old antipathies could be played out in the comparative irrelevance of a race meeting. And so much more than just personal ambition and financial benefit was poured into what the two horses seemed to embody. Mill House came to characterise the big, bruising English yeoman, the sort to be found grinding the opposition down in the second row of a scrum. Arkle on the other hand was a more mercurial will-o'-the-wisp fly-half, light on his feet in evading the big bully. Typical of the intricate nature of the history of these islands, though, the reality was much more complicated than the portrayal.

For one thing Mill House was just as Irish as Arkle. Bred in Kildare, he was actually much more familiar to Pat Taaffe than Arkle was. Broken in by the jockey's father Tom, early schooling on the strapping bay was carried out by the man who would later engineer his downfall. Then came some hunting and Taaffe remembered, 'He loved every minute of it. Nothing daunted him. If I put him at a gate, a wall or whatever, he would prick his ears and go. No questions asked. And, running free across the land, you can believe me he was something to fill the mind of a man.'

Mill House's fledgling racing career contained a number of races for Tom and Pat Taaffe in Ireland, including a win at Naas, before he was sold to the English businessman Bill Gollings. The horse ended up with Fulke Walwyn, possibly the leading English jumps trainers in the middle of the twentieth century, but his jockey would be Willie Robinson, a hugely talented and versatile rider who is one of the select band to have won National Hunt racing's triple crown – the Gold Cup, Champion Hurdle and Grand National. None of the others, though, managed to also finish second in an Epsom Derby.

When Mill House arrived at Walwyn's, Robinson received a letter from Pat Taaffe informing him that he would be riding 'the best horse in Britain – and possibly the world'. Famously it wasn't long before he got another letter from his friend – 'You are now up on the second-best horse in the world!'

So it was that the horse born and raised in Ireland, and ridden by an Irishman, became a veritable John Bull, the best seen in Britain for a generation. Already a Gold Cup hero, Mill House's full potential still looked to be ahead of him, maybe enough to threaten Golden Miller's Gold Cup record of five in a row. With the world at his feet, the big horse's only problem was that an even more accomplished horse's feet had entered the world at the same time.

It's a misfortune that happens occasionally, truly outstanding horses being trumped by those even more exceptional who've just happened to be foaled at the same time. Alydar, runner-up to Affirmed in all three of the 1978 Triple Crown races in America, would be remembered as a true champion were it not for such synchronicity. More recently, how more highly rated would Fame And Glory be except for having run into Sea The Stars during his three-year-old career? What Mill House ultimately did achieve was to show just how good Arkle could be. But what can never be forgotten is that Round One in this super-heavyweight struggle very definitely went the way of Mill House.

The greater options for today's steeplechase elite means it is rare for the top ones to venture into handicap company any more. In 1963 it was a different story, and Newbury's Hennessy Gold Cup was the major pre-Christmas target. Arkle went into it with two easy warm-up victories. Mill House was having his first start of the season and had to concede 5lb to his rival. Despite everything, he won. Arkle managed only third, nearly nine lengths behind.

To the Mill House fan club, the verdict was a decisive verdict. Their hero had won, and conceded weight into the bargain. What many didn't realise was that Arkle had been right in the winner's slipstream at the third last fence when slipping on the landing side and losing all momentum. Thick mist at the track meant many didn't see the incident and the BBC's cameras failed to pick it up. Taaffe's report to Dreaper the following day was full of conviction: 'Coming to the third last I gave him a kick and I had no idea he was going to accelerate like he did. If I'd sat quietly he'd have beaten Mill House as he wouldn't have slipped when he landed.'

Christmas saw both horses winning: Mill House a three-runner King George VI Chase at Kempton and Arkle a handicap at Leopardstown. Two weeks later Arkle conceded 31lb to Loving Record in the Thyestes Chase at Gowran and won by a dozen lengths. In February Arkle scooped the Leopardstown Chase in a canter after Flying Wild's fall at the second last. Despite conceding masses of weight he started a 4–7 favourite. That ability to defy monster weights was already proven. However, beating Mill House in the 1964 Gold Cup was another matter entirely.

In the days leading up to the most eagerly awaited race for decades, there was a reminder that no favourite is ever past the post until actually standing in the winner's enclosure. Three thousand miles away in Miami Cassius Clay managed to relieve Sonny Liston of his heavyweight title in what remains one of boxing's greatest ever upsets. Arkle wasn't as big an outsider as Clay for the Gold Cup but for most British racing experts, Mill House was Liston-like in his status as title-holder. It might now be regarded as treachery to assert that more than a few in Ireland believed the same, but history is often rewritten by the winners.

What will never be disputed is the anticipation that wrapped around a Gold Cup that for the first time in its history was run on a Saturday. For almost twelve months, a clash of steeplechasing's two young superstars had been awaited with the sort of enthusiasm that all too often means the event itself is an anticlimax. This was one of those rare occasions when it wasn't. No funny step, or malevolent stone bruise, or strained muscle came between the perfect match-up. Two other horses lined up. King's Nephew, the last horse to beat Mill House, was joined by the veteran 1960 Gold Cup hero Pas Seul. Both were top horses in their own right but dismissed as also-rans on 7 March 1964. Nothing got in the way of racing's most famous head-to-head.

Mill House started the 8–13 favourite, while Arkle was a 7–4 shot. That reflected the majority of pre-race coverage, which suggested that the English champion would simply be too powerful for his Irish rival. It is hard now to process how shocking it was that Arkle was not only able to beat Mill House, but to do it so impressively.

On a bitterly cold but bright day, Mill House led from the start and at halfway had built up a lead that had Irish feet shuffling uneasily in the stands. Pat Taaffe admitted later it was the most nerve-wracking race of his long career but it was impossible to tell as he almost casually manoeuvred Arkle to within a couple of lengths of his rival approaching the third-last fence. If the impression of confidence had been illusory then the couple of lengths that Mill House made at that obstacle could have been crucial. The momentum gained by the favourite on the downhill run to the straight would normally prove hard to make up. Arkle managed to make it look easy, so much so that at the second-last the pair of them were locked together.

One of the most remarkable transformations that fences provoked in Arkle was raw speed. A horse that looked downright slow when running in three-mile hurdle races possessed over the bigger obstacles a turn of foot that almost convinced Taaffe of his superiority to anything else he ever rode. That acceleration, allied to boundless stamina, convinced many that the great chaser would make an impression on the flat too if ever he campaigned seriously on it. In fact Arkle won the sole flat race of his career when he began his 1963–64 campaign in a two-mile maiden at Navan under the classic winning rider T.P. Burns. The 1960s saw many top Australian riders ply their trade in Europe and one of them, Des Lake, then riding for Paddy Prendergast, declared that Arkle would win a Melbourne Cup – carrying ten stone!

Time would eventually prove that an Irish jumper could win Australia's greatest race, but in 1964 it was that raw speed which sealed the most famous steeplechase ever run. Taaffe sent Arkle to the lead before the last. One final lunging leap briefly flickered some hope back into the Mill House challenge but it quickly died out. Arkle spurted clear up the hill to win by five lengths. On the BBC, commentator Peter O'Sullevan uttered the famous line: 'This is the best we've seen for a very long time.' He was right, but that didn't stop both Robinson and Walwyn from being 'shattered' by the defeat. Both men subsequently got over it. The argument about whether Mill House ever did still rages. Many feel it was subsequent defeats by his rival that broke the big horse's spirit. Some, though, trace it back to the 1964 Gold Cup. Whatever the truth of it is, the aura of invincibility that surrounded Mill House was gone, transferred to a horse that carried it with such aplomb over the next thirty-three months that his status as the best has never been seriously challenged.

That Arkle was different in his range of abilities was proven just twenty-three days after the Gold Cup when he carried twelve stone to victory in the Irish Grand National. It was the first occasion on which the Turf Club used a different handicap for when Arkle raced. On soft ground Height O'Fashion got to within a length and a quarter of the champion in what kicked off a series of phenomenal weight-carrying performances.

The following season's Hennessy at Newbury was billed as the 'rubber' match between Arkle and Mill House, but in reality it became another coronation. This time the Irish champion conceded 3lb and when Taaffe elected to match Mill House stride for stride rather than using those 'pounce' tactics employed at Cheltenham, the home team's hopes grew. By now, though, Arkle could win any way. He pulled clear from the cross fence at Newbury to win as he pleased. There are those who still maintain it was his finest performance, though some argue that actually came just a week later at Cheltenham, where Arkle actually finished only third.

Over two miles and five furlongs in the Massey Ferguson Gold Cup, the champion carried 12st 10lb, giving an enormous 32lb to the top mare Flying Wild and 26lb to the champion novice Buona

Notte, but failing by just a short head and a length to pull off an all but impossible task. Arkle didn't start again until February's Leopardstown Chase when he successfully managed to give 35lb to Scottish Memories. In the circumstances, meeting just three opponents, including Mill House, in the 1965 Gold Cup seemed like a piece of cake – and so it proved. An easy 20-length defeat of his old rival preceded a return to handicap company in the Whitbread Gold Cup at Sandown when he again made carrying twelve and a half stone look nothing.

The following 1965–66 campaign consisted of a perfect five for five, with three handicap successes in the Gallaher Gold Cup, the Hennessy and the Leopardstown Chase, all under 12st 7lb, and victories in both the King George and the Cheltenham Gold Cup. The impossibility of tackling Arkle off level weights was obvious to everyone. But the dangers of even trying to became painfully clear in the King George.

What threatened to become another small-field formality was enlivened when the owners of the brilliant two-mile champion Dunkirk decided to chance their arm on the famously level three miles at Kempton. After just three fences, Dunkirk was a couple of hundred yards clear. It was some start to give any horse, never mind one as talented as this, but Taaffe patiently bided his time and when Arkle took the lead at the fifth-last the writing was on the wall. Dunkirk's final attempt to wrest the lead back resulted in a fall that broke his neck and killed him instantly.

Mercifully the only dramatics in the Gold Cup centred on Arkle's own attempts to part the eleventh fence. It was such a shock that the famously articulate Peter O'Sullevan was reduced to 'Ohh!' when it happened. Taaffe later reasoned that the 1–10 favourite was so bored against four vastly inferior rivals that he was looking at the crowd rather than the obstacle. Despite the blemish, Arkle completed his Gold Cup hat-trick without breaking sweat. And on St Patrick's Day, he carried a sprig of shamrock in his bridle.

Such touches only made him more popular with the general

public in Ireland. At the height of his career, there seemed to be no limit to the fascination with the horse, even down to his dietary requirements. The fact that Arkle got outside a couple of bottles of Guinness a day tickled public curiosity to such an extent that the managing director of the famous brewing company wrote to Tom Dreaper to thank him for the publicity. And that gratitude extended to committing Guinness to supplying 120 free bottles of their brew to the yard every week.

The animal at the centre of it all genuinely seemed to revel in the attention. It's hard to imagine now complete strangers turning up at a major racing yard and having the most valuable racehorse in the sport pulled out for inspection, even having children popped up on his back for pictorial posterity. But Arkle thrived on it all. Public appearances were selective but hugely popular and they mixed with domestic duties that would seem incongruous in a modern training establishment. It wasn't unknown for Dreaper horses to be pressed into service helping to herd sheep on the trainer's farm. The greatest steeplechaser of them all was no exception.

At the start of the 1966–67 season, everything seemed set for Arkle's dominance to continue. He was still only nine, the age when most chasers are regarded as being at their peak. The belief that Golden Miller's five-in-a-row would at least be equalled before the stumps were drawn on Arkle's career was gathering more and more credence. Mill House's credibility as a viable rival was just a memory and there was no new plausible threat visible on the horizon. Soundness had never been an issue with the horse and his enthusiasm for the toughest game of all remained intact. And yet just three races later, before 1966 was finished, Arkle's career was over.

The first of his three remaining contests resulted in another Hennessy defeat at Newbury. Making the running under 12st 7lb, Arkle looked set for another phenomenal weight-carrying victory on the run to the last, but Stan Mellor on the grey Stalbridge

Colonist, later to be placed twice in the Gold Cup and in receipt of 35lb, was shadowing his every move. A flamboyant leap at the last gave the English horse enough momentum to lead but he was being hauled back all the way to the line and only held on by half a length. There was no mistake at Ascot in the SGB Chase, although Taaffe couldn't help noting how Arkle jumped to his left over the last three fences. Afterwards, a cut on his near fore-foot was discovered. It looked a simple over-reach. The King George would be next up.

However, as early as the second fence at Kempton, Taaffe felt something was wrong. 'Arkle jumped to the left, and that was very strange,' he remembered. 'But after he seemed OK, at least till the seventh from home. But he was never jumping brilliantly.' Instead of the usual dominance there were early signs that something was different this time. The 2–9 favourite was having to struggle to repel horses he would normally treat with disdain. That resulted in mistakes. Woodland Venture emerged as a viable threat, so much so that on the run to the second-last Terry Biddlecombe was convinced he was going to win. But Woodland Venture came down. That left Arkle clear of Dormant, apparently with the race in his pocket. But on the run-in he slowed so dramatically that his demonstrably inferior rival was able to overhaul him in the last fifty yards.

Initial disbelief that Arkle had been beaten quickly dissolved into concern at how badly lame he was; it was remarkable that he managed to finish at all. X-rays revealed that the great horse had broken a pedal bone in his off-foreleg. Taaffe reckoned it happened early in the race, which if true meant Arkle had run almost three miles in pain that must have been especially terrible when landing over the fences. And yet not once did he stop trying to run and jump and defeat the opposition.

'Going to the last he did start changing his legs. I knew then something was wrong. But he was not pulling up. Even then he was not pulling up,' Taaffe recalled. 'We came to the last and he still jumped it and made for the line. It was only in the last fifty yards that he started to stop.'

Beaten for just the fourth time over fences, it was a defeat that revealed a champion's courage. Recognition of that resounded throughout the racing world and beyond. Arkle remained at the Kempton racecourse stables for nearly two months and every update on his condition was eagerly reported. The chances of his racing career resuming were no more than fifty-fifty but the prognosis for the horse's long-term health was favourable. When Arkle eventually returned to Ireland, a large crowd was waiting at Dublin airport. His convalescence continued at Bryanstown Farm and ten months after leaving Dreaper's Greenogue yard for Kempton, Arkle was back home.

Early 1968 was dominated by feverish speculation as to when he might race again. Even a Gold Cup victory for his stable companion Fort Leney couldn't dilute it. Racecourses queued up to stage specially framed races. But a racecourse school over hurdles at Naas squashed those hopes. Taaffe ventured he felt the horse would never be fully right again. A final decision was postponed to the autumn but the Duchess of Westminster eventually bowed to the inevitable. By the 1969 Gold Cup, Arkle would be twelve. Expecting anything but a pale shadow of his imperious best would be wishful thinking. He was retired.

Sadness was a rare visitor to the Arkle story while he was racing but if ever a horse deserved better in retirement it was him. Throughout 1969 his physical condition deteriorated. Arthritis was suspected in his hip. His hind legs became increasingly stiff and he spent more and more time lying down. Lesions developed in his hind feet. When Taaffe visited his old ally at Bryanstown, he knew there was no hope. All that could be done was to help the horse avoid any further suffering. On 31 May 1970, Arkle was put down. He was buried in his field at Bryanstown.

As he was during his racing career, so the great chaser was front-page news in death. Some of the coverage verged on the maudlin but there was no denying how genuine the emotion was in Ireland and beyond. Another *Irish Times* editorial reflected that when declaring:

> 'Only a horse' is the dismissive remark of the rationalist who may not always analyse closely the value in eternity of some of his own favourite preoccupations . . . Were any bard to sing the praises of Arkle, there would be nothing unfitting in the exercise. That horse added to the lives of thousands. His instinct, which allowed him to put his power under human control – men are suffered by horses – had about it something that did honour to horses and to man.

Of course bards had by then already composed many songs about Arkle. In recent years other champions have had dirges tied around their neck but most have reeked of opportunism rather than the genuine depth of feeling that inspired those in thrall to the 1960s champion. Maybe that's appropriate. The idea that a racehorse might capture the public imagination again to the extent that Arkle did is all but impossible to take seriously. In an age when television's insatiable time-filler demands can turn even the most one-dimensional attention-seeking wannabe into a celebrity, there is little space left for anything that doesn't come complete with a sound-bite story, cartoon characterisation or plastic-boobed sheen. Arkle was as much of his time as any shaggy-haired hippy.

And that's the propulsion driving those who can't bring themselves to quite believe any horse can be as good as the myth suggests. Cheltenham's Gold Cup remains steeplechasing's ulti-mate prize but the route there has changed immeasurably. Tom Dreapar had no choice but to run Arkle in handicaps. Bar the Hennessy there was nothing else realistically to target in the first half of the winter. Even the King George wasn't a level-weights contest. Now there are any number of conditions events throughout the season and the appearance of a horse like Denman carrying topweight in the Hennessy is an oddity.

That's not good for the stats brigade. Handicapping is so much more tidy when horses actually run in handicaps. It means levels of ability can be clearly parsed into figures. A top-notcher such as Kauto Star might have been capable of successfully conceding masses of weight but no one will ever know. Was he really a stone and a half inferior to Arkle? No one will ever know that either.

National Hunt racing has been transformed in the last four decades. Training methods are infinitely more professional. Veterinary and scientific aids would be unrecognisable to Tom Dreaper, who trusted his eye because there was little else to work with. Now a horse will hardly have finished a piece of work before he's scoped, scanned and had blood samples taken. Professionalism has made the figures more exact and maybe that famous 212 isn't as precise as it might be. But what remains is the certainty of the people who saw him race.

There are no ifs and buts about Arkle. In twenty-six steeple-chases he was never less than excellent, even in defeat. Whatever the quibbles about how handicaps were formulated in the 1960s, the facts remain that he could concede colossal amounts of weight and still manage to win easily. And it's not as if he was conceding to mugs. His 1967 Gold Cup successor Woodland Venture was stones inferior on a form line through the runner-up Stalbridge Colonist. Fort Leney in 1968 was rated three stone worse. The 1969 winner What A Myth must have been over three stone behind Arkle. Mill House, the one horse who presented him with a threat, still rates as one of the best of the rest in terms of Gold Cup winners.

And Arkle did it all with a brio that meant a nation took him to their hearts. It's hardly any wonder, then, that in a much more complicated world, the myth remains so powerful and peculiarly real.

Vintage Crop

It might not be correct to get all *Pinta*, *Nina* and *Santa Maria* about Vintage Crop and the 1993 Melbourne Cup, but neither should the challenges of that most famous of international racing achievements be underestimated. In many respects it really was a plunge into the unknown. At a time when the internet was still largely theory, mobile phones the size of bricks and digital communications right on technology's cutting edge, there was an undoubted touch of the exotic about the first European raid on Australia's most famous sporting event. Certainly it didn't take long to find out that when it comes to racing's place in the Aussie public consciousness, the Melbourne Cup is in a different league to anything in this part of the world.

As part of the small, but, ahem, select group of Irish and British journalists prepared to bravely venture down under, it was this scribbler's fate to discover first-hand the level of interest in 'the race that stops a nation'. Stepping off the plane at Tullamarine Airport, dishevelled, sleep-deprived and feeling more than a little seedy after spending over twenty hours sitting next to a friendly but mouthy Aussie taking a few years off Europe to do college, it came as quite a cold shower to be on live radio before even clearing arrivals. 'Mouthy' had sold the newcomer as a racing 'expert' from

Ireland who was in Oz to cover the Cup. I didn't even have time to consider why a radio station was broadcasting from an airport in the first place before I was desperately trying to field questions about how a failed hurdler like Vintage Crop could possibly win the greatest race in the world. And how come he'd no form on fast ground, mate?

It wasn't long before the tiny hack pack was swamped in a wave of prodigious generosity and uncomplicated curiosity. Accustomed to a mixture of distrust and barely concealed disdain from racing professionals at home, it was startling but more than a little intoxicating to be included in a great swathe of events featuring the great and the good of the state of Victoria in the week leading up to the big event. Speeches at a ball at the Governor General's house contained exclamations about how the 1993 Melbourne Cup was the beginning of a new age in international racing. They mixed with more pious declarations of the traditional links between the countries involved.

At another merlot-soaked event, there was a 'phantom call', a determinedly raucous pretend commentary on what might happen in the Cup a few days later. People bet on the outcome. An early visit to Flemington racecourse revealed how there is no parade ring in Australia but rather a 'mounting yard', while grooms were 'strappers' and everyone's big ambition was to get up the 'Quinella' – to pick the first two horses home. Most of the major home hopes for the Cup ran just three days before the big race, almost falling over themselves in attempting not to try too hard. It all seemed very different from back home, a racing world separated not just by thousands of miles but by an entire culture.

Swamped by hospitality as we were, there was also no getting away from the fact that the European challenge was commonly believed to be little more than a curio. The Melbourne Cup could sometimes be temporarily exported to a Kiwi but in a country not noted for a lack of self-confidence, there was no mistaking the rampant scepticism that either Vintage Crop or the British-trained Drum Taps could get anywhere near to winning. Certainly any idea that a horse that hadn't run for six weeks – and had travelled 12,000 miles from the other side of the world – could get the better of the top Aussies was plainly ludicrous. The beer and the wine were chilled but not as chilled as the locals were about keeping Australia's most coveted sporting prize at home.

Such a status was obvious in the run-up to the first Tuesday in November 1993. Trying to describe the Cup's pervasive impact to those who haven't experienced it for themselves is all but impossible. Plenty of people in Britain and Ireland bet on the Aintree Grand National but that race is not even near the scale of the Melbourne Cup. A state holiday in Victoria, race day is an unofficial national holiday throughout the country. And if that's unofficial, what is a damn sight more official is the requirement for everyone to have a bet on it. Not doing so would be almost unpatriotic.

That level of public involvement is reflected in media coverage that steadily builds for weeks in advance to saturation level. Just think Grand National, World Cup Final, All-Ireland Final, Grand Slam decider and whatever you're having yourself – then double it. On the Saturday beforehand, the centre of Melbourne is closed down to hold a parade of past champions, both human and equine. In 1993, Black Knight, the Cup winner from nine years previously, pranced past the huge crowds, clearly the most popular member of the state constabulary. Following retirement from racing, he had been retrained to join the Victoria Mounted Police. It seemed a perfectly Australian combination of the practical and the sentimental.

Perhaps not coincidentally, the one visitor familiar with the intoxicating environment was Vintage Crop's trainer Dermot Weld. As a young man learning his trade he had spent time in Sydney and experienced this obsession first-hand. On his return home he had quickly become one of the top trainers in Ireland while also maintaining a world-view that distinguished him from most every other trainer anywhere.

In 1990 that ability to think outside the traditional box paid off spectacularly. No horse trained outside North America had ever won a leg of the famous US Triple Crown, but Weld's audacious attempt with Go And Go came off in style. A horse that was Group 2 standard at best in Europe but who could operate on the dirt surface thrived over the mile and a half trip that is often a step too far for America's ten-furlong specialists. Go And Go won the Belmont Stakes easily and Weld's ability to identify opportunities overseas was clearly established.

However, taking a horse 3,000 miles across the Atlantic was, if not commonplace, already eminently achievable. Attempting to travel to Australia with a fully tuned-up racehorse and take on the best of the home team was taking the vision thing to extremes. Many felt it couldn't be done. Weld had long held the belief that it could. It just needed an exceptional horse.

In Vintage Crop he felt he had such an animal. What the tall, burningly ambitious Irishman with the fluent tongue didn't have was a route to Melbourne that offered even a slim chance of success. A Cup attempt in 1992 had to be abandoned due to stringent quarantine regulations that made a raid impracticable. But by the following year, with the co-operation of a Victoria Racing Club desperate to market their greatest asset to a wider audience, enough had changed to make a challenge possible.

What tends to be forgotten about the 1993 Melbourne Cup now is that Vintage Crop was to most people very much the second-string of the European party. Drum Taps, twice an Ascot Gold Cup winner, was the northern hemisphere's champion stayer. He was also trained by a man who started out as William Hastings-Bass but morphed into Lord William Edward Robin Hood Huntingdon. Having an English Lord who trained for the Queen arrive on their doorstep was manna from heaven for a ravenous local media. That Drum Taps was set to be ridden by the flamboyant Italian jockey

Frankie Dettori just added to the cream. It wasn't long before every move by Drum Taps turned into, if not quite a circus, then definitely something of an event. In comparison, Vintage Crop was overlooked, something that might normally have irked the press-savvy Weld but which suited him perfectly in such circumstances.

Both horses were quarantined at Sandown Racecourse on the edge of Melbourne. Whereas Drum Taps ventured to Flemington for a pre-race work-out, Vintage Crop remained at Sandown, doing little more than gentle canters under his lad, David Phillips. Weld's public face presented a rather gloomy picture. The 38-hour journey from the Curragh to Melbourne had taken a lot out of the horse, causing him to lose weight and generally feel less than great about this new experience. In contrast the Drum Taps team were making encouraging noises.

Flying under the radar suited Weld perfectly. What he needed now to boost his already growing confidence was some rain. It almost seemed to be fate that the night before the big race Melbourne was soaked by a downpour accompanied by thunder and lightning. After two inches of rain the result was going rated heavy by home standards but nicely yielding by Irish ones. The scene was set for Weld's smash-and-grab raid on the blue riband of Australian horse racing.

Vintage Crop's rider Michael Kinane flew in from Hong Kong just before the race — a move that irked some Aussies, who regarded such a late arrival as casual — walked the track and pro-nounced himself satisfied with conditions. Ireland's champion jockey was very un-Dettori-like in his public behaviour but, even though he was used to the fanaticism that racing generates in Hong Kong, the man who was normally an oasis of calm on the eve of a big race could feel this was something different. A hundred thousand people showed up at Flemington and the unusually wet conditions couldn't dampen everyone's determination to enjoy the day. With Drum Taps one of the favourites, Vintage Crop was initially a 20–1 shot with the on-course bookmakers. That was cut to 16–1 by the off-time but in Hong Kong, where Kinane enjoyed huge popularity, the Irish horse was extremely well backed in Tote pool betting.

The unique demands of the Melbourne Cup were soon apparent. Used to slugging it out over two and a half miles at Ascot, Drum Taps found the stop-start tempo of the race too much to cope with. Starting like sprinters for the first half-mile, typically once around the first bend everyone slows down and, by European standards, the field crawl through the middle part of the race. Then comes an increase in tempo again for the run to the line. Ideally a horse has to have enough speed to secure a position while possessing sufficient stamina to thrive when the going gets tough towards the end. It's a curious mixture but Weld's conviction that Vintage Crop had it was borne out in style.

The chestnut gelding with a physical quality that matched his ability hardly got a silky-smooth passage through the race. But once the horse got a clear run up the long straight, Weld's vision came true in devastating fashion. Vintage Crop powered three lengths ahead of Te Akau Nick, and the only bum note was struck by a stunned race-caller who shrieked as the Irish horse passed the post: 'And the Cup goes to England!'

The Australian reaction overall to the Cup result was similarly stunned. As a noticeably calm and collected Kinane, who earlier that year had won the Epsom Derby on Commander In Chief, returned waving a small tricolour, there were spluttering attempts on television to explain what had just happened. If the pre-race view of the European invasion had been mildly scornful, after - wards some apocalyptic visions were painted for the future. Dismissiveness turned to fear. If European stayers were so superior then the Melbourne Cup could be picked up almost at will in the future. What if the real top-notchers travelled? Derby and Arc winners, even?

Time would prove such fears to be unfounded. Some high-class runners did venture down under, who on paper were far superior to the home team. Oscar Schindler went to Melbourne in 1997 after getting placed in an Arc and finished nowhere. Aidan O'Brien sent both Yeats and Septimus and ended up receiving barrages of flak from the locals over tactical foul-ups. Delta Blues did win for Japan in 2006 but the only other European runner to crack the Cup code was Media Puzzle in 2002. And he coincidentally just happened to be trained by a certain D.K. Weld. Ultimately time has only reinforced the view that Vintage Crop's success was a truly special moment in world racing, perhaps worthy of being described as the greatest single achievement in racing history.

But such perspective was for the future. In the immediate aftermath one Aussie reporter shook hands with yours truly as if I had had some hand or part in Vintage Crop's victory. Dolefully he attempted to make the best of a bad situation: 'At least the Pommie horse didn't win.'

Weld was in his element. There were no wild celebrations. Instead, now that victory was in the bag, he presented a calm, almost patrician face to a racing world that would never be quite the same again. He briefly outlined his links with Australia and regaled the media hordes with tales of how he'd grown up fascinated by the country and its famous poet 'Banjo' Paterson, who wrote the lyrics to 'Waltzing Matilda'. His audience treated this as the visitor schmoozing the locals only for Weld to start reciting verses of 'A Bush Christening' off the top of his head. With so many Aussies claiming Irish heritage it was no surprise to see Weld and Kinane swamped by well-wishers.

'This is as good a feeling as an Epsom Derby,' said Kinane to general bemusement that anything could equal winning the Melbourne Cup. 'It's historic. To do the two in the same year is unreal.'

While the winning connections partied into the night in Melbourne city centre, the medium of all the drama was back at Sandown, stretched out in his box, fast asleep. Vintage Crop was a top-class horse, a double winner of the Irish St Leger on the flat and good enough over jumps to finish fifth in a Champion Hurdle. He was also an advertisement for patience. Despite being well enough bred he was four before he even made it to the racecourse. That he won that debut when completely unfancied at 20–1 indicated he was just a little bit different. Without Melbourne he would have had a career that was thoroughly admirable if not remotely sufficient to earn a ranking among the greats on racing merit alone. But he will always be the first horse from Europe to win the Melbourne Cup.

His ultimate reward for such a singular achievement was a retirement to the Irish National Stud. There might not have been a breeding career but he has spent a lengthy life there exerting an almost magnetic hold on hundreds of thousands of tourists – not all of them Anzacs – visiting Ireland. In his own way Vintage Crop continued to make the world a little bit smaller long after waving goodbye to Flemington.

His final farewell actually came in 1995 with a performance that handicap experts rate at least on a par with his display two years earlier. Like the Grand National, the Melbourne Cup is a handicap, theoretically allowing all the runners a chance to win. It suits the Aussie temperament to invest so much in such a race, the whole 'fair shake' egalitarian spirit that so characterises Australians' view of themselves. After carrying 8st 10lb to victory, Vintage Crop returned in 1994 and, carrying topweight of 9st 7lb, finished seventh to Jeune. But in 1995 he ran a storming race under 9st 4lb to finish third to Doriemus, conceding the winner 10lb. By then he was eight years old, geriatric in terms of top-class flat racing. Weld and owner Michael Smurfit took their cue and retired their champion on the high of that last Cup effort.

It was an appropriately positive note to end on although the distance between the two racing cultures could never be fully bridged. Kinane felt the full force of an Australian media determinedly set in their ways as to how horses should be ridden. Any fancy European rider attempting something different was fair game and in 1994, circumstances conspired to leave the Irish jockey wide open. A week before the race, Vintage Crop shied away from some paper swirling in a breeze and caught a leg on an exposed piece of steel rail. It was touch and go whether the horse would be able to race at all and Weld's instructions to his jockey understandably included a brief to stay out of trouble.

'I got heavily criticised for that ride, which pissed me off. Vintage Crop had seventeen stitches in an elbow and really shouldn't have even run, and it was all because of carelessness on their part out on the training track,' Kinane later remembered. 'Dermot told me to stay on the outside and not have him knocked about . . . the Aussies don't like horses being ridden on the outside. It's their way. And their way is the only way. They castigate their own so they loved having a go at an outsider. The Aussies are great. They tell you straight what they think. But they turn on you quick. They probably just didn't like us taking the Cup off them the first year.'

The jockey had no doubt about what made Vintage Crop the horse to overcome all the logistical difficulties, and the demands of the race itself – courage.

'A great horse had to have attitude, who'll want to go to the pain barrier for you. Vintage Crop was one of the handful I've ridden who was willing to do that. The third year he ran in the Cup he finished legless in third. He went out on a limb for us,' Kinane said. Weld put it succinctly in a book he wrote in 2009 outlining the story of that famous 1993 victory called *Vintage Crop – Against All Odds*. The trainer described him simply as 'The bravest horse I had ever trained.'

Even famously astute horsemen like Weld and Kinane could hardly have guessed that such reserves were inside the two-year-old son of the disappointing sire Rousillon and Overplay, a talented racemare trained by Weld for the American owner Bert Firestone. Vintage Crop was extremely backward and was sent back to Gilltown Stud to mature. By that time the Firestones had sold all their horses in Ireland to the Japanese businessman Yoshiki

Akazawa. It was from him that Weld bought Vintage Crop in 1991 for the Irish businessman, Michael Smurfit. The latter sponsored the Champion Hurdle and was looking for prospective jumping talent. But it was on the flat that Smurfit's new purchase first appeared in October in a two-mile race at Thurles. He was not expected to win. Kinane rode a better-fancied stable companion called Padiord, who started second favourite. Weld's No. 2 rider Pat Shanahan was given instructions to make sure the newcomer got a positive first experience of racing.

'In the weeks before Vintage Crop's first race we increased his work on the gallops. He still looked very immature and unfurnished but his talent shone in his first serious work-out about three weeks before the race. He really impressed me with the pace he showed over nine furlongs,' Weld wrote later. 'Horses show ability from an early stage if they possess it. If they don't, you can't put it there. My belief is that the good get better and the bad get worse.'

Some stables have form when it comes to second-strings coming out on top. Weld, however, prides himself on knowing what he is dealing with and it was that as much as Vintage Crop's performance at Thurles that indicated this horse might be out of the ordinary. That winter he set out on what looked to be his future career. Vintage Crop was no natural jumper. Extensive schooling under jockey Brendan Sheridan revealed he was fine meeting a hurdle long. But when he had to fiddle a jump he didn't seem able to adjust himself very quickly. Nevertheless when he made his hurdling debut at Fairyhouse there was enough natural ability there to allow him to beat decent opposition. That Christmas he appeared again at Leopardstown and, in a tight finish, Sheridan had to get serious with Vintage Crop for the first time. He responded well enough to win but afterwards Weld noticed some lameness. The horse also didn't seem totally happy in himself. It was no surprise.

A bad back can impact on every facet of life for those afflicted with it. Vintage Crop was plagued with back problems throughout his life. It was never established how he damaged it but Weld later revealed the horse often had to run and work in some degree of pain. Vintage Crop's sacroiliac joint was the problem and that made it a continual problem because the one thing guaranteed to prolong the problem is extensive movement. Jumping hurdles could be painful and Weld decided to postpone any more jumping in an attempt to get the horse right. Throughout the rest of his career Vintage Crop received weekly physiotherapy while also getting regular acupuncture. A special nonslip floor was also put in his box.

Vintage Crop could be a narky customer sometimes, which was hardly surprising as in addition to back problems, he also suffered from stomach ulcers. The stresses of training often lead to racehorses suffering from the ailment but only a small percentage are affected as much as Vintage Crop was. It meant he had to receive more care and attention than a lot of his stable companions, but Weld began to believe that getting him right could result in a real pay-off.

In May 1992 the former patient was starting to bloom with some sunshine on his back and easily won a fourteen-furlong handicap at Gowran with just 8st 5lb on his back. He didn't appear again until August when finishing third to a stable companion, Sharp Review, at Leopardstown. By now, Weld's Melbourne Cup ambitions for that year had evaporated. Significantly, he had already entered Vintage Crop for the 1992 race but quarantine problems – involving a month in England before then enduring another month under wraps in Australia – as well as transport difficulties made a trip impossible. Weld had previously hoped to send Rare Holiday for the race but had come to the conclusion that the Australians weren't ready to entertain visitors just yet. Instead he picked out a prestigious target closer to home.

First of all, though, Vintage Crop easily won a valuable handicap at Tralee before running fifth to Mashaallah in the Irish St Leger, a race sponsored by his owner. It completed a remarkably quick rise through the ranks to Group 1 level. Not surprisingly, the still-maturing horse found the Leger pace altogether different from what he was used to, but ultimately he wasn't beaten far. And it set him up perfectly for the big target, which was the Cesarewitch at Newmarket. The two-and-a-quarter-mile handicap is one of the most coveted handicap prizes on the English calendar. After his Leger effort, Weld's belief that Vintage Crop was handicapped to win it was shared by many. Michael Kinane had left to begin a six-month contract riding in Hong Kong, so Walter Swinburn was engaged for the ride.

The man who steered Shergar to a memorable 1981 Derby victory was one of the best, and most subtle, big-race riders in Europe at that time and was also the son of Weld's former stable jockey, Wally Swinburn. The new partnership gelled immediately and Vintage Crop sailed through from the back of the 24-strong pack to win by eight lengths. Swinburn was impressed, especially with the winner's exceptional pace. Not many stayers could quicken like that and the jockey was so confident he said he was singing 'When Irish Eyes Are Smiling' at the two-furlong marker!

It would be a while before Weld's eyes were smiling about Vintage Crop again. Not surprisingly for a horse with a bad back, the big chestnut reacted badly to the winter cold. As always he did his work and tried hard but there was little enjoyment in it for him. After a schooling hurdle in December 1992 he was inter-mittently lame, and although Cheltenham's Champion Hurdle was what Michael Smurfit wanted to win more than anything else, the signs weren't encouraging. The ground remained heavy throughout, which ruled out a preparatory run, but the decision was still taken to run at the festival.

Despite having run just twice before over hurdles, Vintage Crop started only 9–1 for the Champion Hurdle in March. He was travelling well enough just behind the leaders coming down the hill until meeting the second-last hurdle all wrong. It was a mistake waiting to happen. His back was never going to allow Vintage Crop to be a naturally fluent jumper. Typically, he didn't chuck the towel in and was only a couple of lengths off the winner Granville Again when another mistake at the last finished any chance he had of winning. Afterwards Weld and Smurfit ruled out ever going jumping with him again.

'Jumping is the name of the game and Vintage Crop was never a natural jumper. He was brave and true and would take on anything but his back prevented him from jumping with fluency,' Weld concluded.

That spring the horse was plagued again by ulcers and also picked up an infection that took him some time to shake off. Instead of thriving Vintage Crop was eating pickily and generally looking less than pleased with life. On his return to flat racing in the Listed Saval Beg Stakes he started odds-on but could only struggle into third. He did win back at Leopardstown afterwards but a tilt at the Ascot Gold Cup over two and a half miles failed. Soft ground didn't suit a horse never quite able to get home over such an extreme distance and Vintage Crop finished only fifth behind a rival he was to get to know quite a lot better before 1993 was over. Drum Taps dominated the Gold Cup throughout to win it for the second year running. He was unquestionably the top stayer in Europe.

By then the Melbourne Cup also figured prominently on Drum Taps' agenda. Recognising that a month's quarantine in the UK before another month tied up in Australia was impractical, the Victoria Racing Club and government authorities eased up on the restrictions. Instead of a month, horses could be isolated for a fortnight at home before being quarantined for another two weeks at Sandown racecourse. Crucially, that would allow them to exercise rather than just being restricted to walks. Although still expensive and a huge ask in terms of adapting to different seasons and racing styles, a Melbourne Cup attempt was now theoretically possible. After Ascot, Drum Taps became a headline contender. In the early summer Vintage Crop hardly featured on the radar.

Weld was desperately worried. The array of ailments looked to be catching up with his horse. But where medical science floundered, a few days on grass under some rare Curragh sunshine seemed to do the trick. Suddenly there was an appetite again, and not just for his grub. Vintage Crop's work picked up to such an extent that he was able to run in the Group 3 Curragh Cup on Irish Derby day. Commander In Chief may have completed a Derby double that day, but Vintage Crop's victory in the main support race was a hell of a pick-me-up for Weld's Melbourne ambitions. A few more weeks break back in the paddock with his pal Bobby the pony seemed to transform the horse. A return race in the Meld Stakes over an inadequate ten furlongs yielded a hugely encouraging second to Lord Of The Field, leaving some high-class middle-distance runners behind him. Vintage Crop might not have been able to land the Smurfit-sponsored Champion Hurdle but he was now a prime contender to recoup his owner's money in the Irish Leger.

Melbourne will always be what Vintage Crop is remembered for but in terms of raw handicapping achievement it's quite possible to argue that his greatest success was the 1993 Irish Leger. Drum Taps was there as was Snurge, the 1990 English Leger hero who was chasing an all-time earnings record. There was also Assessor, the previous year's winner of the French St Leger, the Prix Royal Oak, and who just a few weeks after the Curragh would go on to win France's Gold Cup, the Prix du Cadran. The line-up, however, didn't prevent a gamble on Vintage Crop, cutting his odds from 8–1 to 9–2. It was not surprising as he had been buzzing at home, revealing how good he could be with a stretch of physical wellbeing behind him. Snurge started favourite but Weld was looking for nothing but a win.

Kinane was on board and remembered: 'Frankie Dettori sent Drum Taps straight into the lead but the pace he set was too steady for some of us and just under halfway Johnny Murtagh took over on Shrewd Idea. I went past him early in the straight and I reckoned if I could get a length or two clear of the rest Vintage Crop would be hard to catch. And that's just how it proved.'

The victory was a perfect morale-booster for Weld's audacious attempt to turn accepted wisdom – that a European horse couldn't win the Melbourne Cup – on its head. Even a simple element such as the actual flight-path to Australia had to be changed. Previously horses flown to Australia couldn't land in the Middle East due to concerns about mosquito-borne infections. Instead horse planes flew via Canada, Hawaii and Fiji. Months of negotiations, including at European level in Brussels, meant by 1993 Vintage Crop and Drum Taps would be allowed to land in Sharjah and Hong Kong before flying on to Melbourne. Five weeks' worth of feed for Vintage Crop was flown out ahead of him. The horse initially found his two weeks of quarantine isolation at the Curragh very strange. Instinctively he seemed to know something different was about to happen. But he didn't let it get him down. What nearly wrecked everything before it started was some good old-fashioned fog at Dublin Airport. The plane that would take Vintage Crop to his connecting flight at Heathrow couldn't land. Weld was devastated. Nature appeared to have wrecked years of preparation in a few minutes. But for the pilot deciding to make one last attempt at landing in Dublin, it would have.

Australian trainer Bart Cummings, the irascible 'Cup King', had four runners in the 1993 Cup, including the heavily backed favourite Our Pompeii. Typically they had all run three days before at the track and Tennessee Jack had won the Dalgety Stakes. He would be ridden by the top young Aussie rider, Damien Oliver. To a veteran local trainer like Cummings, the European method of training, which meant a six-week break since last turning out was no big deal, was incomprehensible. There was also the question of a European rider like Kinane taking on the local jockeys, a startling concern to the eyes of the visitors who hadn't been overly impressed with the virtuosity of some of the riding at Flemington, some of which verged on the agricultural. Certainly for someone with an Epsom Derby and an Arc already under his belt, navigating the Cup was no big ask.

Vintage Crop was stretched to go the early pace but although Te Akau Nick made an early move, it was only the Irish horse that ever looked like hauling him back in. As Our Pompeii, Drum Taps and all the other fancied horses started to back-pedal, it was noticeable how Vintage Crop seemed to be eating up the ground as his proven stamina came into play. At the line he had three lengths in hand.

There is ample evidence to back up a popular theory that any horse has only a certain amount of time at its peak. The eighteen-month period between the summer of 1993 and winter 1994 saw Vintage Crop at the height of his powers. When he reappeared in the 1994 Saval Beg Stakes, despite carrying 10st 1lb he won easily. It set him up for another crack at the Ascot Gold Cup. A furlong out it looked like Vintage Crop was set to score but after a scorching gallop on very quick ground, the extreme distance eventually took its toll and he came up half a length short of Arcadian Heights. Just eight days later he appeared again in the Curragh Cup under a monster weight of 10st 4lb. Weld admitted later he shouldn't have run but he only failed by a length to Witness Box.

The big targets for 1994 were for Vintage Crop to retain his Irish Leger and Melbourne Cup crowns. A warm-up race at the Curragh saw him beat George Augustus (a horse that had beaten the top German runner Monsun in a Group 1 the previous year only to be disqualified by the stewards) in comfortable style. Traditionalists might have been appalled at a classic being won more than once but when the Irish Leger was opened up to older horses, it was to encourage stars like Vintage Crop to come back. The horse more than lived up to his side of the bargain. The best of his opposition was the previous year's English Leger winner Bob's Return. He never landed a blow and it was left to Rayseka to chase the 7–4 favourite home. Ireland had its very first dual-classic winner.

If suspicions remained in Australia that Vintage Crop had been handicapped relatively leniently the previous year, with a view to encouraging him to travel, there could be no similar suggestion in 1994. Topweight of 9st 7lb left him facing a massive task. Then came his pre-race collision with the unpadded running rail at Sandown. As if that wasn't enough, the Irish star was handed a wide draw, which left Mick Kinane with a tactical quandary that he was never able to solve in the circumstances. Vintage Crop didn't travel with the same fluidity he had when at his physical peak and it was impossible to avoid the conclusion that his injury played a role in him recording the worst finishing position of his career. He finished seventh to Jeune.

That winter Weld and Smurfit decided the 1995 season would be the horse's last. It opened with another impressive victory at Leopardstown before a final attempt at the Ascot Gold Cup yielded a fourth to Double Trigger. Then came a hugely courageous success in the Curragh Cup under 10st 4lb. Kinane dismounted and told Weld: 'You will never train another like him.'

Another success at Leopardstown preceded a final Irish Leger attempt but this time Vintage Crop could manage only fourth to Strategic Choice. It looked like age had caught up with the top stayer. Back in Australia he thrived in the sunshine but there was as much sentiment as hard cash riding on the Irish star to make him an 8–1 shot. That he ran up to those odds said everything about the horse's determination.

Vintage Crop was not a champion in the awe-inspiring sense that Sea The Stars or Nijinsky was. He may not even have been the best stayer trained by Dermot Weld. A sound case can be made that that was Vinnie Roe. As a four-time Irish Leger winner he trumped Vintage Crop in home achievement and it is unlikely the latter could have finished fifth in an Arc as Vinnie Roe did. And while Media Puzzle may have won the Melbourne Cup in 2002, possibly the greatest Flemington performance of all by a Weld horse came the following year when the Aussie legend Makybe Diva needed a perfect passage through the race to beat Vinnie Roe by just over a length while getting 5lb from her rival.

The scale of that run can be calculated from the fact that last year the Victorian Racing Club got their senior ratings personnel to formulate a handicap of the top twenty-four Melbourne Cup winners in the race's 150-year history. The legendary 1930 winner, Phar Lap, got topweight of 60kg. Makybe Diva was rated third best of the lot on 58kg. Vintage Crop was ranked thirteenth.

What can never be taken away from Vintage Crop is the historic nature of what he achieved. And while being the first European to win the Melbourne Cup will always define him, few things became him more than the way he bowed out. Age not surprisingly had caused him to lose some pace, but considering the ground was heavy it was still shocking to see him trail the whole field as they went by the winning line with a circuit to go. Unusually there had been a constant and true pace throughout and, as others dropped back, Vintage Crop made up a little ground until badly baulked six furlongs from home. He had any number of excuses to chuck the towel in but that was never his style. Kinane delved into those famous reserves one last time and the response was staggeringly brave. Doriemus was ultimately a dominant winner but the top-class 'Nothin' Leica Dane' was running on empty in the final furlong and another fifty yards would have seen Vintage Crop claim the runner-up spot. It was the final flourish of a true champion.

Sentiment is not obviously abundant among many racing professionals in Ireland when it comes to horses past their productive best. It's not that it isn't there but there is an under-standing that the beast is a working animal and not some expensive pet. Despite that there are paddocks throughout the country where ageing racers live out happy retirements under the blustering care of many otherwise hard-headed people who wouldn't in a million years admit to a horse having got under their skin.

Vintage Crop could have been kept under wraps on home property by Michael Smurfit but instead he was sent to the National Stud near Kildare town in a gesture that reflected his unique status. Visitors walking through the grounds are treated to the sight of the Melbourne Cup winner messing around with his friends, the former steeplechase favourites Danoli and Florida Pearl, while characteristically minding his arthritic back. Public appearances were limited but in 2000 he made the long trek back to Melbourne and led the parade of champions through the city. In Ireland he has had a Listed race in Navan named after him and a statue of the horse commissioned by his owner is situated outside the weighroom at the Curragh racecourse.

Dermot Weld has had thousands of horses go through his hands. Some of them were more talented than Vintage Crop. None, however, got to the great trainer like Europe's first Melbourne Cup winner.

'I went to visit him at the Irish National Stud. He knew me immediately and came straight over and whinnied at me,' he wrote. 'I talked to him, praised him and gave him a pat on the neck. He never took his eyes off me as I left. He stood and gazed until I was out of sight. A truly amazing horse.'

Monksfield

Plenty of the horses listed here were hardly equine paragons. The young Arkle, for instance, as Pat Taaffe famously remarked, had a set of back legs through which a wheelbarrow could be driven. Vintage Crop was plagued by a chronically bad back. Flyingbolt's temper was sulphuric. However, the most unlikely success story of all must be Monksfield's. Physically there was so much wrong for the job he had. And yet a better hurdler has yet to come out of Ireland.

Those who buy and sell horses for a living would have initially looked at the paltry 740 guineas it cost to buy the yearling Monksfield and told the vendor they'd done well. Maybe it's not surprising that Des McDonogh, the man who bought him and subsequently moulded one of the most memorable racing careers of all, was a comparative novice at the bloodstock game. Certainly any 'expert' would only have needed to see Monksfield walk to have them quickening their own pace in the opposite direction.

From a purist's perspective, a horse's front feet should work symmetrically, travel straight through in an efficient manner that places a minimum of stress on the joints. When Monksfield moved, his front legs rotated like a pair of radar dishes. They swung outwards and back in a motion known as 'dishing' that might not be harmful but is unsightly to those who worry about such things. And whatever you might think about cosmetics, the waste of energy involved in such an action is no plus. But if the front legs were a nightmare, it was what resided between the back ones that makes the Monksfield story even more remarkable.

Horses still in full possession of their stallion equipment have run over jumps in the past and some have even prospered. The 1947 Gold Cup winner Fortina himself sired a pair of Gold Cup winners, Fort Leney and Glencaraig Lady. Battleship, the 1938 Grand National hero, spent some time at stud afterwards too. More recently, the 1995 Champion Hurdle winner Alderbrook carved out a breeding career for himself. Other names such as Sula Bula and Baron Blakeney have also managed to race while remaining entires. But they are very much exceptions to the rule in the jumping game, for obvious reasons. Racing over long distances when your instincts are telling you to indulge in less exacting and more pleasurable alternatives makes it more difficult to concentrate on passing the post first. There are other more practical considerations too, such as the ticklish problem of brushing through the tops of birch fences. Monksfield's career was confined to hurdles but his stature – oh, yes, and he was tiny – often made negotiating them look a struggle. However, rarely have obstacles of any kind been overcome with such obvious zest and enthusiasm. In a world of mostly dour geldings, the resolutely extravagant horse known as 'Monkey' stood out in every way.

That he did so only emphasises the reputation Monksfield carved out. Most sports have a golden generation, a time when excellence and competition seem to collide into a dramatic period that nostalgia makes only more remarkable. If Brazil's 1970 World Cup-winning side remains international soccer's benchmark of excitement and quality, then the 1974 Lions serve a similar function in rugby. As for tennis, will there ever be a more consuming time than when Messrs Borg, McEnroe and Connors were swaggering their way through Wimbledon? The coincidence of all those stars appearing at a time when colour television first became the 'norm' for many of us, and so unfolded an impossibly exciting first impression, is no doubt a fascinating subject for psychological debate.

In sports terms, though, the reasoning will always take second place to the images, and in hurdling terms the 1970s formed the bulk of a golden period that lasted from 1968 to 1981. In that fourteen-year span, there were just seven winners of the Champion Hurdle. Persian War won three between 1968 and 1970, while Bula (1971–72), Comedy Of Errors (1973, 1975), Night Nurse (1976–77) and Sea Pigeon (1980–81) were all double winners. And in among them is the sole Irish representative, little Monksfield, whose back-to-back victories in 1978 and 1979 were sandwiched in between two runner-up placings.

The strength of competition at that time was such that animals of the quality of Bird's Nest, Dramatist and Beacon Light, horses that were officially rated superior to many later Champion Hurdle winners, never got on the roll of honour. Bird's Nest, a three-time winner of the Fighting Fifth Hurdle, and an instantly recognisable figure at the time under jockey Andy Turnell's frighteningly short riding style, is rated among the top ten hurdlers ever. From that mid-70s period, Monsksfield, Night Nurse and Sea Pigeon also feature among that top ten. Between 1975 and 1981, at least two of that quartet met in twenty-seven races, a rate unheard of now when opportunities for the top horses to avoid each other are so much greater.

But the lack of alternatives resulted in a bunch of horses becoming household names and pushing each other's capabilities to the utmost. That they were instantly identifiable and different in terms of character only added to the mix. If Sea Pigeon was a comparative Flash Harry, full of flat race speed and a flamboyant style that threatened to engulf all opposition, his stable companion Night Nurse was the opposite, a roundhead professional that looked a little goofy while being fearsomely difficult to pass.

Monksfield combined the two, a bit flash in terms of personality but full of spit-in-your-eye determination when it counted. Between them they produced years of drama that have yet to be replicated. And at the end, they each possessed perfectly rational arguments as to why they were the best.

As if the Monksfield story hadn't enough in itself, there was also the flavour provided by the humans involved with him who brought a dash of little-guy-made-good, plenty of against-the-odds struggle and more than a hint of aggro that kept everyone enthralled even when the great equine rivals weren't out there taking on each other.

And happily, at the end of it all, there was no sombre finale. The eight-year-old Monksfield retired in 1980 in full health and soundness. Not for him an anonymous retirement out in a field. Instead he went to David Pim's Anngrove Stud in Co. Laois where he enjoyed nine seasons as a stallion before passing away in 1989. He didn't sire a dynasty or anything like it. There was certainly no danger of him outbreeding, or getting one better than himself, but it was typical of Monksfield that one of his most high-profile winners turned out to be an otherwise unexceptional horse called It's A Snip. In 1995 he ventured to the Czech Republic for the famous Velka Pardubicka Chase and carried his trainer Charlie Mann to victory around the notoriously difficult track with its massive obstacles, ploughed fields and twisting route that above all else places a premium on courage. Not all Monksfield's progeny had talent, but rare was the one that lacked for guts.

If pressed to plump for one over-riding characteristic in the little horse with the revolving legs and the incongruously handsome head, it would have to be the raw courage he showed throughout his career. As well as a pair of Champion Hurdles, Monksfield notched up three victories in Liverpool's major hurdle prize, now known as the Aintree Hurdle. The confines of the Irish programme book at the time meant home efforts usually involved conceding impossible amounts of weight in handicaps but never once did he waver. Presented with umpteen opportunities to sour in the face of ridiculous odds, Monksfield kept on galloping and jumping and, even more remarkably, rarely if ever gave the impression it was anything but right good fun. Winning distances were never extensive but when it came to producing the goods during his favourite time of the year in spring, none of his rivals relished a scrap more.

Timeform rate Monksfield and Istabraq as their joint-best Irish hurdlers ever. Only Night Nurse is rated above them. Istabraq was clearly superior to his opposition and put in the figures in terms of distances to confirm that. Monksfield's greatest moment came when he just edged out Sea Pigeon for a second Champion Hurdle victory that is still regarded as one of the greatest Cheltenham Festival eyeball-to-eyeball scraps the famous old course has ever seen. It wasn't by much, but it was Monksfield's courage that won out. Des McDonogh has always maintained his horse only needed a target to pitch himself against, for in a scrap there was none better. And Monksfield's contemporaries were so good there was never getting away from a fight.

If the diminutive champion always seemed a little different from his peers it only fitted in with his background. Not many horses have a tie-in with the 1969 moon landings, but the man who bred Monksfield wrote a book soon after Neil Armstrong, Buzz Aldrin and Michael Collins did their 1969 lunar gig and made enough on the back of it to cement a somewhat tenuous link with the bloodstock industry. An unintended trip to the sales ring in Ballsbridge a year previously had resulted in Peter Ryan paying out £1,700 for a mare called Regina who had only produced one foal in the previous six seasons. Well bred as a daughter of the Derby winner Tulyar and a Coronation Stakes heroine in Tambara, Regina was pretty useless as a racehorse, as well as having a dubious breeding history. Peter Ryan's cousin Arthur agreed to stable Regina at his farm in Co. Tipperary, where the mare surprised everyone with two foals in succession. Then she visited the

American-bred sire Gala Performance, who had been imported to Coolmore Stud in the days when it was still owned by Tim Vigors. On 7 June 1972, Monksfield was born. Arthur Ryan's first impressions were not positive.

'As he began to trot and gambol around the field I spotted his appalling action,' he later recounted. 'At a walk his movement did not show up too badly. But he had a terrible action when he started to go faster. His two front legs went out and round in a great big circle.'

The yearling Monksfield went to Goffs Sale and didn't attract a single bid. The following year he returned to Ballsbridge with a reserve of just 800 guineas on his back. After a brief spurt of bidding, the offers stopped at 740. Arthur Ryan decided to take it and offload the little colt with the funny legs. He was on his way to Co. Meath and surroundings a long way from the equine luxury of Newmarket or the Curragh.

Des McDonogh's horse pedigree was all but nonexistent. Born and raised in Limerick, the son of a clerk at nearby Shannon Airport, his grandfather ran a livery business, but McDonogh's initial interest ran to singing and amateur dramatics. He learned to ride during summer holidays at a cousin's farm and accompanied his father to the Limerick races when they were on. On leaving school a succession of jobs failed to enthuse him but riding out at a nearby stables did. Soon he was riding in point-to-points and at a hunt ball he met Helen Bryce-Smith, whose racing pedigree was extensive. Her parents trained successfully in Co. Meath and she was a formidable horsewoman in point-to-points. McDonogh followed Helen to Meath and started working at the Bryce-Smith yard. In 1971 the couple married and moved into a small dairy farm, Billywood Stud, which they received as a wedding present. Practically over-run, with only a few cow barns and a shed, it seemed an unlikely setting for training thoroughbreds.

McDonogh's first winner as a licensed trainer came in early 1973 and two more winners followed that year. When he went to

Ballsbridge Sales in 1974 the fledgling handler was trading at the bottom of the financial barrel. But with Monksfield it was love at first sight.

'I opened the door and that was it, the way he looked up at me from the corner of his box. He perked up as if to say, "What the hell do you want?" I loved that head the instant I saw it,' McDonogh remembered.

Monksfield's box at Billywood was built from spare bits of material. A small gap in a wall was filled with an old window. The walls themselves were so crooked that building on them threatened to bring the whole thing down. Only when the horse won his first Champion Hurdle was the inside plastered. But if the niceties were sparse, individual attention was abundant. The trainer 'did' Monksfield and rode him in his work. The first stages of learning his trade proved so easy to the bright little colt that he was nicknamed 'Smarty'. Finding an owner for him proved to be much more tricky. After a couple of people turned him down, Des McDonogh ran into an uncle at Roscommon races who introduced him to his friend, Dr Michael Mangan. Galway born but based in St Johns, Newfoundland, as a radiologist, Mangan was home on holiday and suddenly found himself with the opportunity to fulfil a long-held ambition to own a racehorse. After visiting 'Smarty' to inspect him, although he admitted to not having a clue what he was looking at, the Canadian-based doctor paid out £1,125. Mangan named him Monksfield after the guesthouse his mother had run in Salthill in Galway.

McDonogh later said that the right man had bought the right horse. Mangan was impressed with the young couple's ambition and care for their horses and left the business of training Monksfield to them. Since he was based in Canada, there was plenty of distance between him and rural Co. Meath anyway – but interfering owners have been known to make their presence felt from further than 3,000 miles away.

By the end of October 1974, Monksfield was ready for a run.

McDonogh picked a seven-furlong maiden at Punchestown where the debutant was dismissed as a 647–1 shot on the Tote. Winning was the last thing on the trainer's mind but under jockey Ken Coogan the little horse carrying the maroon and white colours powered through a large field to win by a length and a half. Coogan was as surprised as anyone and exclaimed, 'This could be one hell of a horse. What a hurdler he'll make.'

As forecasts go, this was a remarkably prescient one. Especially since Monksfield's three-year-old career on the flat yielded no victory from thirteen starts. There was, however, a third in the Irish Cesarewitch that provided promise for when he began jumping. Home schooling provided even more hope. 'He was like lightning. He got only the minimum height over his jumps from the word go,' McDonogh said. Sure enough, at Navan in November 1975, Monksfield made a winning debut over hurdles. The following month he won again at Fairyhouse. Five more races yielded a couple of seconds before he won again back at Navan under the jockey who came to play a central role in his career.

McDonogh had engaged some of Ireland's top jockeys for Monksfield such as Bobby Coonan and Frank Berry. Tommy Kinane was not in that league. Already well into the veteran stage, he was initially engaged as a natural lightweight for a handicap Monksfield finished second in. The man whose family is steeped in racing, and whose son Michael would become a world-famous flat jockey, was a forceful personality, not afraid to call a spade a shovel and whose appetite for a scrap never wavered no matter what kind of injury he incurred. Not surprisingly, he took to Monksfield's way of racing: 'He felt a super tough horse under me. Jump? He'd jump right out of jail!'

When the pair lined up for the Triumph Hurdle at Cheltenham, it was the fulfilment of another dream for Michael Mangan, who had been visiting the festival for years. It was all completely new to McDonogh, and Kinane was hardly a headline act in Britain. Monksfield started a 28–1 shot and initially looked every bit of that price as he was carried off his feet by the early pace. But in the grinding style that was to become so familiar he progressed through the pack to challenge for the lead on the run to the last. Jonjo O'Neill on Peterhof also came through and veered right across the Irish horse's nose in the closing stages, forcing Kinane to snatch up. At the line there was just a length and a half in it and the jockey was convinced he would get the race in the stewards room. O'Neill was worried. Mangan and McDonogh were stunned to have got so close, so much so that the trainer wasn't surprised and not too disappointed when the result was allowed to stand. Kinane made no attempt to hide his disappointment and said, 'Justice was not done that day. Anyone looking at the film could see what happened.'

Afterwards, what became possibly even more clear was that springtime brought the best out of one of the best juvenile hurdlers of 1976. Monksfield ran in an apprentice race on the flat at Naas in April and a certain Michael Joseph Kinane, the sixteen-year-old son of his regular rider, was engaged. The partnership won by a head. Eleven days later, Kinane Snr was back in the plate for a valuable handicap hurdle and the horse won easily. One more start on unsuitably hard ground at Punchestown brought a remarkably busy and successful season to a conclusion.

By now the hurdling colt was attracting attention from buyers but Mangan wasn't tempted. For a man who regarded Cheltenham as the centrepiece of racing, Monksfield promised to take him back to Prestbury Park again, maybe even for the Champion itself. Three warm-ups on the flat preceded another busy winter, running mostly in handicaps and conceding vast amounts of weight. In January he ran twice in forty-eight hours. That attracted some criticism that the horse was being over-raced, but McDonogh knew him better than anyone and was aware that the little horse with the beautiful head and appalling action was cut out of granite compared to most of his rivals. The more work he gave him, the more Monksfield came back for extra. A third to

Comedy Of Errors and Master Monday in the Irish Champion was enough to earn a ticket for Cheltenham, but typically he needed one final handicap start to put him right. It had taken fourteen races but Monksfield was ready for the 1977 Champion Hurdle, a race that is still rated the best ever run.

The reigning champion, Night Nurse, was back for more. A pair of future champions, Monksfield and Sea Pigeon, also lined up. But none of them even featured among the first three in the betting. Bird's Nest was heavily supported to 6–4 favourite due to the heavy ground conditions. Master Monday, a 20–1 winner of the Irish Champion, was 11–2 and Dramatist's price was 6–1. Night Nurse was 15–2, Sea Pigeon 10–1 and Monksfield's chances were rated only at 15–1. It reflected a depth of quality that few races at the festival have ever even come close to.

At the third-last, Bird's Nest's stable companion Beacon Light came through to head Night Nurse as Monksfield started to angle to the outside near Sea Pigeon. Fears that Night Nurse wouldn't cope with the going proved unfounded. He was back in front at the second-last. Suddenly Bird's Nest dropped away and it was Dramatist and Monksfield that were the big threats. The trio attacked the last, where a mistake by the Irish star proved decisive. He fought tigerishly up the hill to peg back Night Nurse but the mistake cost him. At the line the winner had stretched his lead to two lengths.

'He's such a great fighter. He showed rare courage to come back like that,' Kinane said. 'But I think if I had taken Night Nurse on earlier I would have beaten him.'

Within a month that theory would become credible to everyone. But Kinane wouldn't be able to prove it himself. On the first day of the Aintree Festival, a fall over the big National fences in the Topham Trophy left Kinane with a painful shoulder injury. The following day McDonogh chose Dessie Hughes, one of Ireland's top jockeys, to replace him for the Aintree Hurdle. Kinane showed up at the track, however, insisting he was fit enough to ride. Hughes remained on board but the incident was the first in a series of cracks in McDonogh's relationship with Kinane. In the race itself Monksfield and Night Nurse raced up the final straight almost together in an epic struggle that still counts among National Hunt racing's greatest. From the last flight Monksfield held a slight advantage, but Night Nurse kept fighting. Fifty yards from the line, Hughes appeared to momentarily look up and stop riding. Night Nurse rallied one final time and had his nose down at the crucial time. A lengthy wait for the judges verdict ended with an announcement of 'dead heat'.

The result confirmed the arrival of a significant new force at the top of the hurdling tree. Ireland's previous Champion Hurdle winner had been the one-eyed Winning Fair back in 1963. Night Nurse might have held the title but he was looking over his shoulder for 1978. In the interim, Monksfield again won the apprentice race he'd landed the previous year and ran a fine fourth under a monster 12st 4lb in a Punchestown handicap.

The build-up to his 1977–78 campaign progressed normally at the start. 'He loves his work,' McDonogh said. 'I've never known him say "no" to work, racing or anything. If he was a human being he would be far too willing to be a trade unionist. He's a very independent person, relishes his work and enjoys his grub and his sleep. Most of all he loves his sleep.'

That was possibly a contributory factor to both McDonogh and Mangan reacting with horror to the idea of gelding Monksfield. 'The horse had such a terrific temperament that the idea did not arise. I did not want to see him cut. He was eminently trainable,' Mangan insisted. McDonogh agreed and said, 'He never bothered looking at mares. He has always had the most superb tempera-ment, and have you ever seen a horse try harder than him?' Nevertheless, the temptation to see him on to stud was always there. In many racing operations, there wouldn't have been much persuasion needed. But Mangan and McDonogh were different. After his 1978 Champion Hurdle victory, John Magnier of the then burgeoning Coolmore empire sent a couple of brief letters requesting he be kept informed of plans for Monksfield. McDonogh didn't bother replying, describing Magnier's approach as rude. 'We don't like the idea of such a fine, brave horse being exploited for monetary gain by a syndicate who might buy him solely for that purpose,' he said at the time. Towards the end of 1977, however, Monksfield didn't look to have much of a future in any activity.

Lameness is a reality for most horses but when one of Monksfield's legs swelled up dramatically it looked long odds that he would make it to Cheltenham that season. His condition deteriorated so badly at one stage there were fears he was going to die. A lot of carefully nurtured condition disappeared and the horse appeared to be in pain. McDonogh despaired and asked for other veterinary opinions. One hit the jackpot. Monksfield was, to all intents and purposes, anaemic. Folic acid was added to his diet and the signs of recovery were dramatic. At around Christmas, the horse that had appeared to be fading away in front of people's eyes was back to his boisterous self. Tentative work-outs suddenly increased into sessions more like the real thing. By the end of January 1978 he was ready for a race. Dessie Hughes wasn't available to ride so Tommy Kinane was back on. Monksfield beat only one home at Navan but considering his situation a couple of months previously it was as good as a win. A month later he tackled top opposition in the Irish Champion Hurdle at Leopardstown, a track where he never seemed entirely happy. But this time he only weakened after the last to finish third to Prominent King and Mr Kildare. Cheltenham was now very much back on the agenda.

Monksfield's work on the run-up to the festival was sensational. McDonogh reckoned he was fitter than ever, so much so the trainer was even moved to bet a hundred pounds on him. Since a fiver was McDonogh's usual stake, it was a confident statement to make on the eve of a race that could define Monksfield's career. Night Nurse was back attempting a hat-trick. Sea Pigeon was there too, as were Master Monday, Dramatist and Bird's Nest. But considering Monksfield had been almost at death's door just three months previously, the 1978 Champion Hurdle turned out to be remarkably straightforward. Night Nurse's attempt to make all was continually harried by the diminutive horse just behind him. After the second-last Kinane made the decisive move of the race, punching Monksfield into the lead with only Sea Pigeon to worry about. A fantastic leap at the last sealed the deal and Ireland had its first Champion Hurdle winner in fifteen years.

Irish winners at Cheltenham always get rapturous receptions, but the one accorded to Monksfield testified to his extraordinary popularity. That never-say-die spirit, allied to the unlikelihood of his success, caught the public imagination. A downside to that was the commensurate rise in public interest, and there was no getting away from the reality that most anything to do with the little horse with the white blaze was now news. That would become a real issue the following season when jockey arrangements threatened briefly to take over the story. But after Cheltenham '78, everything on the racecourse remained relatively straightforward.

Kinane took a heavy fall in the Irish Grand National which ruled him out of Liverpool, so Hughes took over again for Aintree. Once again the evidence that spring sunshine rather than winter cold could transform 'Monkey' was obvious. Despite having to concede 5lb to Night Nurse, he won in what for him was easy fashion, by a couple of lengths. Not content with that, he ran three more times that season. A third victory in the apprentice race was followed by a much more prestigious success in the Saval Beg Stakes, where even quality flat horses and his relative dislike of Leopardstown couldn't prevent another victory. Conceding stones in weight to Royal Gaye proved just beyond him in Haydock's Royal Doulton Handicap Hurdle before he spent another summer out at grass.

While Monksfield indulged his famously prodigious appetite, a new Billywood inmate arrived. Strandfield would prove to be a top-notch novice before the new season was out. As for his famous stable companion, there were the usual series of next-to-impossible tasks set by the handicapper that McDonogh had to tackle in the absence of anything else. With age, though, it was proving even harder to get Monksfield fit. Everything was again geared to Cheltenham and so a winter handicap at Fairyhouse was not a priority. Kinane's instructions were to ride a patient race and the trainer was incensed as the jockey went to the front four hurdles from home. Communication was starting to break down between the young trainer and the jockey fifteen years older than him. McDonogh contacted Mangan and the outcome was that Hughes agreed to be on standby to ride Monksfield in the Champion Hurdle.

Significantly, though, Kinane was still on the horse in his next start when finishing third in the Sweeps Hurdle and was also legged up in the Irish Champion Hurdle. His instructions were again to be patient. But a funereal early pace in the race presented the veteran rider with a dilemma. Stamina was Monksfield's strong point. Turning the race into a sprint finish was completely against him. And yet he knew what had happened before when he took things into his own hands, so he sat and suffered at the back. After the race there was a heated discussion between jockey and trainer outside the weighroom, followed by a regrettable lack of any communication at all. Michael Mangan told McDonogh he would back him if he felt a change of jockey was required, but it was only a week before the Champion Hurdle itself that the trainer told Kinane he'd been jocked off.

Michael Kinane's steely resolution became one of the most recognisable features in world racing over a number of decades. As the old saying goes, he didn't lick that off the ground. His father also possessed a quick tongue and a fondness for an audience. Racing's notorious rumour mill had been alive about McDonogh's decision for days before Tommy Kinane was told. He was bitterly disappointed and wasn't slow about expressing it. For Hughes it was an unenviable situation. The only way he could come out of it ahead was to win the Champion Hurdle, otherwise the 'if only' merchants would have been in their element. Typically, there was another twist to the story to come.

Stranfield had been ridden by Kinane that season and McDonogh magnanimously decided he had done nothing wrong on that horse and left him on for the Supreme Novices Hurdle, the first race on Champion Hurdle day. Kinane rode a brilliant race, coming from last to first to win by five lengths on the 16–1 shot. It was a remarkable success for McDonogh. Only the second horse he had ever brought to Cheltenham had won too. The winning jockey returned to the winner's enclosure shouting, 'I'm not beat yet. They can't keep a good man down.' Plenty in the crowd let it be known they agreed with Kinane, who later said, 'I rode Stranfield in a temper. I wanted to show them they were wrong to take me off Monksfield. I answered my critics. I did it out of temper and I made Stranfield a super horse on the day.'

Dessie Hughes was beaten in the Supreme but then landed the Arkle on Chinrullah. Nevertheless, there was real pressure on the jockey as he prepared for the Champion Hurdle. That didn't stop Monksfield from being backed into 9–4 favourite as Sea Pigeon drifted with Kybo backed into 4–1.

Hughes quickly grabbed the initiative and led down the hill, with Kybo and Sea Pigeon travelling ominously well behind Monksfield. Despite the heavy ground Sea Pigeon travelled supremely well under Jonjo O'Neill. After Kybo's fall two out, Sea Pigeon eased up alongside Monksfield as if he could accelerate away any time he liked. O'Neill certainly thought so and said afterwards, 'I was sure Sea Pigeon would win. I let my fella stride on perhaps half a length into the lead and I was going so easy it was unbelievable. I was just smiling.' Alongside him, Hughes was getting down to some serious work and said, 'I gave Monksfield three smacks before the last and he met it spot-on, went into it faster than Sea Pigeon, and landed back in with a chance, even though Jonjo was going to beat me for the first fifty yards after the hurdle.'

Sea Pigeon didn't fold up the punishing final hill. No horse capable of winning an Ebor Handicap off topweight could be accused of a lack of courage. All that flat class merged into real determination to come out on top. But few if any Cheltenham champions have ever exhibited the terrier-like grit that Monksfield did to win the 1979 Champion Hurdle. Neck outstretched and never flinching at Hughes's vigorous use of the whip, he kept Sea Pigeon to that half-length and then remorselessly gathered his rival back in. The surprise is that at the end he passed the line three parts of a length up, because for the previous two miles everything had been at, or close to, 100 per cent full-on.

'I've never ridden in a race for everything to go so well,' Hughes remarked to Jonathan Powell for his book *Monksfield*.

> Insignificant things can happen that cost you half a length or so but that day everything worked perfectly. He met every hurdle spot-on. If the race was run again I don't think I would have won on him because surely something, however minor, would have gone wrong. He could not have done it perfectly again and only his unique brand of courage enabled him to do it at all.

If that success became the one most associated with Monksfield there are plenty who still believe his best performance of all came the following month back in Liverpool. Conceding 5lb to Sea Pigeon and Kybo, the horse added an unmistakable dash of class to all that courage and for once won without having to go all-out. A Welsh Champion Hurdle victory followed that before another fruitless attempt at Haydock's Royal Doulton Handicap.

Any temptation to retire the horse to stud was understandably shelved with the prospect of a Champion Hurdle hat-trick in the offing. Ultimately those hopes were to be disappointed as Sea Pigeon finally secured the title he had so tantalisingly lost out on in the previous couple of years. Monksfield finished runner-up, but the fact he made it to Cheltenham at all in 1980, and started a 6–5 favourite into the bargain, was surprising considering he was all but written off earlier in the season. He was never at his best during the winter anyway, but there were plenty willing to believe the fairytale was over.

At Navan in December 1979 Monksfield finished last of eight in an amateur hurdle under Ted Walsh, prompting the *Irish Times* to headline: 'Has Monksfield called it a day?' The correspondent recorded beneath McDonogh's view that the ground conditions were awful but added: 'That does not excuse a rank bad performance and it is, I'm afraid, possible that Monksfield is on the way out.'

A month later McDonogh was recorded in defensive form, insisting: 'If he wasn't right, I'd retire him . . . few stallions can run and maintain their form in mid-winter.'

There were plenty of sceptics but they were tucking into sizable portions of crow after Monksfield bounced right back to something like his best in February's Erin Foods Irish Champion Hurdle at Leopardstown. Leading two out, he didn't meet the last perfectly and ultimately failed to concede 9lb to Twinburn. It was, however, a hugely encouraging run with Cheltenham in mind and the little horse was quickly made a 6–4 favourite to win again at the festival. Sea Pigeon was also prominent in the betting but problems with a poisoned foot were not helping his trainer Peter Easterby in the build-up. Bird's Nest was back for another crack at the title, but there were big hopes for a new contender, Pollardstown. There was also a top French horse in Paiute. However, there was nothing in the race to dilute the rising confidence among Irish supporters that Monksfield would emulate Vincent O'Brien's Hatton's Grace, who completed a Champion Hurdle three-in-a-row (1949–51). Distel (1946), Another Flash (1960) and Winning Fair (1963) had been the only other Irish-trained winners of the great race.

Ground conditions at Cheltenham were better than in the previous three years but that didn't concern McDonogh unduly.

His confidence in the little horse remained intact. There were differences, though. The Champion Hurdle would be run on Day One of the festival. More significantly, though, there was also a change in the layout of the big racecourse that placed slightly less emphasis on stamina. For a battler like Monksfield any alteration that made it less of a struggle could hardly be an advantage. But confidence remained sky-high and the Irish star started a 6–5 favourite.

Monksfield went to the front at the fifth hurdle, followed by Pollardstown and Paiute. Sea Pigeon was ridden with typical patience by O'Neill but on the better ground there was a fluency to his challenge that looked ominous for his old rival. Delaying his challenge slightly longer than the previous year, O'Neill brought his 13–2 shot to challenge at the last and this time there was no way back for Monksfield.

Afterwards McDonogh said so much time had been spent getting him right that no way was immediate retirement on the cards. Instead Monksfield went back to Liverpool. Hughes had broken his arm at Cheltenham so Jonjo O'Neill was booked, but despite starting a 1–2 favourite to secure an Aintree Hurdle four-in-a-row, Monksfield again had to settle for second, this time behind Pollardstown. One final crack at Haydock's Royal Doulton became the plan, but in between the former champion was kept typically busy. An amateur hurdle at Down Royal provided Monksfield with what proved to be the final victory of his career under the trainer's wife, Helen. It felt an appropriate touch for a horse that had transformed the lives of the McDonogh family. The winning jockey appeared game to take the reins too at Haydock, but instead that provided another nicely symmetrical touch. Tommy Kinane was engaged and, although Monksfield finished unplaced, the sight of the teak-tough little stallion and his veteran jockey looked to provide the story with an appropriate full-stop.

It being Monksfield, of course, such neatness came with a twist. He went on to a stud career, enjoying rewards for his racing excellence denied to the vast majority of jump champions. But the little horse was always a bit different. Ultimately his glory was in illustrating how different doesn't automatically mean the same thing as wrong.

Nijinsky

On a cold February day in 1965, a young stallion attempted for the first time to have sex. He pranced nervously into a barn in the Canadian province of Ontario and was met with a mare a full hand higher than his own diminutive 15st 1lb. After a number of failed attempts to do the deed she became fed up and lashed out with her back legs, catching the novice lothario in the ribs. No doubt there have been more unhappy cherry-popping attempts in the history of the world, but it was still an inauspicious start. A couple of days later, though, the engineering dilemma presented by a tall mare and a small stallion was solved by the simple expedient of digging a shallow pit into which she could be backed.

It would be nice to neatly conclude the story with a happy ending. In fact the result of their brief union was a dead foal. But a year later the mare, Flaming Page, returned again to meet her by now considerably more experienced partner, whose name was to become the most famous in the history of the bloodstock industry – Northern Dancer. In 1967 their foal was born, a strapping bay with a heart-shaped splodge on his forehead that only hinted at the romance that would accumulate around his own name.

Three years later, on the other side of the Atlantic, Nijinsky became the popular embodiment of what we expect a top-class thoroughbred to be. Highly strung but physically magnificent, the colt that became the first winner of the English Triple Crown in thirty-five years combined fragility with a hauteur that could make even the most powerful human feel just a little more insignificant. For much of his career he came to represent an ideal, that of the perfect, unbeatable racehorse, possessed of enough speed and stamina to make even the possibility of defeat seem ridiculous. So much so that when defeat did eventually come, there were any number of reasons and excuses reached for as to why it had. No one, it seemed, wanted to tarnish the ideal in their heads.

Of course, there was also the name and the emotional baggage that came with it. Vaslav Nijinsky was a Russian who considered himself Polish. After being diagnosed with schizophrenia he spent years in and out of asylums and psychiatric hospitals. It was a largely unhappy life that ended in 1950 at the age of sixty. But for a few years leading up to the Great War, Vaslav Nijinsky was the most exciting ballet dancer the world had ever seen. Prodigious leaps seemed to defy gravitational laws and technical virtuosity merged seamlessly with intense characterisation. Les Ballets Russes, the company set up by the producer Sergei Diaghilev, who was also Nijinsky's lover for a time, toured Western Europe as well as North and South America to ecstatic reviews. The name Nijinsky became synonymous with grace, style and a hint of dangerous unpredictability that seemed to chime perfectly with his reported deathbed prediction that he would be reincarnated as a thoroughbred racehorse.

Saddling horses with grandiose names can backfire spec-tacularly. There have been Napoleons who couldn't have caught a cold on St Helena, Alexanders that wouldn't conquer their way out of a paper bag and Platos whose relationship with the winning post was purely philosophical. However, never has a name been as evocatively appropriate as the one given to Flaming Page's 1967 foal.

When it comes to horses it is usually wise to be wary of those who claim to have known all along there was something different about an animal. But with the horse that would become Nijinsky, there really did seem to be something about him from the start. In Canadian terms he was thoroughbred royalty. Both his parents had won the Queen's Plate, Canada's most prestigious prize. Northern Dancer's impact, though, had also stretched to the US, where he won both the Kentucky Derby and the Preakness before failing to land the Triple Crown in 1964's Belmont. Retired to owner Edward P. Taylor's Windfields Farm in Ontario, Northern Dancer's physical stature was initially held against him by breeders, just as it had been by many racing experts. He overcame that prejudice with aplomb. The little bay with the broad sash became the most important sire of the twentieth century, transformed the face of world breeding and left a legacy that will remain for as long as man still gets a thrill out of finding out which horse can run faster.

In 1968 the first inkling that Northern Dancer might be an exceptional stallion was starting to emerge. With Flaming Page for a dam, the strikingly handsome yearling being prepared for the Canadian Thoroughbred Horse Society Sale was always going to be a catch for North American buyers. But the youngster's fate was settled a month before that sale when a famous visitor arrived at Windfields Farm.

Vincent O'Brien had just saddled Sir Ivor to win the Epsom Derby, confirmation that the Irish trainer's gift with horses had safely negotiated the leap from National Hunt to top-flight international racing. Already adept at cultivating rich American owners, O'Brien was never likely to spurn the opportunity to train for the enormously wealthy industrialist, Charles Engelhard. With horses in England, France, the US and South Africa, the rotund Coca-Cola-swigging product of Princeton and America's social elite had enjoyed significant success with sons of the great Italian horse, Ribot, and asked O'Brien to check out a Ribot yearling at

Windfields with a view to buying him. The Irishman flew to Toronto solely to see the Ribot colt, which meant it was something of a let-down when the horse turned out to have a crooked foreleg. But another yearling on the farm caught the visitor's eye in a big way. O'Brien recommended Engelhard buy him and the owner promised to send a representative to the sale. That startling first impression made by the yearling can be gauged by the amount of fretting that went on in Tipperary while, 4,000 miles away, a few seconds of bidding resulted in racing never being quite the same again.

'His man was entirely inexperienced where the buying of horses was concerned. So I was worried he might make some slip-up and I'd lose the horse,' O'Brien remembered. 'But we got him anyway. He cost Can$84,000, a Canadian record.'

The reverberations of that winning bid are still being felt around the racing world. When Northern Dancer died in 1990 it was estimated that up to 75 per cent of the globe's thoroughbred population had his blood in their veins. Such an impact is backed up by statistics that at one stage of the finance-crazed 1980s his cover nominations were changing hands for a million dollars each. Over 23 seasons, Northern Dancer fathered almost 700 registered foals, 80 per cent of which ran, and of those 80 per cent four-fifths were winners; 146 were Stakes winners and 26 were champions. When he was a veteran of twenty years old, the syndicate that owned him turned down a $40 million offer to buy him. Confined to books of little more than forty mares a year, produce that came on offer at public auction became collector's items. That in turn produced a series of bidding wars in the 1980s that provoked prices still unsurpassed today, and which resulted in a shift of racing excellence back across the Atlantic to a European turf scene transformed for ever by the influence of the little Canadian dirt horse.

The catalyst for such a global phenomenon was Nijinsky, and O'Brien's first impression of him. His racing record blended seamlessly into a subsequent career as a seminal stallion influence himself. Even other legendary sons of Northern Dancer that produced dynasties of their own, such as Danzig, Lyphard and Nureyev, couldn't surpass Nijinsky as a genetic influence. But so much revolved around what could have been an abortive trip to Toronto. O'Brien liked to explain what he was looking for in a young horse by talking of 'a look of eagles', an outlook that spoke of a superiority that could be transferred to the track. No other son of Northern Dancer had it more than Nijinsky.

The great horse's distinctiveness was there from the start. He was anything but the 'Northern Dancer type' that came to be so famous. Instead of the elegant, medium-sized horses that dominated Europe's racecourses in the 1980s, Nijinsky was a massive 16.3-hands lump of a horse that managed to combine class with a physicality that dwarfed much of his racing opposition. Later at stud he produced his own 'type', rangy horses that could be tricky temperamentally but always carried the potential for brilliance. Very much his own character, he was always 'treated as something special' when he arrived at O'Brien's Ballydoyle stables in the winter of 1968. It was that individuality that also threatened to scupper his career before it had even started. Hot-headed impatience is often indulged in the artistic world but the new Nijinsky often seemed to be too impatient and wilful for his own good.

Those who don't 'get' racing often dismiss it as barely being a sport at all. 'It's all about the horse' is the argument and of course ultimately it is. Talent can't be injected into an animal, although the scurrilous have been tempted for centuries to try. There is also no way for a tiny person in colourful silks to make half a tonne of thoroughbred do anything if it really doesn't want to. Often when it comes to equine talent, the best contribution humans can make is to stay out of the way and simply let it bloom. The hoary old chestnut about nobody being able to make a horse but plenty able to break one is still as relevant today as it ever was. But it was human perseverance and intuition that allowed Nijinsky to turn into the phenomenon he became. Left to his own devices all that talent could have dissolved into a pool of sweaty anxiety, the result of a mind soured against what hundreds of years of genetics encouraged him to do.

'Early on as a two-year-old he was in two minds about the whole thing,' O'Brien remembered. 'If I hadn't had really first-class horsemen to ride him I don't believe we ever could have succeeded with him. Also I think if he had been trained on public training grounds like Newmarket or the Curragh he could easily have gone the wrong way.'

O'Brien's habit of referring to his stable staff as 'boys' was a habit of its time but it required real men to handle Nijinsky. Johnny Brabston and Danny O'Sullivan were never household names. The pair were ex-jump jockeys but the glamour of the racecourse turned instead into the daily grind of stable work. In rural Co. Tipperary a job of any kind was valuable and there was always the not inconsiderable plus at Ballydoyle of going to work at one of the most beautiful training establishments anywhere in the world. There was also the chance every year of being around an exceptional athlete.

But working with horses at the coalface is not a job for the faint-hearted. Outside in all weathers, handling horseflesh that is capable of unintentionally hurting you, never mind intentionally, and always bobbing along in a rigidly hierarchical system that often requires sensitivity of any kind to be parked outside the gate. Yet there are thousands around the world who can't imagine any better way to make a living.

Even at Ballydoyle, where working conditions were good, that living was hardly high-on-the-hog, but the work done by O'Brien's staff with Nijinsky was priceless. The trainer himself acknowledged the horsemanship that allowed the big headstrong colt to relax into doing the job he was bred for — 'if it were not for two very capable work riders, Johnny Brabston and Danny O'Sullivan, Nijinsky could easily have been spoiled. They had the strength to handle him and the patience not to knock him about.'

Vincent Rossiter was a fixture at Ballydoyle from 1962, riding work on all of O'Brien's great champions and securing a number of high-profile winners on the track over the years. He too experienced Nijinsky on the gallops.

'He was such a good mover, very athletic,' he says. 'He could be strong, but not over-keen. Once you got him onto the gallop he was no problem. It was only when he got to April/May of his two-year-old career that he really became a handful. He got fresh, and stronger, and bolder. That used to make him rear up or stop sometimes. Sometimes he wouldn't go down the gallop. I remember Maurice Callaghan, the head man, used to follow him down on a bike, or a motorbike, with a long-tom, just to give him a clip on the heels.

'He was no problem in his box. He had a good lad, William Burke. There might be a nip sometimes but he wasn't going around with his mouth open like you might think. And he was genuine. He was just so good that he'd get above himself. That's why Vincent ran him so much as a two-year-old.'

It's fascinating now to see pictures of Nijinsky on the gallops, all the flamboyant power and grace kept under control by Brabston perched on his back, bareheaded and without a back protector or a health and safety instruction leaflet in sight.

Overseeing it all, however, was O'Brien, the quiet Cork man whose abilities with horses were close enough to genius as makes no difference. By the late 1960s he was firmly established as one of the world's great flat trainers, having only finally left behind a stunningly successful National Hunt career just over a decade before. There are still plenty who maintain that that famous hat-trick of Aintree Grand National victories with three different horses — Early Mist, Royal Tan and Quare Times — remains the summit of training achievement. And in such a short period of time it ranks right up there. But the residue of what O'Brien did on the flat transformed an entire industry, not just in Ireland but worldwide. It was he who twigged the force Northern Dancer would become and he who masterminded the careers of so many of his sons, who in turn altered the face of the bloodstock world forever. What O'Brien never forgot, though, was that it all came down to each individual animal and what was required to get the best out of it. It's impossible to ignore on any piece of film how he is constantly looking at the horses, seeing in even the tiniest detail something only he could imagine using to try and make a difference. In interviews the proof that such gifts were intuitive and explanation-proof came in often haltingly shy answers that revealed little or nothing; so much came down to that maddeningly imprecise word 'feel'.

The feel Nijinsky gave his riders on the gallops that spring was enough for his name to be on the lips of those in the know even before his racecourse debut at the Curragh at the start of July. He could still be desperately impatient and was usually worked alone ahead of his stable companions. But the tendency to rear up was going away and once he was galloping it was noticeable how he settled and actually seemed to stop sweating. Nijinksy easily won first time up and returned to the Curragh to also land the Railway, Anglesey and Beresford Stakes. The latter race was run over a mile on soft ground and it was the first time Nijinsky had more than a stroll on his hands. Decies, who would become an Irish Guineas winner the following year, made him work for it. Any serious mental fragility rather than just plain edginess could have been uncovered by such an experience but, significantly, O'Brien didn't hesitate to send Nijinsky to Newmarket for his final two-year-old start in the Dewhurst Stakes. The outcome was a hugely impressive four-length success. Liam Ward had ridden Nijinsky in Ireland but Lester Piggott rode the colt for the first time in the Dewhurst and the new partnership scythed through the field in imperious fashion.

They seemed made for each other, Piggott and Nijinsky. One

eminently combustible, the other cocooned in his own socially awkward, coldly focused world-view which consisted of little else but getting to the finishing post first. It didn't hurt that they looked great together. Piggott's arched figure on a horse, perched precariously before uncoiling into an elemental force-of-will in a tight finish, seemed to hawkishly prey on his rivals. Nijinsky's push-button acceleration was tailor-made for those lethal final bursts that Piggott loved to deliver. Never one for even the faintest glimmer of emotional incontinence, the rider nevertheless left Newmarket after the Dewhurst, convinced he had just ridden his greatest prospect ever. Since illustrious names like Crepello, Petite Etoile and Sir Ivor already figured on Piggott's CV, it was clear that Nijinsky was something else again.

Afterwards O'Brien put the winter classics favourite into a paddock every day to gain some R and R before the winter began. The few weeks of simple grazing with a pal seemed to work wonders for the big colt. He relaxed noticeably more when ridden out and that habit of rearing up quietly stopped. The signs for an epoch-making 1970 were all in place during the spring. Nijinsky thrived, both physically and mentally. No one could ever accuse him of being a soft touch. But there was no getting away from how impressive his work became. He reappeared on the racecourse when travelling to the Curragh again for the Gladness Stakes. It turned into a routine victory that set him up perfectly for the 2,000 Guineas.

Rarely if ever has a classic appeared to be more predictable. The *Sporting Life* headline captured the general mood on the day of the race when asking: 'Who's Going To Be Second To Nijinsky?' He started the hottest Guineas favourite for thirty-six years. Timeform noted: 'In the paddock he outclassed his rivals as seldom a classic field can have been outclassed before.' It was the same in the race itself. Piggott had Nijinsky closer to the pace than many thought he would and travelling down to the bushes after the three-furlong pole they were in third, sitting on Yellow God's flank. Outside the furlong pole, Piggott bustled up the favourite who went two and a half lengths clear of Yellow God and Roi Soleil to win comfortably.

If the Guineas run-in was smooth in every respect, it was a very different story for Epsom. Five days before the Derby, O'Brien rushed Nijinsky to Sandown racecourse on the outskirts of London due to an outbreak of coughing in Ballydoyle. The move was made under intense secrecy, such was the concern about the classic favourite getting nobbled. A couple of days before the race, he was moved to Epsom; he was allowed to lob around to get a feel of the unique roller-coaster track on the day before the Derby. Everything seemed normal after the light piece of work but as Nijinsky was being rubbed down in his box afterwards, he started to sweat and paw the ground. Then he lay down. They were the unmistakable signs of colic.

Since horses can't vomit, stomach obstructions can be extremely dangerous and sometimes fatal. Anyone who has spent any time working with horses can spot the signals immediately but often even surgery isn't enough to save the victim. However, some horses are prone to little bouts of colic and recover quickly on their own. That the Derby favourite was behaving like this on the eve of the race was the worst nightmare for any trainer. O'Brien was determined to not let word of this potential disaster out until he had some definitive news. Vets were consulted. If it was just a twinge, then the Derby attempt would still be on. But if it got worse the priority would be to save the horse. For everyone watching, the hour and a half it took to establish that Nijinsky would be all right must have seemed like an eternity. Some grass was eventually gathered and offered to the patient. When he ate it, the exclamations of relief alone might have tipped the outside world off. As it was, nobody else knew until after the race.

Hindsight has allowed the theory to take root that Nijinsky was way superior to a very average crop of three-year-olds in 1970. It is correct that some of his rivals didn't set the world alight after running into him but before that year's Epsom Derby the general consensus was that it would be a vintage renewal. So much so that Nijinsky would start odds against (11–8) for the first time in his career. The giant chestnut Gyr was rated so good by the legendary French trainer Etienne Pollet that he postponed his retirement to handle his classic campaign. And Pollet had steered Gyr's sire, Sea Bird, through the 1965 season. Gyr, he told friends, would be invincible at Epsom. Another French star made the trip too. Stintino had landed the Prix Lupin in impressive fashion on his previous start. The main British defence looked to come from Approval while Meadowville also came into some calculations. Anticipation was huge as the stalls opened. Even years later, O'Brien would admit, 'Nijinsky's Derby victory is probably the most treasured memory I have.'

Cry Baby cut out the running, closely followed by Approval and Gyr with Piggott settling Nijinsky in midfield. The Irish superstar was perfectly relaxed. In fact he was taking things too leisurely. Around Tattenham Corner and into the straight, Joe Mercer secured a dream run through the field on Great Wall which took him into the lead alongside Gyr. On the outside Stintino made an ominous move that took him past Nijinsky, who momentarily looked to be in trouble. 'He'd got too relaxed so I had to give him a couple,' Piggott remembered. The response was instantaneous. Pre-race stamina doubts that a North American-bred son of a horse that failed to stay the mile-and-a-half Belmont disappeared as all that acceleration came to the fore. Nijinsky cut through a gap between his two French rivals and swept past the post as if only just joining in the race. Despite the ease of the victory, the winner's time only just missed out on the 1936 hand-clocked course record.

A sport and industry always keen to applaud a new superstar tore off its sceptical gloves and pondered if Nijinsky might be the best ever seen. Just two years earlier Sir Ivor had completed the Guineas–Derby double too but his reputation suffered after four subsequent defeats, including in the Irish Derby, Eclipse and Arc de

Triomphe. It was only five years since Sea Bird had sauntered to the Derby and then beat a vintage field in the Arc. And yet, nothing had ever made an impression like Nijinsky. Invulnerability is a mistaken concept when it comes to something as fragile as a thoroughbred but during the summer of 1970, the son of Northern Dancer and Flaming Page looked as close to it as any horse ever has.

Back at the Curragh for the Irish Derby, even a recurrence of the anxious sweating in the preliminaries that sometimes happened at home couldn't stop him winning easily. Just as with Sir Ivor, O'Brien's jockey in Ireland, Liam Ward, was on board Nijinsky. The Irishman had fielded some stick for getting beaten on Sir Ivor but this time there were no concerns.

Ward later recalled to the *Racing Post*:

I was never beaten on Nijinsky and winning the Irish Derby on him was probably my greatest day as a jockey. Saying I was never beaten on him isn't meant to be a boast. Every time I rode him he was a steering job. He was an amazing horse who would blow Vincent's sprinters out of the way on the gallops. His best trip was probably a mile and a quarter and his sheer class enabled him to get a mile and a half.

I remember being scared going to the start of the Irish Derby as he sweated up a lot. When I got to the start, Michael Kauntze, who was assistant to Vincent at the time, was there and he could see I was worried. He told me I needn't be as Nijinsky had done the same at Epsom. He was right and by the time I pulled him up after the race there was hardly a drop of sweat on him.

Riding him was easy. He would stand in the stalls like a disinterested donkey and when the stalls opened he would drop the bridle. You could put him anywhere you wanted in a race.

It was that ability to cruise off any sort of pace, and then quicken off it, that so excited racing fans. If anything Nijinsky seemed to be getting better, a hardly unreasonable development as he matured even further into that magnificent frame. Next up for him was the King George at Ascot and his first meeting with older horses. He was the only three-year-old against Blakeney, the previous year's Derby hero, and the winners of the French Oaks and the Washington International. In truth it wasn't a vintage King George field. But the great race has never been won easier. Piggott hardly had to move as Nijinsky sauntered disdainfully past Blakeney to win with any amount in hand. Afterwards there was something of a collector's item as O'Brien was pictured leading Nijinsky back in. It was something he rarely if ever did and it wasn't to be repeated until 1993 when he led back College Chapel, his last Royal Ascot winner, ridden by Piggott. That he did it after such a remarkable King George display seemed only apt for such a special talent.

The King George was the pinnacle of Nijinsky's career. It shouldn't have been, but with horses if the racecourse doesn't get the better of you then any number of other imponderables can. With Nijinsky it was ringworm. Within a week of coming back from Ascot a bout of the fungal skin infection hit him hard. Some of his hair fell out. It wasn't possible to put a saddle on him. As well as being irksome for the patient, it meant a serious hold-up in his work. And then Charles Engelhard let it be known he would love it if his star could attempt to become the first since Bahram in 1935 to complete the English Triple Crown.

In the last three decades, the prestige of the one mile and three furlong St Leger, the oldest classic of all, has gradually declined to where it has become almost a black mark against any horse's breeding prospects. Potential National Hunt stallions now win the Leger, something of little or no use at the high end of the inter - national bloodstock market. When Sea The Stars landed the Guineas–Derby double in 2009, only the most pea-green innocents even considered for a moment he might try and emulate Nijinsky by going for the Leger too. But even in 1970, there was general surprise that the Doncaster classic would be used as a warm-up for the following month's Prix de l'Arc de Triomphe. The old adage about the fastest horse winning the Guineas, the luckiest the Derby and the best landing the Leger seemed quaint even then. A horse with the necessary speed to win the Guineas would have to be exceptional indeed to also last out in a fourteen-furlong slog. But the owner pays the bills and O'Brien felt Nijinsky needed a run before Longchamp anyway. The problem was that the ringworm bout had left him short of work.

Nijinsky won the Leger, all right, but it wasn't as easy as he and Piggott made it look. On the surface everything seemed as smooth as ever. Inside the final two furlongs the partnership cruised past Politico and Piggott barely had to nudge Nijinsky to repel his old rival Meadowville and pass the post pulling up. Everything seemed set for a note-perfect career finale a month later in the Arc. However, the Leger had taken its toll. Nijinsky lost a lot more weight than normal after the race. A Triple Crown had been secured but in European racing no race means more than the Arc and O'Brien fretted that the Leger had compromised his chances of getting to Paris in A1 shape.

The Leger got some of the blame for Nijinsky's Arc defeat. So did the French. Piggott got most of it, though, and there was even a tincture left over for the horse himself. Decades later it seems safe to say that it was that unfortunate case of ringworm that ulti-mately removed some of the lustre from that momentous season. Just a couple of months after seeing his hair fall out, and with a classic win in the interim, it was a huge ask for the charismatic colt to land Europe's all-aged highlight. But he still came agonisingly close to pulling it off.

O'Brien was in no doubt about Piggott's culpability. Beforehand he instructed his jockey, 'The records show that the winner of the Arc invariably holds a prominent position throughout the race. You must lie up. Few horses further back than fourth turning into the straight go on to win the Arc.' With supreme confidence, Piggott replied, 'I don't care if there are one hundred horses in front of me!'

Before the race there was the not inconsiderable job for the Ballydoyle team of keeping Nijinsky cool in the face of feverish interest from the Longchamp crowd. Access to the pre-parade ring, and even the stable yard, is a much looser affair in France than in Britain or Ireland and it seemed every Parisian turfiste was anxious to get a look at or snap a picture of the unbeaten Irish phenomenon. The parade-ring atmosphere fairly hummed and Nijinsky's fragile nerves started to fray, though he settled down once out on the track and in the race itself was typically professional.

At that time Piggott's Arc pedigree was questionable. He had never won the race but had managed to get Park Top beaten by Levmoss the year before. In 1968 he also had to settle for the runner-up spot on Sir Ivor. Any anxiety, however, was well hidden. Nijinsky turned into the straight with most of the field in front of him.

O'Brien went to his grave still fuming that Piggott gave the horse too much to do but view the race again and despite the grainy black-and-white pictures, it doesn't appear that Nijinsky was given the enormous amount of ground to make up that the legend might suggest. Sassafras is a few lengths in front of him a furlong and a half out but Piggott angles out and gets to him quickly. Half a furlong out and Nijinsky looks sure to overhaul the French Derby winner. He could even momentarily have got his head in front, depending on the camera angle, but then came the unexpected. Piggott pulled his whip through to his right hand and Nijinsky ducked left. It was too late to correct the move and Piggott threw everything into one last desperate lunge. It didn't come off. The unbeatable champion was only second.

The blame game afterwards was played out against a backdrop of bitter disappointment that months later still had O'Brien bitterly criticising his jockey. Significantly, though, a strict reading of the formbook suggested Nijinsky's Arc performance was right up there with anything else he produced in his career. Gyr was fourth at Longchamp, beaten further than he was at Epsom. Piggott's view, years later, was characteristically wry but also succinct.

'The St Leger left its mark,' he reflected in the *Observer*.

> He didn't have the same feel at Longchamp. In the straight Sassafras was in the lead and I went after him. We got to the front 100 yards out, but then he went a bit to the left – he hadn't done it before – and Sassafras got back up on the line. At the time it was a catastrophe! Seriously, though, it was disappointing. He was unbeaten in 12 races. Everybody expected so much. The public were disappointed, but so was I. We all wanted him to win and it hurt.

Piggott was a famously hard man in the saddle and typically valued toughness in the many champions he rode through the decades. But despite the mental fragility that haunted the 1970 Triple Crown hero, he still declared in the same *Observer* interview:

> In terms of raw ability, Nijinsky was probably the best. He got nervous before his races, and I was always anxious until he had jumped out of the stalls. Then he'd drop the bit and you could put him anywhere in a race. Soon after the King George he got ringworm, and ran in the St Leger, probably before he'd really got over it. It was the Triple Crown and no horse had landed it since Bahram in 1935, so you can understand why they wanted him to go. He won all right, but not as easily as people thought.

In the circumstances it was hardly surprising that Nijinsky was given a final chance to end his career on a winning note in Newmarket's Champion Stakes. The opposition was demonstrably inferior and the colt hadn't lost much weight despite the exertions of his trip to France. Above all, it would allow him to bow out on a positive note. The Arc would always be a regret but Newmarket provided a more appropriate way for the great horse to end his racing career. It seemed a formality, but the task that O'Brien and his team always had in controlling Nijinsky's temperament became all too obvious before the race. On the way out of the parade ring, an outburst of cheering from an admiring public, as well the attentions of a phalanx of photographers, sent the colt over the edge. Before he cantered to the start he seemed to be physically trembling. Even a mile and a quarter away at the start, people milled around the horse before he was loaded into the stalls. Nijinsky seemed only a shell of the great horse he'd been in the summer. Lorenzaccio made all the running to beat him.

'I saw on the film afterwards that he was a sorry sight,' O'Brien recalled. 'It was a sad day, really dreadful.'

It was a downbeat end but the impact of the great horse, even beyond racing, was considerable. A documentary film – *A Horse Called Nijinsky* – was written and directed by Jo Durden-Smith and released in 1972. The narration was provided by the legendary Hollywood actor-director Orson Welles. At the time it was unheard of for a racehorse to receive such highbrow treatment but, as had been repeatedly proved, this was no ordinary racehorse. At the end of the year, the team around Nijinsky received the BBC Sports Personality of the Year Team Award. Nijinsky's career had pushed so many evocative buttons for racing fans that his name is still a byword for excellence. Mick Kinane recalled travelling back after winning the 1993 Epsom Derby on Commander In Chief for one ride that evening at the Curragh on a 1–4 favourite. The horse duly went to the lead, only to be passed by a newcomer who, Kinane exclaimed, '. . . went by me like Nijinsky!' It wasn't the first time, and it certainly won't be the last, that somebody reaches for such a simile. Even a young jockey like William Buick, born almost two decades after the Triple Crown, said after winning the 2010

Leger on Arctic Cosmos: 'I knew I was always going to hold on –
unless Nijinsky came in from behind!'

But if it was on the racetrack that the Nijinsky legend was made,
then his influence stretches far beyond that. Immediately after the
Champion Stakes an attempt was made to organise a syndicate
that would keep the horse in Europe for a stallion career.
Engelhard, however, was determined to breed his own mares to
him in America and so a deal, which valued Nijinsky at $5.5
million, was set up for him to stand at Claiborne Stud in Kentucky.

It would have been almost shocking if Nijinsky hadn't been a
success at stud and sure enough he carved out his own dynasty,
part of the Northern Dancer legacy but still distinctive. He
stamped his stock with size and quality and if some of them could
be difficult to handle, then it was a small price to pay for the chance
to tap into genuine brilliance that could always turn up some-
where. A champion sire, Nijinsky fathered 156 individual Stakes
winners and became a significant broodmare sire whose influence
still continues in breeding lines throughout the world. Most
notable of all, though, he equalled Northern Dancer's record of
siring three winners of the Epsom Derby – Golden Fleece (1982),
Shahrastani (1986) and Lammtarra (1995.)

Mainly an influence for turf racing, Nijinsky outdid Northern
Dancer by also siring the 1986 Kentucky Derby winner Ferdinand,
a top-class dirt performer who wound up also landing the Breeders
Cup Classic. Ferdinand entered stud in the US but was sold on to
Japan where he met a regrettable end, being sent to a slaughter -
house without any notification being given to any of his former
connections. The outrage that greeted this news provoked a series
of measures in America designed to protect and care for retired
thoroughbreds.

The most exciting of Nijinsky's sons to enter stud was probably
Golden Fleece, whose racing career was brought to a premature
end by injury after he maintained a perfect four-from-four record
at Epsom. The giant colt overcame claustrophobic tendencies, as

well as a boisterous temperament, and was highly rated by Vincent O'Brien, for whom Golden Fleece was a sixth and final Epsom Derby winner. Instead of retiring to stud in America he was kept in Ireland at Coolmore, only to suffer a tragically premature death in 1984.

Other star racing performers that failed to shine at stud included Shadeed and Royal Academy. Probably the best of Nijinsky's sons as a stallion was Caerleon, a top-flight racehorse in 1983 for O'Brien. The son of the Round Table mare Foreseer won the French Derby and the York International before retiring to Coolmore where he was champion sire in Britain and Ireland both in 1988 and 1991. The best of his progeny was the outstanding dual Derby and King George winner Generous. He died in 1998, aged eighteen.

Even among the equine nobility that lived at Claiborne, Nijinsky managed to stand out. That was no mean feat, since the farm is possibly the most famous and distinguished in the American thoroughbred industry and a contemporary of Nijinsky's at Claiborne was the great US Triple Crown champion, Secretariat. The latter was understandably the centre of attention for home visitors to the farm outside Paris, Kentucky. But Nijinsky was usually the first stop for European callers. They included Queen Elizabeth II, who visited the farm twice. Nijinsky lived until April 1992 when, at the age of 25, he was put down after three years of battling the hoof disease laminitis. At the end, the onset of the circulatory disease phlebitis made the decision to end his life inevitable.

Claiborne's burial ground near the farm office is the final resting place of some of the most illustrious names in thoroughbred history. Already there before 1992 were the champion sires Buckpasser, Nasrullah, Bold Ruler and Round Table. Nijinsky's final resting place is exclusive by any standards. He is buried between the Kentucky Derby winner Riva Ridge and the legendary sire Mr Prospector. Just a few feet from his headstone is the one for Secretariat.

England's last Triple Crown winner was registered in the USA as Nijinsky II. However, just like the famous dancer he was named after, there could never be any mistaking him. All his life he continued to represent an ideal of what the thoroughbred is. For a couple of days in October 1970, that mantle of perfection slipped a little, but perfection is illusory anyway. It's enough that there had been another couple of days earlier that year when the illusion seemed very real indeed.

Dawn Run

Sport is littered with those who looked to have every attribute necessary to succeed, bar perhaps the most important of all. The motivational industry has made a packet out of trying to define 'will to win', trite phrases tumbling over one another in a futile attempt to compress an unfathomable part of an individual spirit into a snappy one-liner.

Dawn Run didn't have many of the more obvious weapons in her armoury. For one thing, as a mare, she was a rare female able to compete against the best males in the brutally hard world of National Hunt racing. On the flat, it is much more common to have champion fillies at the very top level. Over jumps, though, there is no doubt that Dawn Run was unique, by general consensus the best mare ever to race, and still the only horse of either gender to bring off the greatest double in jumping history.

There will be those who point to Golden Miller's Gold Cup-Grand National double and quibble with such a statement. That 1935 achievement remains the Holy Grail of steeplechasing, but Dawn Run's successes in the 1984 Champion Hurdle and 1986 Cheltenham Gold Cup crossed a disciplinary divide.

Arkle was an ordinary horse over hurdles. Night Nurse, rated in some quarters as the greatest hurdler of all, could finish only second in the Gold Cup. It's akin to the difference between rugby union and rugby league: they both involve an oval ball, fierce tackling and a try line, yet for all their similarities they remain resolutely different. The nearest racing analogy is between running on turf and dirt. The basic requirement to run fast is still the same and yet how many have been able to show up with their A-game on both? Some shrewd veteran hardboots in America still believe the great Triple Crown champion Secretariat was actually better on grass than on dirt but there remains a sense that 'Big Red' wasn't so much foaled as anointed by the racing gods. Dawn Run's enduring appeal, however, lies in her apparent ordinariness.

A tall, angular individual who almost died as a foal, Dawn Run had never stood out as a youngster. She wasn't one of those talents whose potential was immediately obvious. The gallops at Paddy Mullins's yard in Co. Kilkenny never had to be treated for scorch marks after Dawn Run worked. As with the vast majority of National Hunt mares, success could have been measured in a victory or two before being packed off to the paddocks to breed, hopefully producing male offspring that could be profitably sold on.

But this one was different. Dawn Run was beaten twice before winning her first race but it quickly became obvious that she had ability. What made her special, though, was that indefinable and unidentifiable ability to combine talent with, not so much will to win, but a hatred of losing. Max Schmeling, the legendary German boxer, when asked to explain why he won came up with the beautifully succinct explanation: 'Because I didn't want to lose.'

It's that hatred of giving best to an opponent, rather than any pseudo-psychological stuff about will to win, that best sums up those rare equine athletes who appear to want to win more than others. By definition, Dawn Run didn't know where the finishing line was better than any other horse, or the importance of what-ever race she was running in, or the depth of public sentiment tailing her every step. What she had in bucketfuls was the instinct to be ahead of the herd and in charge.

Observers of wild horses believe that herds are dominated by 'boss mares' rather than the old cliché of the swaggering, snorting stallion. And those mares lead from the front. It isn't so quixotic to reckon on a genetic quirk inside Dawn Run that made her an equine Boadicea, determined to lead at all costs.

It's certainly the way she expressed herself on Europe's racecourses; from the front, there to be shot at and just daring anything to try and get past her. Of course, the most memorable race of her career, and indeed one of the most remarkable in racing history, was when not just one, but two opponents managed to overhaul Dawn Run before the final fence of that fateful Gold Cup. It's hard to think of any other horse that could have retrieved the situation from where she was. Three years later Desert Orchid rallied too in the Gold Cup, but he had a glorified handicapper to overhaul. Dawn Run had the previous year's blue riband winner Forgive N'Forget as well as a triple King George champion in Wayward Lad ahead of her. However in possibly the most emotion-wringing run-in of all time, that dogged refusal to lose shone greater than ever before.

Even now it's hard to credit that Dawn Run does manage to get back up. Between the final two fences, her goose didn't look so much cooked as pulleted, plucked and pooped. Jonjo O'Neill is working overtime, the mare underneath him apparently extend - ing every sinew, neck stretched out, ears flat back. And yet, despite having three lengths to make up on Wayward Lad, she gets back up. It seems unachievable but the gap from impossible to possible is bridged by that famously raw, dogged, spit-in-your-eye deter - mination. As O'Neill punched the air passing the post, there were plenty at Cheltenham who couldn't believe what they were seeing. And yet they had to believe. It had just happened in front of their eyes.

'Incredible' was the following day's headline summary in the usually determinedly sober *Irish Times*: hard to believe, then, that within three months Dawn Run was dead, that resolute neck broken in a fall in Paris, her carcass destined for a French abattoir amid layers of rancour and recrimination strewn among a legacy that still reverberates today.

It's hardly a fate she deserved but it remains a reality that the peaks of National Hunt racing are so rarefied precisely because the lows can be so dreadful. Dawn Run's story is also the sort of multidimensional one that rules out any attempts to over-sentimentalise it. Mind you, if sentiment is your game, the bare facts contain enough to keep the country music industry ticking over for quite some time. The mare her trainer reckoned might be too placid to compete was owned by a tiny grandmother whose desire to race ride led to the inevitable sobriquet of the 'Galloping Granny'. Together they provided an irresistible tale. That it isn't quite so straightforward as history's first draft indicates just illustrates the depth of feeling behind the headlines.

Charmian Hill was hardly a stereotypical Irish granny. Her own grandfather was the distinguished historian G.H. Orpen and she had a well-to-do Anglo-Irish upbringing that included a boarding school education in England, a school for 'older gels' in Germany and studying at Dublin's Trinity College. It was there she met her husband Eddie, a doctor, who quickly had to learn to cope with his elfin wife's near-obsession with horses, hunting and point-to-points. Based near Waterford city, the couple had four children. But when the children were at boarding school, Mrs Hill didn't reach for either gin or golf clubs. Instead, in 1959 at the age of forty, she started race-riding in point-to-points.

Usually the Hill horses were kept at home for their owner to ride. If one was too much of a handful, it could end up with the trainer Willie O'Grady. One such animal was Knockadoon, whose only notable feat in 1969 was to deposit a young Dermot Weld in the Cheltenham water jump on his sole ever festival ride. But mostly the oldest and, at no more than eight stone, the lightest jockey in point-to-points galloped her own horses at home and rode them in competition. In the early 1970s, however, the Turf Club decided to allow women to ride in amateur flat races, or bumpers. On New Year's Day 1973, 54-year-old Mrs Hill became the first woman to take advantage of the new situation. There followed eight memorable years of riding under rules, although not always memorable for the right reasons. In 1980 she broke her neck in a fall that resulted in three months of treatment at various hospitals. Her weight dropped to six and a half stone, but most of it seemed to remain heart. By the following year she was looking for a new horse; her son Oliver agreed to buy one with her. Between them they had £6,000 to spend.

They secured the three-year-old daughter of Deep Run and Twilight Slave for £5,800 at Ballsbridge Sales. 'She just *walked* out of the box,' Charmian Hill recalled later. 'I said to myself, "Wow, here we go." It was the *way* she walked out.' After taking her home, the new owners had to decide on a name. Hill's daughter, Penny, was in training for a marathon and was getting up at dawn to practice. Dawn Run was a perfect fit. The following spring, the four-year-old filly arrived at Paddy Mullins's yard in Goresbridge.

Mullins's reputation as a master horseman and a shrewd exploiter of equine talent whatever the arena was already established. Quietly spoken to the point of diffidence and suspicious of any kind of media scrutiny – 'they all talk through their pockets' – he had showed an expert touch both over jumps and on the flat. Four Irish Grand Nationals, plus a handful of Cheltenham Festival triumphs, had been added to in 1973 by Hurry Harriet's memorable success in Newmarket's Champion Stakes where the 33–1 Irish outsider defeated the glamorous Arc champion Allez France. The Mullins family were steeped in racing. All five children, including the subsequent champion trainer, Willie, have ridden winners. Mullins himself had been a winning amateur rider and his wife Maureen won on her sole racecourse start. After two encouraging starts in the summer of 1982, Mullins struck the first of many blows with his new mare at Tralee in the £692-to-the-winner Castlemaine Flat Race.

Ridden by her now 63-year-old owner, Dawn Run made most of the running, apart from when briefly headed by Espeut at halfway. Not for the first time though, the large mare, with the little woman on her back, reacted as if personally affronted. She fought back to beat Espeut by a length. But the focus afterwards was on a rather irate winning jockey.

Just a week before the Turf Club had decided to withdraw Hill's riding licence. They gave no reason. Previously questions about when the galloping granny might retire had been rebuffed with a brisk 'when my nerve goes'. That was still intact and Mrs Hill was not one to react well to having her mind made up for her. Dawn Run's victory was a slap in the face to any suggestion the venerable rider was not up to the job and she shrilly decried the Turf Club decision as 'archaic'. The regulatory body's reasons have never officially been given but unofficially it appeared that they wouldn't have given a licence to a professional jockey of similar age so they weren't going to make an exception for an amateur. Hill may have fumed but the Turf Club's view was that they had to take into account their responsibility to the betting public and the rider herself. As final rides go, however, it wasn't a bad way to go out.

In media terms the story wrote itself – a wronged granny not being allowed ride her own horse by a male, self-elected establishment. The Turf Club still even had some retired generals and other ex-army types just to reinforce those cartoon portraits of right and wrong. As with most things, however, the reality was more grey than black-and-white.

For one thing, Dawn Run was hardly any 'cuddly horsey' cliché. It had already been noted at the Mullins yard that when she was at race-fitness, only the brave, the reckless or her regular groom, John Clarke, entered her box without reckoning on the chances of a bite or a kick. The other female in the partnership hardly lived up to any cosy tabloid representation either. The single-mindedness that had Mrs Hill riding winners at an age when many of her contemporaries were doting on their grandkids didn't make her everyone's cup of tea. 'A miserable oul' bitch,' Ted Walsh once described her with typical bluntness. Since there has hardly been a subject invented that the television pundit doesn't reckon his opinion is relevant to, such a summary is hardly gospel but it is still one that plenty within racing wouldn't quibble with. Hell would freeze over before Paddy Mullins came out with something as colourful, but even he could be driven to cheek-puffing exasperation by the sexagenarian owner who regularly rode out her mare around his small circular gallop.

Hill's resentment at the Turf Club decision never wavered but ultimately proved futile. A month after that first victory, Dawn Run won easily at Galway, ridden by Mullins's youngest son, Tom. Then she landed a race at Tralee that confirmed this was a mare well out of the ordinary. So much so that a tilt at the November Handicap on the flat at Leopardstown was next for Dawn Run. She beat one home. Restrained in behind horses, Dawn Run resented the alien tactics and sulked. A fortnight later, however, she began the career over jumps she was bred for and which would reach heights that would beggar belief among the general racing world. The man who bred the future superstar would be no different.

Dawn Run grew up at John Riordan's farm in north Co. Cork, a product of a mare, Twilight Slave, that never raced and a champion sire in Deep Run. Breeding horses was very much a hobby for Riordan but when Twilight Slave's 1978 foal was just eight weeks old there came a sneak preview of that legendary toughness.

An abscess in Twilight Slave's foot didn't look nearly enough to prevent her owner from heading on a golfing trip for a few days. She would just be confined to her box. But stress caused the mare's milk to dry up and suddenly her foal had no nourishment. When Riordan returned she had diarrhoea and a high temperature. Put on a drip, veterinary advice was that she would not survive. But every three hours over a number of days, Riordan's wife Prudence tried to coax the foal into eating a mixture of Complan and glucose. Her perseverance paid off. The little animal started to eat. Within a week she was back in her paddock.

Some neat conclusions could fit nicely on the back of such a tale, an inevitability that in hindsight makes sense, but which would be fanciful in the extreme. If the hardy foal had grown up into an unknown broodmare that followed in the unraced footsteps of her mother, then no one, least of all John and Prudence Riordan, would have been surprised. In fact it would have seemed a damn sight more likely than what started to unfold when obstacles were put in front of Dawn Run.

Fourth on her jumps debut, she won three of her next five starts over hurdles, earning a trip to Cheltenham for the Sun Alliance Novices Hurdle in the process. Another of Paddy Mullins's sons, Tony, a promising young professional, had been riding Dawn Run in Ireland but for Cheltenham Charmian Hill resolved to get somebody more experienced. The ride was reportedly offered to the Irish champion jockey Frank Berry but he turned it down. Instead it was Ron Barry, the veteran former champion jockey in Britain, who rode Dawn Run. Twenty-seven runners might have gone to post but none of them were able to shake the Irish mare out of her customary position at the head of the field until Sabin Du Loir eventually powered ahead. Dawn Run, however, was rallying again at the line. Barry argued if he had known her better, she would have won. On its own terms it was a magnificent performance for a mare in open company. But it was two races over a 24-hour period the following month that really opened people's eyes.

A two-mile-five-furlong novice hurdle turned into something of a procession, so much so that Paddy Mullins toyed with the idea of turning her out again for the following day's Templegate Hurdle. But that would mean a clash with the new champion hurdler Gaye Brief and the previous year's championship winner

For Auction. Even on soft ground, the general consensus was that Dawn Run would be out of her depth. Mullins decided to go for it. Sent straight to the lead, however, that dogged refusal to yield made nonsense of such an argument. Only Gaye Brief could overhaul her on the run to the last, but Dawn Run kept fighting and at the line there was only a length between them. For Auction was a full twenty lengths back in third.

'It was the runner-up who stole the limelight,' opined the *Sporting Life* newspaper, who caught a new consensus in stating that fences lay in her immediate future.

Jumping might have been the name of the game, but the techniques required to jump hurdles and fences are subtly different. With both the secret is not to spend too much time in the air, but the bigger obstacles demand a horse is able to bend its back and exhibit more flexibility than when jumping hurdles. Over the smaller and flimsier jumps, the trick is to barely break stride, flick the top of the obstacle and emerge at the other side without having reduced speed. It places different demands on horses and with Dawn Run growing all the time into an imposing physical presence, there was an assumption that her size would be better suited to fences and that racing back over two miles would catch her out for speed.

Tony Mullins had ridden the mare at Liverpool and also on her first start over hurdles at Down Royal when easily justifying 2–5 odds. However, an otherwise routine victory included a bad jump to the left at the last that meant nothing in the context of Down Royal but which the Hill camp believed boded ill for the future. Mullins's style was hardly in the mould of that uber-stylist John Francome, who was at the height of his powers in the mid-1980s. The young Irishman was much more upright in the saddle and rode with a loose rein. He also was prone, like many Irish-based jockeys, to using his whip in the forehand position down the shoulder. It could look ungainly but what Mullins did have was the priceless gift of getting horses to run for him.

Charmian Hill, however, was afraid of her mare 'getting into bad habits' and considered the Down Royal exhibition to have been 'a terrible ride'. She decided on a change of jockey. She later recounted that when telling Paddy Mullins that she was jocking off his son, he 'seemed almost relieved'. The trainer's sphinx-like inscrutability must have been particularly stony that day. There was little likelihood of Mullins Snr talking the owner out of a decision that must have cut deep. Four days before Dawn Run was to run at Ascot in November 1983, Mullins phoned the former British champion jockey Jonjo O'Neill, asking him to ride.

O'Neill's reaction was understandable. If the Corkman didn't accept the ride, someone else would. On unsuitably quick ground, Dawn Run struggled to a short-head success over Amarach. Hill was thrilled, telling the press: 'It was only the ground, she wouldn't let herself go. But Jonjo taught her a lot.'

The scene was now set for a rematch with Gaye Brief in Kempton's Christmas Hurdle. The champion had the aid of a pacemaker and for once Dawn Run didn't lead in the early stages. Instead of sulking she raced generously to the third-last before taking it up, with Gaye Brief sitting on her tail. Try as he might up the long straight, he couldn't get to grips with the Irish mare. At the line there was only a neck in it but the impression given to many was that the pair of them could have done another circuit and the older horse wouldn't have got past. The score was one-one and Cheltenham seemed likely to be a perfect decider. Before that, the Irish Champion Hurdle at Leopardstown provided a perfect warm-up. And then, a week before Cheltenham, came news that Gaye Brief was out of the race because of injury. Suddenly Dawn Run was the only Champion Hurdle story, despite a mare not having won the race in forty-five years.

The full force of media interest converged on Goresbridge, a nightmare for Paddy Mullins who willingly conceded the limelight to his owner, who in turn was happily still leading the string during morning work-outs on her mare. Acres of newsprint were devoted to the granny and her star racer, especially in Britain where the story provoked the usual torrent of stereotypical caricatures. There were even stories about 'secret tactics' that might be used by the Irish team.

However there was nothing secret about the way Dawn Run went about winning. She quickly went to the front, but turning away from the stands the odds-on favourite was joined and briefly led. Desert Orchid didn't turn into a bad front-runner himself, but at halfway in his Champion Hurdle attempt he was a spent force. Coming down the hill it was another Irish challenger, Buck House, that ranged alongside. There was a slight collision between the two at the second-last flight but ultimately it fell to the outsider Cima to lay down the final challenge. A slight mistake at the last, not the first of Dawn Run's career, helped Cima range alongside, but yet again O'Neill never looked anything but confident about holding on.

'I have never seen such a reception or more popular winner since the days of Arkle,' said the BBC commentator Peter O'Sullevan. Two days later, Jenny Pitman won the Gold Cup with Burrough Hill Lad but took time to declare: 'If Dawn Run can win the Gold Cup then she's a champion the like of which has never been seen before.'

Already anticipation was growing about this unique mare having the credentials to complete the Champion Hurdle-Gold Cup double, not a bad achievement for a horse who was still just six. Despite her young age, though, there was no question of easing off. Dawn Run returned to Liverpool for the race in which she had been runner-up to Gaye Brief the previous year. Twenty-four hours before it, however, O'Neill took a nasty fall over the big National fences that ruled him out of riding the champion. Tony Mullins was back on board and it was impossible to ignore how easily Dawn Run won. No one disputed that O'Neill was the more accomplished jockey but the mare seemed to run more kindly for Mullins. Then it was announced that Dawn Run would be prepared for the French Champion Hurdle at Auteuil in June.

No non-French horse had ever won the Grande Course De Haies D'Auteuil before. Only Mandarin in 1962 had broken the home domination of the French Gold Cup. This was virgin territory for a young mare after a strenuous season. Both Paddy Mullins and Charmian Hill were accused of greed, of asking too much of their horse. At the end of May she was given a warm-up in the Prix La Barka. Dawn Run took to the very different Auteuil obstacles with élan, making all the running to win easily. A month later she returned to France's premier jumps track for the big race over an extended three miles and one furlong, further than she had ever raced before.

It was a huge ask for any horse to win the English and Irish Champion Hurdles over two miles, then tack on the French version over such a different distance, and do it almost as a season-concluding afterthought. Dawn Run, however, made it look effortless. By the first jump she was already clear and after the first mile she had her opposition spread-eagled. If Tony Mullins had any stamina doubts he disguised them well with a display of front-running brio rarely if ever seen before at Auteuil. On a couple of occasions he allowed her to fiddle jumps in a way that might have had purists tut-tutting, but there was no mistaking the class that Dawn Run exhibited for him in addition to all that toughness. She completed a unique Champion Hurdle treble, pulling up, by six lengths.

'The horse she beat that day (Mister Jack) came out next time and won a Group 3 on the flat. I'm telling you, that day she'd have beaten Arkle,' Tony Mullins later declared.

It would be four months before what was now generally accepted to be the finest mare the sport had ever seen would race again. And this time it would be over fences. Paddy Mullins's instinct to remain hurdling for another season was over-ruled by Charmian Hill. Instead Dawn Run was schooled over fences that autumn, including racecourse sessions at Dundalk and Limerick Junction. She proved to be a natural. Each outing only seemed to make her jockey's lopsided grin even wider. But it wasn't just the jumping. There were now plenty willing to accept the mare ran more kindly for Tony Mullins than Jonjo O'Neill. France had illustrated how devastating that could be when allied to all her toughness. To the trainer there was no doubt; his son would remain on board Dawn Run. Little wonder, then, that her jockey could be seen laughing as they cantered to the start of the Nobber Novice Chase at Navan at the start of November.

Hardly a championship event, and worth only five grand to the winner, the race named after the provocatively named Co. Meath village remains an indelible memory for those who were there. Those prone to dismissing Dawn Run as merely a tough old bird had to contend with possibly the most visually impressive display seen over fences in years, certainly by a novice. Up against her was her old rival Buck House, already a winner over fences, who was installed favourite by the bookmakers. It wasn't long, however, before the pair flip-flopped in the market, and then Dawn Run showed why. It was a perfect debut over fences. A slight peck on landing over the first was the only semblance of a mistake. Meeting the fifth all wrong, the big mare skipped her legs so adroitly it hardly looked like anything was amiss. Buck House stayed with her over the two-mile trip as long as he could but the final two fences were more coronation than competition.

Afterwards Paddy Mullins declared the Sun Alliance Chase would be her Cheltenham target. The Gold Cup could wait until 1986. He was right, but not according to plan. A month later, Dawn Run strained a ligament under a pastern during exercise. Initial relief that it wasn't the tendon disappeared when the injury was slow to respond to treatment. By Christmas she was sound but it was decided to exercise caution. Jump racing's greatest star was finished for the season.

A summer at her owner's farm preceded more schooling,

including a couple of post-race work-outs at Navan and Fairyhouse. At the start of December Punchestown's Durkan Chase saw Dawn Run take on established stars in Bobsline and Royal Bond, making all to beat the latter by eight lengths. 'It was just like a school,' Tony Mullins reported. Later that month, she returned to two miles at Leopardstown. The Christmas Festival fans got a glimpse of the future as Dawn Run and Buck House duelled down the back straight. The little chestnut gelding jumped noticeably better than his rival, and touched down ahead at the second-last. But the mare was only getting going. Despite being awkward at the last, she eventually won easily by four lengths.

'She needs more education,' was Paddy Mullins's reaction. Despite that, and on the back of Burrough Hill Lad's King George defeat four days previously, Dawn Run was suddenly a 5–2 Gold Cup favourite. It seemed remarkable that a horse with just three starts over fences under her belt should be favourite for steeplechasing's blue riband but any doubters could have their fears eased by a pre-festival trip to Cheltenham in January. They didn't.

Misty Spirit won the Holsten Distributors Chase at Cheltenham on 25 January 1986, but rarely can any winner have been so ignored in the aftermath. It should have been little more than another school for Dawn Run. She actually was getting weight from her seven rivals, including 11lb from the future Grand National winner Rhyme N'Reason, who was badly out of form. In the circumstances a 4–9 starting price looked a lot more attractive than any Gold Cup odds, despite the fact that one cynical book - maker was betting on which fence she would exit at. No doubt it was Cheltenham's famous downhill fences that the bookie was banking on, but instead it was the sixteenth, six from home, where Tony Mullins's world started to crumble.

Dawn Run almost landed on top of the fence, catapulting her rider out of the saddle. Neither she nor Mullins fell. The jockey landed on his feet, grabbed the reins and ran alongside the mare before coming to a halt. The opposition wasn't brilliant but they were well gone by the time Mullins got back on and rode around for fourth. 'She jumped superbly until that fence which is a bit on the horizon and has been a bit of [a] bogey for us over the years,' his father said. 'Tony said she went for a big one and changed her mind.'

Mrs Hill changed her mind too. Her old suspicions about her beloved mare falling into bad habits with her young jockey resurfaced. Those concerns were reinforced by media criticism of Mullins. His habit of leaving only one hand on the reins while leaving another outstretched – hailing a cab, as it was called – was pointed out repeatedly. Would sentiment towards the trainer's son cost Dawn Run a chance of history, the argument went. Just over a year previously, the Hill team had found out how precarious a steeplechaser's health can be. Would there be another shot at Gold Cup glory? And if there wasn't, didn't they owe it to the horse to give her the best possible shout?

Inside a couple of weeks, the decision was taken. Mullins was off and Jonjo O'Neill back on. Plans for a confidence-restoring run at Punchestown with O'Neill on board were abandoned and so Dawn Run went straight to the Gold Cup. With the benefit of hindsight it seems astonishing that a mare that had raced just four times over fences, the last of them ending in disaster, should even go for the biggest chase of all, never mind be expected to win. But that illustrated the unique place Dawn Run had come to occupy. Mont Tremblant thirty-four years previously was the nearest Gold Cup winner to approach her level of inexperience. She did have a 5lb sex allowance but thirteen seasoned performers lined up against her, including the top-class Combs Ditch, the previous year's first two, Forgive N'Forget and Righthand Man, as well as Wayward Lad, who already had a pair of King George victories to his credit. Also lining up was the vastly improved Run And Skip, who was to play a major role in the race.

The 1986 Gold Cup was no solo-show from the front. Steve Smith-Eccles on Run And Skip was determined to fight for the lead. Dawn Run's jumping was put under the sort of pressure that would expose any weakness. Early on the second circuit came the first crack when her splash at the water jump cost a couple of lengths. Then, at the last ditch, Dawn Run's inexperience cost her again. It didn't take long for O'Neill to bustle her back to the lead, but coming down the hill dangers were queuing up.

Run And Skip grimly hung on to Dawn Run as they faced the final two fences. Wayward Lad was being ridden to close but Forgive N'Forget appeared to be travelling ominously well. Between the last two fences both horses passed their Irish rival. It looked between Forgive N'Forget and Wayward Lad, who a hundred yards from the line appeared to hold a decisive lead. And that was when all that dogged refusal to accept defeat came to the surface.

'It seemed over. But I felt her relax and fill her lungs with a huge intake of oxygen. It was like priming a turbo charge,' O'Neill recounted more than a decade later.

Cheltenham has seen winners get receptions riotous enough to make Marrakech look like Mecca on a slow night but Dawn Run's completion of the Champion Hurdle-Gold Cup double remains in a different league. Much of that had to do with how she had snatched success from defeat, but something extra seemed to resonate with so many people. This wasn't a flawless performance à la Arkle. Instead it was a triumph despite all-too-obvious flaws. Dawn Run's jumping should have caught her out. So too should her inexperience. But still she overcame it all through a combination of talent, guts and pure undiluted will. Only the hardest of hearts couldn't have fluttered at what she pulled off.

For the prize-giving ceremony, O'Neill carried Tony Mullins on his shoulders. Both men displayed a grace that had nothing to do with their gymnastic ability. In the midst of the general celebrations, however, one man struggled to go with the popular flow. Considering he had just performed a minor miracle of training in getting such a raw novice to win the Gold Cup, Paddy Mullins was entitled to feel better than he did. There was no getting away, though, from the hurt he felt for his son. A shy man suspicious of the limelight at the best of times, as the Queen Mother handed out the trophies, all Mullins wanted was to get away.

For Charmian Hill, however, there was a huge sense of vindication. 'A lot of people will have to eat their words,' she said. In a business where results are what count above all else, it was hardly surprising that the tiny figure at the centre of the Cheltenham maelstrom felt entitled to crow. Dawn Run might have run more freely for Tony Mullins but would the younger man have had the raw strength O'Neill showed on the run-in? With the memory of his unseating just a couple of months previously still fresh, would he have managed to gather the mare together after those mistakes in the Gold Cup? The argument was moot: but to the winner the spoils. It just felt wrong that the man most centrally involved of all didn't feel able to relish the moment.

The frailties that endeared Dawn Run to her fans reared up less helpfully at Aintree a few weeks later. Starting odds-on to confirm Gold Cup form with Wayward Lad, she took the first fence by the roots and exited. The 40–1 shot Beau Ranger proceeded to win. O'Neill was soon to have greater worries than a mere fall. Since Christmas he hadn't been feeling right, tired all the time, taking longer than usual to recover from the routine bangs automatic to a jump jockey. It all began to get too much. The prospect of training became more attractive. He called time on a glittering riding career; a couple of months later he was diagnosed with cancer.

Such perspective wasn't available soon after Liverpool when the prospect of a clash between the new Gold Cup heroine and her old rival, Buck House, who had been crowned two-mile champion at Cheltenham, looked likely in a Coolmore Stud-organised chase at Gowran Park. However after what Paddy Mullins described as an 'error of omission' Dawn Run's name didn't figure among the entries. The idea of a match, though, had grabbed the imagination of one significant racing figure.

When Tony Mullins saw Vincent O'Brien approach him at the Curragh races, his immediate surprise was at the great trainer actually knowing who he was. Then the most accomplished figure in the history of Irish racing proposed a meeting of the two champions. 'Vincent was at a stage where he wanted to give something back to jump racing. That had been his stepping stone to where he ended up,' Mullins later recounted. O'Brien contacted the then Racing Board chairman Michael Smurfit and, after both sets of connections were consulted, the idea was firmed up.

The Racing Board put up ten thousand pounds. Punchestown racecourse, Coolmore Stud and the Purcell family who owned Buck House contributed five grand each. The Hills put in nothing, reasoning that Dawn Run was the star attraction anyway. That didn't endear them to some observers and, in the light of the cherished memory that the match has become in Irish National Hunt racing, it is also worth recalling that there was plenty of anger from within the industry at the level of public money being spent by the Racing Board on what was effectively a private race. It would be run over two miles, giving the Buck House camp hope they could reverse the six defeats they had already suffered from Dawn Run. Soft ground, however, suited the mare. Up to 40,000 people attended.

'It could so easily have fallen flat on its face. One could have gone off and won by ten lengths or one could have fallen at the first,' remembered Buck House's trainer Mouse Morris. For Tony Mullins, the stakes were even higher. 'The pressure was immense,' he later said. 'Because if I'd got beat they'd have said it was because Jonjo wasn't riding her. Even by winning it would be only because the mare was great. Losing would have been catastrophic. I knew that was the deal.'

Ultimately hardly anyone could feel cheated. Dawn Run set a

searing pace that Buck House coped with easily. At the second-last fence Dawn Run's habit of jumping left allowed her rival up the inner and into a slight lead. 'I gave him a couple of belts and hoped he'd pull away,' said Buck House's rider Tommy Carmody, 'but I knew in my heart of hearts that she'd go to the line better. She was unique.' Dawn Run pulled away from the last to win so readily that the accomplishment of dropping back from the three and a quarter miles of the Gold Cup to beat the reigning champion at two miles seemed merely routine. Little wonder, then, that the fateful idea of returning to France that summer didn't seem outrageous, just as two years previously the task of taking in the Prix La Barka before the Champion Hurdle had proved to be no trouble.

Dawn Run was older now and more mature: in theory it should have been more than doable. But since her last French raid, the locals had come up with a formidable opponent. Le Rheusois had won the Champion Hurdle in 1985 and was at the peak of his power. He too was getting a prep in the Barka. It didn't look like being a cosy warm-up and so it proved. Dawn Run came up three lengths short of her rival and Tony Mullins returned to the parade ring with an unusually stern look on his face. He made his feelings plain to his father.

'I said if we came back for the next race we weren't going to win. We weren't going to beat the other horse. She'd had a long season. He agreed, but Mrs Hill wouldn't hear of it and because of my negativity she put up a French jockey,' he remembered.

In a sport and an industry primarily based on people's willing - ness to own racehorses, it is a rule of thumb that what the owner wants, the owner gets. Charmian Hill's manner may not have made her particularly popular but she was hardly venturing beyond the pale in demanding her horse run. And the over-whelmingly male racing world of the 1980s could be tough, even for a firm-minded, decisive woman determined to have her way. Insisting that the local jockey Michael Chirol ride Dawn Run in the Grande Course De Haies D'Auteuil might not have been particularly sensitive but 'jocking off' riders is as venerable a racing tradition as throwing on saddles.

If 1984 had been a summer swagger in the Parisian sunshine, then two years later was a very different *tasse de thé*. Try as she might, Dawn Run couldn't shake off her opposition, in particular Le Rheusois. Racing down the back straight, the Irish star put in some extravagant leaps in order to assert her authority but coming to the fourth-last Le Rheusois was right there next to her. Fighting to keep the lead, she stretched for the obstacle but caught the top of it, somersaulted and crashed to the ground. Her neck broke on impact and she died instantly.

Opinion as to what might have happened was divided afterwards. A shaken Chirol told Paddy Mullins that Dawn Run was sure to have won. Others were not so sure. Either way it hardly mattered. A unique talent was dead at just eight years of age. Her carcass was cleared away and taken to an *équarrissage*, a sort of French knackers yard. The rumour subsequently developed that she was sold for meat. In fact the usual outcome in such circumstances is that the carcass is cremated and the ashes used as fertiliser. It was a final touch that only added to the recriminations.

Tony Mullins was at a sale back in Ireland when he heard about Dawn Run's death. 'I'll never forget the feeling, an absolute anger I'd never felt before,' he said. When official confirmation came through from Paris it became front-page news in the following day's Irish newspapers. The impact would continue to be felt for long after those newspapers were consigned to the bin.

Paddy Mullins died in October 2010, almost a quarter of a century after the horse he used to train. Many of his obituaries quoted his oft-repeated statement that winning the Champion Stakes with Hurry Harriet was his proudest moment as a trainer. And yet hardly any of those same obituaries didn't begin without reference to Dawn Run and her unique accomplishments. Both points were noticeable, but Dawn Run came first: as per usual.

Orby

Of the approximately one million people that left Ireland during the Great Famine, not many came back. Richard Eyre 'Boss' Croker did return from America in the early twentieth century, and in many ways he shouldn't have.

Wealthy beyond the imagination of most, and possessed of an independent streak that chimed with the changing political climate of his birthplace, he nevertheless failed to gain what perhaps he valued most which was acceptance from an Anglo-Irish establishment he affected to scorn. It's only one contradiction in a man whose life was full of them.

Unlike most of those that left a ravaged country in the 1840s, Croker was Protestant. And yet in 1907, when the horse he famously owned and bred, Orby, became the first trained in Ireland to win the Epsom Derby, he was famously acclaimed as 'a Catholic winner' during a victory parade through the centre of Dublin.

Years earlier, at the height of Croker's period as boss of the notorious Tammany Hall political machine, he ranked as possibly the most powerful figure in New York politics and yet never held significant political office. Possessed of a mind independent enough to disregard a polite society outraged by his marriage to a Cherokee Indian princess forty years younger than him, he nevertheless tried everything to gain membership of both the Jockey Club and the Turf Club, only to fail each time.

After Orby's seminal success at Epsom, what Croker described as the most memorable day of his life was tainted by the refusal of King Edward VII to fulfil the traditional function of inviting the winning owner to the Royal Box.

Such an action only emphasises the vapidity in the old cliché of everybody being equal both over and under the turf. Whatever the truth about the latter, Croker would have felt in his bones how inane the idea is that money doesn't matter, particularly when it comes to owning racehorses. But due to the efforts of a US Government commission headed by the future President Theodore Roosevelt, which resulted in the boss of the under-investigation Tammany Hall having to leave New York in a hurry, he also experienced an old-world snobbery that no amount of money was seemingly able to conquer.

If Roosevelt's commission hadn't existed, Croker would almost certainly have remained in America, thus preventing one of the most remarkable stories in the history of the turf. There never seems to have been any sentimental longing for the land where he was born but left aged seven in 1848 on board the *Henry Clay*. America suited him because of its still-unfilled canvas, a place where your accent didn't automatically include presumptions about class, education and ability. In America, a guy can still be just a guy. In Croker's time it was even more so, especially a guy with money. But when the government started cracking down, it meant taking a powder back across the pond to where his difference stood out, and where money wasn't enough to blend in.

What can't be argued with, however, is that the US Government might have had legitimate grounds for investigating the Irish émigré, and the organisation he managed.

Tammany Hall wasn't all bad. It started as a form of political debating club with Democratic Party leanings. For arriving emigrants in New York, it provided an unofficial social welfare programme giving out food, coal and other essentials. It was multi-ethnic. Irish, Polish, Italian and Scandinavian newcomers were all catered for, and in return they gave their votes. The big-city machine had only one real purpose, the perpetuation of its own power. A bureaucracy developed second only to the Catholic Church and New York was controlled for the best part of half a century with an almost feudal degree of patronage.

It was in this environment that a teenage Croker grew up. Physically imposing enough to have prize-fighter among his long list of jobs (that also included barman, machinist and blacksmith), it was the Tammany Hall system of the nod and the wink, the sly bribe, the belief that everything and everyone has a price, which moulded the attitudes of the hungry Irish kid.

In his teenage years, Croker led the Fourth Avenue Gang, using his fists when threats and back-handers didn't work. The Tammany machine meant he voted nineteen times in one election. Under the tutelage of 'Honest' John Kelly, probably the originator of the famous phrase 'an honest politician is one who, once bought, stays bought', the boy who left Ireland rose to become boss of an organisation that was almost mythical in its reach and influence. In the process he exhibited plenty of signs that a dubious five-dollar bill appealed to him more than a straight ten.

Once, when a multimillion-dollar contract to repave streets came up, Croker decided to become a contractor and his tender – about half that of bona fide pitches – had to be accepted. The specification called for 'an even surface on the streets and pave-ments', an engineering difficulty solved by the simple expedient of turning the existing slabs upside down.

If the story possesses a rather roguish charm in hindsight, then there is more than enough evidence from modern-day organised crime that the reality of such a life is a lot more sordid. In 1874 Croker was charged with the killing of John McKenna in a fracas on Second Avenue and 34th Street. Some witnesses said they saw the big man with a pistol in his hand. Others denied that. At his trial, ten of the jury voted to acquit and two to convict, so Croker walked free. He avoided prison but William M. 'Boss' Tweed, who was the most visible figure in Tammany at the time, and the man who propelled Croker into becoming an Alderman at just 28, was not so fortunate. After amassing millions from the proceeds of political fixes and protection rackets for brothels, bars and gambling dens, Tweed ended up dying in prison. Croker avoided that fate but the source of his financial fortune was no different.

At the height of his power, there wasn't much that hadn't a price. A judgeship was $25,000 and there were fixed rates for differing police grades. Just $300 got a patrolman's job, it was $1,600 for a sergeant and a captaincy cost $10,000. The result was a private fortune that at his death in 1922 was estimated at almost five million dollars. It was a level of wealth that would have turned the most sober head and Croker's appetite for the finer things in life included a developing interest in playing the ponies.

The concept of international racing might seem modern but the late nineteenth century had its share of transatlantic traffic too, though mostly in the one direction. Its most obvious expression was in the flow of American jockeys attempting to make their way in Europe. The visitors brought their revolutionary 'monkey on a stick' style that contrasted with the more upright local way of riding, as well as a swaggering, almost brazen willingness to disregard the rules and regulations of doping and/or stopping horses.

Danny Maher, Lester Reiff and Tod Sloan – he of the cockney rhyming slang 'on your tod' – were among a hugely talented group of riders that altered the face of British racing and in their wake came some of American racing's most powerful owners, including a certain Richard Croker.

In 1892, the Tammany boss bought an upstate New York horse farm for a reported $100,000, followed by $200,000-worth of horseflesh to put on it. The following year, he shelled out a staggering $250,000 in Tennessee for a half-share in the famous

Belle Meade Stud run by General W.H. Jackson. That got him access to eight stallions and 185 of the best broodmares in the US. It was all a long way from the mean streets of New York City, but even further was Newmarket in England, which saw a team of horses owned in partnership by Croker and another American owner, Mike Dwyer, arrive in January 1895. The link with Dwyer lasted only five more months but Croker continued to race horses in Britain.

The turn of the century saw Croker at the peak of his power and influence. His greatest success could have been the 1897 election of Robert Van Wyck as the first Mayor of greater New York, a move that led to speculation that it was really the Irishman who ran the city. But it wasn't long before leaving New York became an attractive option. It didn't provoke any desire for a return to the auld sod, however, and instead the great fixer ended up in England with a well-publicised fortune to his name and a desire to mix with the quality. The only problem was that the English elite — hardly a breed known for their love of Irish-Americans with shady pasts — didn't return that desire.

Considering the less than morally pristine way much of the wealth of the British Empire was built on, it may have taken chutzpah to peer down one's nose at the stately, if by now portly, figure from across the Atlantic, but an attitude of condescension had come to be almost a birthright for the English elite.

Settling in Wantage, the hothouse of New York politics — and a notoriety that had Mark Twain drawing comparisons between Croker and an infamously corrupt eighteenth-century governor of Bengal — must have seemed a long way off. But it didn't take long for the exotic new arrival to take offence. Importing some of his American mares to Britain hadn't been particularly successful so Croker decided to invest in some local bloodstock. However, his wish to have them trained in Newmarket was quickly rejected when the Jockey Club, and in particular a worthy named Colonel Ned Baird, refused to allow Croker anywhere near the place. Furiously, he upped sticks and moved back to the land of his birth.

There is more than a little irony that the man who had been denounced from the pulpit in New York purchased the Glencairn Estate in South Dublin from a prosecutor, Mr Justice James Murphy, in 1904. There is just as much from the fact that the place is now the residence of the British ambassador to Ireland. Built in 1860 by George Gresson from a design by the well-known architect Sir Thomas Deane, the house and the three hundred acres also bought by Croker overlook Sandyford village and the city of Dublin. It was from here that the new owner set out to conquer the racing establishment.

Another new arrival at Glencairn was the mare Rhoda B and her newest foal. Bought as a foal herself and taken to Belle Meade Farm, she proved to be a talented racemare in England, being unlucky not to win the Oaks. From the famous Hanover line in America, Rhoda B made it into the General Stud Book in Britain, but she was an exception. Weatherbys, who compiled the Stud Book, insisted on pedigrees being traceable 'without flaw' and that wasn't always strictly possible with all of American bloodstock. The rules weren't always so strict, however, and Rhoda B was judged qualified. When she came to Ireland she had her foal by Orme, a product of the first crop of the outstanding Triple Crown winner Ormonde.

Trained by John Porter, Orme was a hugely talented runner, winning the Middle Park Stakes and the Dewhurst Stakes as a two-year-old and strongly fancied to emulate his father as a multiple classic winner. However, while preparing for the 2,000 Guineas, Porter noticed the colt in distress in his stable. A substance had been administered to Orme, either mercury or strychnine, and had it not been for his particularly robust constitution he may have died. Orme took three months to recover and return to racing when he landed the Eclipse and the Sussex Stakes before failing to stay the trip in the St Leger. He again won the Eclipse as a four-year-old before becoming a successful stallion, siring the 1899 Derby winner Flying Fox.

As a product of a champion sire and a talented runner, hopes were inevitably high for the chestnut colt that was given the name Orby. Considering his later reputation as the embodiment of all things Irish and Catholic, it's interesting to note that he had in fact been born in Britain. Croker's immediate task, however, was to identify a trainer for his embryonic champion.

One name dominated Irish training in the early decades of the 20th century. J.J. (Jim) Parkinson was one of those individuals for whom the phrase 'human dynamo' could have been invented. Based at Maddenstown Lodge on the Curragh, he adopted a 'holistic' approach to horses, breeding them, owning them and selling vast numbers overseas while at the same time breaking records for the numbers of winners trained by any one individual in Ireland. In later years he was a member of the senate and almost went bankrupt in a failed attempt to make the new Irish Free State self-sufficient in coal.

A native of Tramore in Co. Waterford, Parkinson graduated from the Royal Veterinary College in London and returned to Ireland to practise at the Curragh. However, after taking out a training licence in 1897 his later achievement seemed unlikely considering an initial period of ill luck that seemed to plague him. In 1902 he was 'warned off', or had his licence taken away, after a race at Leopardstown. As a result Parkinson had to move out of Maddenstown and auction his string, which included the subsequent Irish Derby winner Lord Rossmore. During his suspension, however, the Irish trainer travelled to the USA and became a fan of the American style of riding. The restoration of his licence coincided with Croker's arrival back in Ireland.

In hindsight it is hardly surprising that the alliance of two decisive men used to getting their own way would end in tears. Orby would be at the centre of the falling-out, although initially the partnership was hugely successful. Croker's colours of 'Yale blue with yellow tassel' were carried to multiple big-race victories including the Irish Oaks with Blakestown.

In the spring of 1906, however, another Parkinson owner, Lord de Clifford, died and the trainer arranged for Croker to buy one of the deceased's runners, Electric Rose. It didn't seem a major event because the as yet unraced Orby was already provoking dreams of greatness. His work on the Curragh was spectacular but hard ground that summer meant Parkinson was reluctant to risk what he felt were 'shelly hooves'. Eventually, through pressure from the owner, he relented and ran Orby at Leopardstown in August, but only over five furlongs to minimise the injury risk. The 'talking horse' was beaten. Croker was dismayed and demanded another race in the Railway Stakes at the Curragh, which Parkinson explained was Electric Rose's target. The owner again prevailed.

Both horses ran in September's Railway Stakes at the Curragh and Electric Rose won with her stable companion only third. In the winner's enclosure, though, Croker looked anything but the satisfied winning owner. The big man accused Parkinson of stopping Orby, alleging a contingency of sale with Electric Rose that Parkinson would be paid all prize money won by her that season. It was a scene out of modern-day tabloid heaven and Parkinson, outraged at this slur on his character, provided a perfect denouement. After returning home he sent a telegram to Croker – 'Horses at Kildare Station – Collect!'

Any satisfaction at such a line would have been diluted by the knowledge that, in Orby, Parkinson had possessed a singular talent, so singular in fact that he would never again train a realistic Epsom Derby contender. Despite two defeats, the rangy colt had showed enough on the gallops to suggest the grandest racing ambition of all wasn't totally outlandish.

Orby was taken back to Glencairn, where the training facilities were expanded and a new team appointed. Croker's self-confidence didn't extend to deluding himself that he could develop a horse's potential himself. Instead he appointed two men.

James Allen oversaw much of the work, but the new official trainer was Lt-Col Frederick McCabe, a surgeon and former racing cyclist, who had been medical officer with the South Irish Horse regiment in South Africa. Orby's owner might have been feisty but, compared to the veldt, Glencairn must have seemed paradise itself. Together they plotted a course to Epsom that must have seemed unlikely for a horse that hadn't even managed to win a race yet.

That was put right first time out in 1907, Orby taking the ferry to Liverpool to win, and following up at the now-defunct Baldoyle course on the north side of Dublin. Croker decided to put his money where his mouth was and started backing his colt for the Derby. It didn't take long for many more of his compatriots to take more than a passing interest in Orby's progress, even if it wasn't always financial. Nevertheless, ante-post prices of 66–1 quickly disappeared.

Ireland's political misfortune had always been to be so close to a powerful neighbour and the early 20th century saw the Empire at the zenith of its might and arrogance. Just thirteen years previously the second Irish Home Rule Bill, which would provide Dublin with its own parliament, had passed the House Of Commons only to be shot down in the House Of Lords. In 1907 the build-up to a third Home Rule Bill was already under way. Hardline republicanism through the Irish Republican Brother-hood had stagnated and instead the focus was on the Irish National Party's political manoeuvring in London. The country had a veneer of stability, but underneath were latent antipathies to England that never needed much stoking, and an opportunity to thumb the nose at England's establishment in the world's most famous and important race was one that quickly caught the public imagination.

Croker's political ideals had rarely if ever crossed the rubicon of his own self-interest. He became a notably generous benefactor to various charities throughout the country and especially Dublin, where the depths of poverty that much of the population lived in was shocking. To the Irish media, the story of the rich, bluff 'Yank' with the dubious past and his rapidly developing racehorse was like catnip. Their colleagues across the Irish Sea, however, were more scornful of the uppity challenger.

Any journalist who has ever decided to take a definitive tack and leave no avenue for escape can only have sympathy for William Allison, who had been dismissive of any Irish horse even coming close to visiting Epsom, never mind winning the Derby, in *The Sportsman* a year before.

'The turf in Ireland has no spring in it,' he opined. 'The climate is too depressing and no Irish trainer knows enough to even dare compete for the greatest race in the world.'

If ever there has been a hostage to fortune it was Allison in the run-up to the 1907 Derby. While he undoubtedly had a point about the Irish climate, he clearly didn't row along with the modern view that Ireland's limestone soil is perfect for racing and raising horses. And as for a trainer not daring, well, he can't have been familiar with 'Boss' Croker's habit of getting what he wanted. And what the Boss desperately wanted was a Derby victory.

Croker later denied reports he tried to tempt Danny Maher into riding Orby by offering the top rider $7,000 up front. Maher elected to ride Bezonian instead. The American link was maintained, however, with the owner turning to Ohio-born lightweight, Johnny 'Knickerbocker' Reiff. The darling of racing society, Reiff used to have ladies kissing the top of his head for luck in the parade ring and when profiled for *Vanity Fair* in 1900, the teenage wunderkind presented a picture of cherubic innocence alongside a caption that read: 'He likes sweets and he loves his Mum'. It was a somewhat one-dimensional portrait.

Reiff had followed his older brother Lester, one of the many American riders who revolutionised the jockey scene in Europe, to England. Lester won the 1901 Derby on Volodyovski but later that year he lost his licence after being judged to have stopped a horse at Manchester. The ban all but ended his career in England, so he and his brother moved to France, where controversy started to revolve around Johnny too. In 1902 he looked for $40,000 of damages from the French Société d'Encouragement (the body that then ruled French racing) after police allegations that he had stopped horses too. On his trips back to England, however, Reiff remained a popular figure and the 22-year-old turned up at Epsom on the morning of the 1907 Derby for his first glimpse of Orby.

What he saw in the light rain was a rangy colt trained to the minute but who was reported to have bad feet and didn't appear as 'sleek' as some of the English favourites. Orby had a pipe-opener just to get a feel of the unique track, which places such demands on a still relatively immature thoroughbred. As the throngs of people started arriving after their journey from London, Reiff started to fancy his chances of emulating his brother, even if the Irish horse looked to be up against it.

Only nine lined up for the 1907 Derby and the small field was dominated by the 2,000 Guineas winner Slieve Gallion, who was trained by Sam Darling in Beckhampton. Good enough to win the Champagne Stakes as a juvenile, Slieve Gallion looked a potential superstar at Newmarket, landing the classic after previously scoring a Craven Stakes success. He started an 8–13 favourite at Epsom. Also in the field was Wool Winder, who just happened to be owned by the same Colonel Baird who a few years previously had been among those who signed the documentation keeping Croker out of Newmarket.

It is hard to imagine now the central place the Derby had in the English sporting calendar. Nothing else compared in terms of prestige and genuine public interest from all levels of society. Among the masses packed into the infield there seemed to be an ambivalent attitude towards the Irish-American hope who started a 100–6 shot. Reiff was popular, his owner not particularly so, and Slieve Gallion was going to win anyway, seemed to be the general view.

When the race began, John Bull took the lead from the

favourite, followed in turn by Bezonian, Galvani and Orby. Coming down the hill both Bezonian and Orby made ground and around Tattenham Corner, Reiff made his move to test Slieve Gallion's stamina. It worked. Despite looking less than completely at ease on the unique Epsom camber, Orby stayed on much too well for his big rival, who faded to third. As if to make the day perfect for Croker, it was Wool Winder who ran on to be second, two lengths behind the Irish winner.

The Tammany boss won 6,500 sovereigns in prize money, an estimated quarter of a million US dollars in winning bets and, most of all, the satisfaction of having collected maybe the British establishment's most coveted sporting prize. The impact must have been intoxicating and yet Croker's past refused to loosen its grip. The King, a man whose personal morality might not have stood up to much public scrutiny either – his penchant for bathing in champagne with his favourite Parisian prostitutes was well known in polite circles – refused to invite the winning owner to meet him.

There was a lot involved in the gesture, Croker's dubious actions in New York apart. King 'Bertie' wasn't alone in resenting such a public display of downright uppitiness from across the Irish Sea. An ingrained superiority complex over the Irish was almost ingrained in the English national psyche, and not just among the elite. One newspaper reporter noted at the time: 'Mr Croker gained little of the goodwill of the British racing public.' Another said: 'Orby met with a mixed reception on returning to the scale.' For a man who had invested so much in acceptance, to be snubbed so publicly must have been hard to take. Characteristically, though, Croker made light of it to the *New York Times* reporter who was at the track.

'I have attained the ambition of my life – at least the ambition I have had since taking up the sport of racing,' he said, adding:

It is a great thing to win the Derby and how proud I am to have accomplished this I have not words to express. I am very proud,

> especially as Orby was bred and raced in my stable, having
> brought his dam from America. I can't say I felt sure of winning
> but still I had the greatest confidence in Orby. He is a grand
> horse and if all goes well, he will add many laurels to this.'

Others were more gracious to the Irish winners than the King. Slieve Gallion's trainer Sam Darling said, 'He is a splendid horse. He was well ridden today. Reiff used good judgement in not hanging too close to the favourite in the early stages of the race. Slieve Gallion is also a magnificent horse but he has not the staying power of Orby.'

Orby returned to Dublin to a hero's reception, being paraded through the city behind a pipe band, during which the story, whether apocryphal or not, was told that an old lady pushed her way through to grasp Colonel McCabe's hand and say, 'Thank God, and you, Sir, that we have lived to see a Catholic horse win the Derby!' The Commanding Officer of the South Irish Horse definitely did get a telegram at the time saying: 'Medical Officer authorises the issue of champagne to all ranks!'

Next stop for Orby, Croker determined, would be the Irish Derby, which at the time hadn't a fraction of the prestige it does now. The ground at the Curragh was described as 'rock hard' on the run-up to the race. Colonel McCabe advised against running Orby. Croker declined the advice, saying, 'The Irish public should see their hero in action on home ground.' The controversial owner also sent champagne of his own, to the Turf Club, along with an offer to fund the Irish Derby to the same level as Epsom – in return for election to the regulatory body. The Turf Club declined the offer, but kept the champagne.

'Mr Croker had as much chance of being translated up to heaven alive as he had of being elected to the Club,' McCabe later declared.

Orby duly completed a Derby double at the Curragh in front of a massive crowd, starting at 1–10 in a field of seven and, despite conceding weight, winning easily by seven lengths from his stable companion Georgetown. Croker watched the race from the press box. He only just made it on to the track to lead his winner in afterwards, as Orby was almost mobbed. The suspicion remained, however, that winning the race on such firm going ultimately came at a cost.

Orby's preparation for an attempt on the Doncaster St Leger included a warm-up event in Liverpool. He finished last of four, and injured. The *Irish Field* reported: 'Orby has sprained a sub-carpal ligament in his off-fore leg which practically amounts to a breakdown.' The Leger was off the agenda. It was Orby's old rival Wool Winder that went on to boost the Derby form at Town Moor. Orby was retired to Croker's stud at an estimated valuation of $150,000.

The great Derby winner's stud career was successful but not without its curios, none more so than being mated with his half-sister Rhodora, who had landed the 1908 1,000 Guineas. The resultant foal was deformed and the mare died. When bred along more conventional lines, Orby proved to be a surprising influence for speed, siring the 1,000 Guineas winner Diadem, and being a notably successful broodmare stallion. In 1919, however, he produced a son that emulated his own feat as Grand Parade landed the Epsom Derby, propelling his father to second in that year's leading sires list. Ireland's first Derby winner, though, had died the year before, aged fourteen.

Anyone expecting Orby's owner to fade from prominence and into a low-key dotage clearly weren't familiar with their man. That wasn't Boss Croker's style. Where once public interest had zeroed in on his political influence and financial wealth, not to mention his racing accomplishments, the post-Derby winning years saw his personal life take centre stage.

Croker's first wife, Elizabeth Frazer, had provided him with nine children, although three died young. One son, Frank, was killed in a car crash in Florida, and another, Herbert, had been found dead in a rail car when travelling the West in 1903. A typically colourful family history also included a daughter that married Count Louis San Martini of Naples. However, the turbulence of the Boss's domestic situation was reflected when Croker left America for England and his wife travelled instead to France. Elizabeth died in 1914 in Austria and her widower didn't waste any time in marrying wife number two.

Getting hitched to a Neapolitan Count seemed almost tame compared to Croker's marriage to Beulah Benton Edmondson. The daughter of a Cherokee princess, her father was of Scottish descent and her uncle was a congressman from Oklahoma. A singer and a suffragette, Beulah first made herself known in New York in 1913 during a suffrage parade when riding an Indian pony in full buckskins. She reportedly met the 71-year-old ex-Tammany boss at a Democratic Party convention in Kansas City. By the end of 1914 they were married in St Agnes' Church in New York.

The couple honeymooned in Palm Beach, Florida, where Croker had invested heavily in beachfront property and kept an extensive summer house for himself. He regularly spent some months of the year there, with other months spent travelling though Europe and half the year in Glencairn, where the new lady of the manor must have seemed impossibly exotic. Even in Florida, where she'd been born, Beulah was regarded with fascination. The summer house became known as 'The Wigwam' and the unusual couple entertained and spent on a grand scale. Stories abounded, such as Mrs Croker buying five new automobiles in a week and giving some of them to the servants. However, the Grand Dames of Palm Beach society were never present. Croker and his beautiful new wife remained beyond the social pale.

That didn't matter to the Boss, but the final years of his remarkable life were embittered by a series of law suits brought against the newly wed couple by his children. With Beulah in line to inherit the vast majority of his wealth, three of Croker's children, Richard Jnr, Howard and Ethel, decided to fight their father's will. They alleged he was 'enfeebled by age' and that the second Mrs Croker wielded undue control over him. The suits demanded many transatlantic trips and produced little except substantial legal bills and irresistible copy for a ravenous media.

It seemed set to culminate in the summer of 1920 when a 26-day court case ended with the decision that the old man was 'in full control of his faculties'. Outside he declared to reporters: 'They say I am crazy because I won't give them all my money. My son Richard had to admit on the witness stand that I had given him $150,000 to start him in business. I have given to each of my other children $4,000 a year for life. That was pretty mean, wasn't it? I am going to try and forgive them.'

That process of forgiveness was hardly helped by the appeal quickly lodged by his kids. The dispute ran long after Croker's death and after almost twenty years of litigation Beulah was left almost penniless.

While her husband lived, however, the champagne lifestyle continued, the 'Wigwam' swung to the determinedly upbeat post-war rhythm and the old Tammany chieftain was still news. Asked his opinion of the new prohibition laws against both alcohol and gambling, he left no one in doubt about how silly he felt they were. In racing terms, he felt the sport would be completely neutered in America if betting wasn't possible. The European scene was different, he considered, because more people were willing to invest vast sums of money in what they, and many non-owners, still regarded as a sport. Croker remained a major investor in bloodstock, although in Ireland there were more urgently political considerations to the fore.

The Irish War of Independence that sprang up in early 1919 affected all aspects of Irish life, including the financial. For instance, the New York Times estimated that Glencairn's $400,000 valuation was almost halved due to the fighting. Croker resolutely kept a low profile in Irish politics but he was in favour of the December

1921 Anglo-Irish Treaty that brought the conflict with the British to an end but ignited a bitter civil war.

In 1922, returning from a trip to the US, the ship Croker travelled on was supposed to dock in Queenstown (now Cobh), near Cork city, but the port was closed due the imposition of martial law. Instead it sailed on to Liverpool, where everyone disembarked in a snowstorm. The unscheduled stop provoked more than a little confusion and Croker was forced to stand outside on a draughty pier for longer than advisable for an 81-year-old man. He arrived back in Glencairn with a chill that quickly grew worse. There were also fears of a gallstone problem but an operation was ruled out due to concerns regarding using anaesthetic in his weakened condition. Typically, Croker rallied briefly before relapsing and dying on 30 April.

His funeral was a national event in Ireland. The pallbearers included the President of the Dail, Arthur Griffith, the Lord Mayor of Dublin and the writer Oliver St John Gogarty. However, it also made an impact further afield. At Tammany Hall on Fourteenth Street, the flag on top was lowered to half-mast. Charles Murphy, then Tammany leader, described his predecessor as 'a born leader of men. He had magnetism, force and personality. That he was capable, tolerant, considerate, straightforward and genuine is evidenced by the large measure of affection and goodwill that had come to him during his career. All who knew him will feel they have lost a man of character and worth.'

That latter point is uncontestable. In financial terms, Croker's estate was valued at $5 million. Like him or loathe him, there was no ignoring the gruffly self-possessed figure who hauled his way to the top of American politics through nothing but his own fists and wits, as well a stubborn belief in his own opinion. It was that self-confidence that allowed him to dare of taking on the establishment in Britain through racing and to come up with a truly momentous success with Orby's Derby success. But despite the wealth, fame and success, even as an old man, Croker presented a particularly restless figure. It's not unreasonable to suspect at least some of that could have had something to do with what was happening back in New York.

Even before Croker's death, Tammany Hall's influence had started to wane, its best years becoming just a memory, and in terms of legacy there was little or nothing to show for all those years of power and wealth. Its purpose all along had been self-perpetuating, a classic case of power for power's sake. As one commentator at the time put it: 'In the end it left behind no more than Ozymandius.'

For an old man, split from his children, and still distrusted by many sections of polite society, that must have been a bitter pill to swallow, no matter how much he was worth financially. Politically, Croker embodied much of what people came to despise. The institutional corruption might have been coated in a roguish glamour but ultimately not everything has a price. A modern political concept such as 'the vision thing' would have been completely alien to the Irish-American millionaire.

Just like Orby, the horse that was to become his most lasting achievement, Boss Croker was buried at Glencairn. Not surprisingly for such a restless man, the story quickly developed that his ghost haunted the great house. Other myths quickly surrounded his Derby winner. When Orby died, according to Irish sporting folklore, his hooves were cut off and turned into ashtrays. The resultant numbers of hollowed-out 'antiques' that turned up in various pubs around Ireland would lead one to believe that Orby was more centipede than quadruped.

What might also have seemed to grow legs was the story of the 'Catholic' horse and his resolutely colourful owner – were it not for the fact that the best bits were all true.

Flyingbolt

Larry Holmes was the world heavyweight champion for seven years between 1978 and 1985, successfully defending the title twenty times. Only Joe Louis managed better than that. Blessed with a flawlessly pure boxing technique, and a left jab that could remove a speck of dirt from your eye, the man known as the Easton Assassin was a phenomenon of athletic prowess. But even at the height of his prowess he remained admired rather than loved, more respected than cherished, something that understandably rankled.

'Rocky Marciano couldn't have carried my jockstrap,' he complained once, furious that another former champ, unbeaten but against questionable opposition, and whose skill levels had more in common with a bar-room brawler than Sugar Ray Robinson, should be rated above him. Such bitterness didn't endear Larry to a lot of people. A need for acknowledgement often competed with an attitude of lofty disdain for those whose vindication he craved.

Now Larry Holmes is barely remembered. Or, if he is, it is as the guy who held the heavyweight crown after Muhammad Ali and before Mike Tyson: the guy in between. Holmes fought both men. He sparred with Ali as a youngster, admired him while at the same time fancying his chances. At the end of Ali's sad decline into a shambling shadow of his former self, it was Holmes who delivered the final blows. If it is possible to punch a man's lights out kindly, then Larry got close that night in Vegas in 1980. Holmes himself got a feeling of what it's like to go on too long when Tyson at his most fearsome negated all that skill with raw aggression. The older man was left with his memories, his bitterness and a reported purse of $2.8 million.

It's an unenviable role to fill, that of the underappreciated sporting hero. Ivan Lendl felt its cold embrace in tennis. Set against the raging charisma of McEnroe and Connors, the buck-toothed Czech with the metronomic playing style and halting English was a natural for the role of cartoon villain for those who like their sport to also contain a trace of pantomime. Never mind that in tennis 'personality' usually comes clothed in the sort of gurning, attention-seeking self-regard that only a hopelessly smug, middle-class audience could mistake for entertainment: Lendl's belief in watching tennis for tennis's sake just didn't seem to be enough.

It's ridiculous to suggest that Flyingbolt was ever aware of such resonances in his own career. Knowing him, the idea that any other horse in the world could count against him was ridiculous too. If Arkle is steeplechasing's Babe Ruth, then Flyingbolt is its Ty Cobb, a snarling, ornery, maddening sonofabitch that could, for a couple of years in the mid-1960s at least, make people believe the bad cop might actually be better than the good one.

If he were running these days, Flyingbolt would probably be appreciated more. We like our anti-heroes now. Too many human paragons have had their halos tarnished for us to really believe in the concept of heroism anywhere. Or if we do, it has to come with more than a dash of spit-in-your-eye grit. And Flyingbolt was nothing if not gritty. Neither man nor beast was advised to get too close to him. Anyone venturing into his box at Tom Dreaper's Kilsallaghan yard in Co. Dublin had to be on their toes. If the big chestnut with the broad white blaze didn't bite you, then there were a pair of hind legs that could take your eye out quicker than Larry Holmes's jab. At one stage, the horse was regarded as positively dangerous. But if he was mad, bad and very dangerous to know, then he has also been rated as the second-best steeplechaser in the history of the game. The only one better lived just a couple of boxes up the yard at Kilsallaghan.

However, whereas Arkle remains feted and remembered as the epitome of jump racing excellence, his rambunctious neighbour has been all but forgotten. A Google search for Flyingbolt reveals 21,000 matches: the same for Arkle comes up with ten times that. Yet at the peak of a rivalry that never made it to a racecourse, Timeform calculated there were only 2lb between the two champions. No other steeplechaser has been rated within a stone and a half of Flyingbolt. But it is Desert Orchid, or Red Rum, or Kauto Star who continue to attract adulation of a scale that dwarfs the attention given to the 1960s star.

It's hardly fair that such an immense talent is mostly reduced to a mere footnote in the Arkle story. Whatever you think about Timeform, there are still those around from that golden era who insist that Flyingbolt was Arkle's superior.

Barry Brogan's own story indicates a possible in-built affinity to the bad boy Flyingbolt rather than the cool clean hero that was Arkle. A brilliant jockey who initially rode out as an amateur at Tom Dreaper's yard, Brogan's professional career was heroically wayward as he fought addictions to booze and gambling, not to mention subsequently squeezing in four stretches at Her Majesty's pleasure. But he is also a man whose training career in Malaysia has survived a terrifying accident which left him with a spine fractured in two places. No man who has fought his way out of a wheelchair needs to tailor what he says, and what Brogan says of the horses he used to ride out on is unequivocal.

'For all Arkle's brilliance, I felt Flyingbolt was the better horse. If Pat Taaffe was alive, he'd tell you the same,' he declared.

Sadly Taaffe is no longer with us but his son Tom, a Gold Cup-

Arkle (left) and
Mill House battle
it out for the
1964 Cheltenham
Gold Cup.
Courtesy of Bernard Parkin

Arkle checks out his
reviews! © *Mirrorpix*

The Sporting Life

The old rivals clash again as Gallaher Gold Cup

ARKLE LOOKS UNBEATABLE BAR MISHAP

STIRLING TO HOLD FREEDOM IN THE EMBLEM

In fine trim for big bid

Mould is jined after dropping his hands

STAR MOSS

Run And Skip and Dawn Run (right) battle for the lead in the 1986 Cheltenham Gold Cup. © *Action Images*

The 1907 Epsom Derby winner Orby. © *Press Association Images*

Flyingbolt and Pat Taaffe. *Topical Press Agency/Hulton Archive/Getty Images*

Opposite: Sinndar and Johnny Murtagh return in triumph after winning the Prix de l'Arc de Triomphe in 2000. © *Press Association Images*

Above: Moscow Flyer and Barry Geraghty in full flow. © *Press Association Images*

Below: Alleged (right) is beaten for the only time in his career by Dunfermline in the 1977 St Leger at Doncaster. © *Press Association Images*

Istabraq and
Charlie Swan
secure another
Champion Hurdl[e]
at Cheltenham.

Andy Hooper/Daily Mail.
Rex Features

Sea The Stars
(Michael Kinane)
completes the
2,000 Guineas-
Derby double at
Epsom in 2009.

© *Press Association Image[s]*

winning trainer himself, remembers: 'Daddy always maintained there was nothing between the two of them. He might have liked Arkle more as a character, and he won three Gold Cups, but there was nothing between them.'

Such a view hardly dents Brogan's other standpoint – 'I honestly believe he would have beaten Arkle in the 1966 Gold Cup if Tom Dreaper had allowed him to run.'

Instead the trainer split the two great horses. Arkle duly completed a Gold Cup hat-trick while Flyingbolt came close to completing a ridiculous double. Never have 1–5 odds looked such value the effortless way he won the two-mile Champion Chase, but just twenty-four hours later he was only beaten three lengths into third in the Champion Hurdle. There were many convinced it wasn't Taaffe's finest hour at Cheltenham, either. If the great horseman had kicked earlier than he did and made the most of Flyingbolt's stamina, the argument went, then who knew what might have happened. And there was no doubting the horse's stamina. Just a month later he won the Irish Grand National carrying a monster 12st 7lb. Two years earlier, Arkle had won the same race carrying 12st and beating Height O'Fashion. Flyingbolt beat the same mare more easily, and conceding 10lb more.

The threat to Arkle's supremacy was very real and it's difficult to imagine he could have had Flyingbolt's sheer versatility. Would Arkle have been able to bridge the gap between two miles and three and a half with such apparent ease? We can say with some certainty that getting placed in a Champion Hurdle would have been beyond him. At seven years of age, the range of Flyingbolt's accomplishments were more impressive than his rival and during the summer of '66, even Pat Taaffe wavered about who the better horse might be. Flyingbolt surely had to get only better. But once again the anticipation of an epic clash was the best part.

Arkle's career-ending injury came at the end of 1966. Flyingbolt's racing life was to last for much longer but the brilliance of his youth would never again be replicated. During that summer, Flyingbolt spent his holidays out at grass, sharing a field with some cattle. When he came back to Dreaper's yard, everything seemed relatively normal. He went to Cheltenham in late October for a race where he had to concede a lot of weight but it was generally assumed to be just a routine if slightly strenuous bit of work for the heavy odds-on favourite. However, Flyingbolt started to fade from the second-last and eventually struggled home a poor third. Clearly this couldn't be right, and exhaustive tests were carried out. What they revealed might not have been life-threatening but the results were to effectively dash all the hopes invested in the wayward but magically talented chestnut.

Brucellosis is an infectious disease that causes inflammation of the joints and in 1966 there was little chance of a full recovery. It is transmitted through animal secretions, usually from pig, sheep or cattle, and is also known as undulant fever, such is the wavelike nature of its flu-like symptoms. The assumption was that one of the cattle that shared Flyingbolt's field during the summer must have infected him. That undulating effect meant there were times when the magnificently feisty young horse would seem to be almost back, only for those hopes to be dashed. Once Arkle was on the injury sidelines there was certainly a belief that even a half-right Flyingbolt would be good enough to successfully step into his place. But it wasn't to be. Flyingbolt returned to action in 1967 but was never the same horse again. There were suggestions of a heart problem as well. He was removed from Dreaper's yard and sent to England, where he raced on to age twelve until being retired after falling for the only time in his life as a twelve-year-old in 1971.

Those who even by then had raised Arkle to mythical status, and refused to believe any steeplechaser could be as good, would no doubt have been astonished to later hear Tom Dreaper's son, Jim, a Gold Cup-winning trainer in his own right, say that maybe there was one just as good as him in the same yard: 'It is impossible to tell how fantastic Flyingbolt might have been had he not contracted brucellosis.'

What can reasonably be concluded is that a concentration of such talent will probably never be seen again at the same time, never mind in the same stable. Kauto Star and Denman have provoked comparisons in the late 'noughties' and the Paul Nicholls-trained pair exerted a stranglehold on the major staying conditions chases. But the consensus remains that Arkle and Flyingbolt were of a different breed again. Tom Taaffe told me: 'When you think of what Flyingbolt did; win a Champion Chase, placed in a Champion Hurdle and then carry twelve-seven in the Irish National, that's a hat-trick that's impossible to picture today. I mean, that's class. Horses seem to have been tougher then, more resolute. Horses today are more susceptible to problems. I don't know whether it's inter-breeding a little too closely, or more flat breeding, or that horses today travel so much and intermingle so much that they pick things up. But you can't see something like that happening again.'

The story of Flyingbolt's own origins could hardly differ more from the hugely efficient business of the modern breeding shed. He was also a rarity for a top Irish chaser in that he was born in Britain. His father Airborne won the 1946 Epsom Derby, one of the greys to land the blue riband. But Airborne's already disappointing stallion career looked to be over in the late 1950s when he appeared to become impotent. Robert Way, a small-time stud owner and better-known bookseller based near Newmarket, agreed to give the former racing hero a good home and felt there was nothing to worry about turning Airborne out into a paddock with a nineteen-year-old mare called Eastlock, who had also been retired following a number of barren years. Remarkably they took a shine to each other, and even more remarkably that shine bore some fruit. The chestnut foal that entered the world in the spring of 1959 had already beaten considerable odds.

Way sold the foal at Newmarket December sales for 210 guineas to Larry Ryan from Co. Clare, who in turn sold the horse on as a yearling at Ballsbridge Sales through the Rathmore Stud owned by

the legendary jockey Martin Molony. In the immediate post-war
years, Molony was the most versatile jockey riding in Britain and
Ireland. A champion over jumps, he also regularly rode in the top
flat races, winning three Irish classics, as well as a Cheltenham
Gold Cup and three Irish Nationals. His tally of ninety-four
winners in Ireland remained a record for forty-two years. Veteran
racegoers who saw him in action still swear there has never been a
better jockey. All the more unfortunate, then, that injury stopped
Molony's career at just twenty-six years of age. His reputation was
still stratospheric, though, in 1960 when the Rathmore graduate
was sold for 490 guineas to George Ponsonby, a well-known buyer
who had supplied talented horses to Tom Dreaper before. Later it
was his new owner, Mrs Jean Wilkinson, who supplied him with
his name, cleverly using both the sire and dam.

Flyingbolt's first racecourse start on 13 May 1963 was hardly a
blindingly obvious display of outrageous talent. Over a mile and a
half at Leopardstown, the future champion steeplechaser was out
of his depth and finished unplaced. But it did give him a glimpse of
what would be required.

The signs that he was a quick learner were all over his next start
in an October bumper at Navan. Starting an 8–11 favourite,
Flyingbolt won easily under Alan Lillingston, who remembered:
'The lads in the yard had told me he could really go. He was a huge
horse with a giant stride but halfway down the back, not much was
happening, so I gave him a crack down the shoulder. He took off
like a jet plane. Tom Dreaper came up later and teasingly said –
come a bit soon, did you?'

But in the following day's headlines, there was no competition
with the horse who won his one and only flat race just half an hour
earlier on the same card. Operating in Arkle's shadow was a sign of
things to come. Back on the flat himself, Flyingbolt won at
Leopardstown before returning to the Dublin track for a maiden
hurdle victory. Two more hurdle starts, at Baldoyle and back at
Leopardstown, yielded easy victories and so did Cheltenham's

famous Gloucester Hurdle. Flyingbolt ended the season as a champion novice. But the end of the 1963–64 was all about Arkle on the back of his momentous Gold Cup defeat of Mill House.

What was already obvious was that Flyingbolt was the best hurdler Tom Dreaper had ever handled. Flat bred and possessed of enough speed to be competitive in any race at two miles, the chestnut with the flashy blaze was hardly a typical Dreaper 'type'. They were usually raw, stamina-laden three-mile chasers. This English-bred horse was different, and in so many ways.

For a few years in the mid-1960s, Johnny Lumley's job as a stable lad in the Dreaper yard required him to look after the two best steeplechasers in the world. The quiet young man with dark hair and sallow skin had given up a job in a Dublin jewellers shop to work with horses at the stables near his home, despite never having learned to ride a horse. Since riding out is a major plus in a tough job that requires working in all sorts of weather conditions, a lack of saddle-time might have disheartened some. But not Lumley. Looking after Arkle helped, of course. The Gold Cup champion was famously tractable and easy to deal with. Flyingbolt wasn't.

'A small child could walk into Arkle's box in absolute safety,' Pat Taaffe later remembered. 'No child, no man, would ever willingly step into Flyingbolt's . . . at least not twice.'

Paddy Woods, who rode Flyingbolt at home, admitted: 'I didn't like him. He was nasty enough, he'd bite you. It was his tem -perament, like a fella who wouldn't mind injuring you and think nothing about it.' Jim Dreaper remembered: 'We were warned, myself and my sisters, stay away from Flyingbolt. He was the kind of horse, if he was no good, everyone would say, "Christ, he's an ugly brute".'

The temperamental quirks of racehorses is a limitless subject. Often they can be connected to early experiences in their lives but sometimes making excuses for bad behaviour can be as futile as with humans who can be just plain odd. An impulsive nature feeds into the popular image of the fiery racehorse but, more often than not, obvious signs of temperament are a negative in terms of winning races. Clearly there was nothing wrong with Flyingbolt's desire to win, but he was just as clearly a nightmare to deal with. It's in such situations that the horsemanship of the stable staff becomes vitally important and in Lumley, headman Paddy Murray plus work riders Paddy Woods and Liam McLoughlin, Dreaper had some of the best.

Flyingbolt started to thrive over fences as a novice, winning all five races of his 1964–65 campaign, notably the two-mile Cotswold Chase at Cheltenham that is now known as – what else? – the Arkle.

It was around then that a private duel took place which steeplechase fans would still give anything to have seen replicated on a racecourse. Regular schooling was the rule at Dreaper's Greenogue stables and one typical such morning turned into a memory that never faded for the tiny few present to watch it. Taaffe later recounted in his autobiography *My Life and Arkle's* what happened.

> Flyingbolt was hacking along with Paddy Woods on his back
> and a funny look in his eye. Upsides on Arkle, I was thinking to
> myself that I would never see a prouder horse than this. Then
> he turned his head and slowly looked us over. You could
> almost see the curl of the lip. This was the 'Who are these
> peasants?' look of his that I was to come to know so well and I
> suppose I should have been forewarned. Next thing I knew he's
> taken a strong hold and was away. Not to be outdone, Arkle
> took an equally strong hold and got up alongside. And so these
> two young chasers who were then potentially the best in the
> world staged their own private race during what was supposed
> to be a normal session of morning schooling. They took the
> next four fences, neck and neck, flat out as though their lives
> depended on the outcome, while Paddy and I held on to

them for dear life and waited for the fires to die down. Well, they cleared them all right, but it was a bit too close for comfort and Mr Dreaper never allowed them to be schooled together again.

Woods later recalled the morning, principally for the shouts of 'Pull up, pull up!' from Tom Dreaper. 'It was easier said than done. They were going some speed and didn't want to stop. We were going an unearthly speed. I think the boss man nearly had a seizure. But they were so good at jumping, you didn't give a damn what speed they were going at.'

As well as not working together again, during the 1965–66 season, the trainer didn't allow them to race together either. From a logical point of view that made perfect sense. Arkle was rated stones clear of anything else and a Gold Cup hat-trick was just waiting to be completed. But it is tantalising to ponder what might have happened had the pair gone head-to-head. Woods was always an Arkle man and said later, 'It was never going to happen. The boss wouldn't allow it. I think he knew in his heart he'd be killing the younger horse for nothing. There were some people who thought Flyingbolt was better but he knew himself there would only be one result.'

Of course, such confidence comes laced with the benefit of hindsight. During the 1965–66 season, there could be no such certainty. After a hurdling warm-up, Flyingbolt won all six of his chases that season. He began in a handicap at Gowran, winning easily, before winning the Black & White Gold Cup at Ascot even easier. It was in December's Massey Ferguson Gold Cup that he gave what for many was his greatest performance, conceding at least 25lb all round in very heavy ground and winning by fifteen lengths.

'The ground at Cheltenham had been very heavy when we arrived, but by the time of the race unceasing rain had turned it into a sea of mud. For Flyingbolt, with twelve-stone-six to carry, you just couldn't imagine anything worse,' Taaffe wrote in his autobiography.

> I had Flyingbolt settled down nicely in the middle of the field, relaxed, jumping superbly and biding his time . . . Then, as planned, I made my first move going up the hill at the far end of the course and Flyingbolt, unleashed and free, began to fly through the field . . . At the top of the hill only Solbina and Scottish Memories were still in front. Flyingbolt went past and away from them, a man running against boys.
>
>   Rounding the final bend, he was going so easily that he found time to jump a path across the course. He stormed up the hill, increasing the distance between him and his pursuers with every stride, to win by fifteen lengths from Solbina with Scottish Memories third. It was the manner of his victory, rather than the victory itself, that caused the furore. Men remembered that Scottish Memories had met Arkle twice in the previous season and stretched him on both occasions. In this self-same race, the Massey Ferguson, there had been thirty-three pounds and two lengths between them. And in the Leopardstown Chase, thirty-five pounds and one length. Now Flyingbolt had given him twenty-six pounds and left him sixteen and a half lengths behind. Didn't this prove that Flyingbolt was now every bit as good as his more illustrious stable-mate?

That question seemed even more relevant after January's Thyestes Chase back at Gowran. In hock-deep ground, the chestnut favourite beat Height O'Fashion by a distance. Flying Wild, who was getting 29lb, was further back in third. In the 1964 Massey Ferguson, Arkle had failed to give 32lb to Flying Wild. Formlines are rarely so straightforward, but even Arkle's most fervent fans couldn't ignore the fact that he had a genuine rival whose statistical record at the very least stacked up against 'Himself'.

It could have been settled in the Gold Cup but Dreaper was never going to pitch both horses against each other when separating them promised a Cheltenham bonanza.

Flyingbolt started the shortest-priced favourite ever (1–5) for the two-mile Champion Chase and won in a canter by fifteen lengths. The aura that now surrounded the seven-year-old can be gauged by how Dreaper pulled him out again the following day for the Champion Hurdle, but more especially that he also started favourite to beat the specialist two-milers in a field of twenty. 'Flyingbolt not disgraced in finishing third,' was the *Irish Times* headline the following day. The report outlined how Taaffe felt he was going to 'trot up' coming to the fourth-last only for Flyingbolt to make a mistake. Despite that the horse took the lead at the second-last.

'Out of the corner of my eye, I saw the very horse I feared, Salmon Spray, coming along to tackle my fellow and Salmon Spray went half a length ahead at the last,' Taaffe told the reporter, while insisting the earlier mistake made no difference to the result. Salmon Spray, ridden by the stylish English jockey Johnny Haine, had fallen at the second-last in the 1965 Champion Hurdle and he held off Sempervivum in second.

Flyingbolt wound up his campaign with an attempt to secure Dreaper another Irish National. Just six lined up but Flyingbolt had to carry 12st 7lb with everything else on 9st 9lb or less. What the race would prove was whether the three and a quarter miles trip, the same as the Gold Cup, would be a problem. It wasn't. Flyingbolt veered slightly to left in the straight, giving Height O'Fashion a brief glimmer of a chance but Taaffe said later he was always confident of victory.

'Flyingbolt won the 1966 Irish National very easily from Arkle's old rival Height O'Fashion. He settled down beautifully and I was surprised how well he stayed,' he wrote later. 'If top weight worried him, it never showed. He made winning look an easy thing that day. Once again I was reminded that I was alternating between the king and crown prince of chasing. More than ever, it now seemed only a matter of time before he took over from Arkle.'

Unbeaten in eleven chase starts, there was no getting away from the suspicion that by the age of seven, Flyingbolt had actually achieved more than his more famous stable companion. Little wonder, then, that Taaffe always maintained there was nothing between the pair. However, thanks to that fateful summer holiday with Dreaper's cattle, the intriguing speculation as to how good Flyingbolt could have been began pretty much immediately afterwards. What was certain was that his best was behind him.

Two starts in the autumn of 1967 yielded a third at Punchestown and a seventh in the Mackeson Gold Cup back at Cheltenham. It was obvious that the bout of brucellosis had taken its toll. Tom Dreaper's instincts were to retire Flyingbolt there and then. Pat Taaffe felt the same. That powerful frame could hint at a return to its former glory but joint pain was never far away and it was impossible to get a proper run of preparation. However, his owners disagreed. Flyingbolt left Greenogue stables for Hawick in Scotland. Barry Brogan had moved to Britain and was riding for trainer Ken Oliver. Renowned for an attitude to life he summed up himself with 'win or lose, we'll have the booze', Oliver was a more than capable trainer, but any hopes that 'The Benign Bishop' would return the new arrival to his former level were doomed to failure.

Flyingbolt ran twice in the 1968–69 season, winning under Brogan at Haydock, but ended up back on the sidelines. After missing another year, he returned to race again and finished runner-up to Titus Oates in the 1969 King George VI Chase. There was also a third in the Cathcart at Cheltenham. Finally, however, the inevitable retirement came when, while carrying topweight in the 1971 Topham over the huge Aintree National fences, Flyingbolt and his jockey David Nicholson fell at the fourteenth fence. It was the only time he ever fell in thirty-four starts.

It was Berkshire trainer Roddy Armytage who oversaw the final races of Flyingbolt's career. Despite being stones short of his best, the horse left a definite impression, as he told the *Racing Post*.

> I rode him work one morning and just for a couple of furlongs you could feel what an astonishing machine he must have been. But after he worked, his joints used to swell up – there was nothing you could do about it . . . He was tall and angular and never looked well. We used to call him 'Nutty' because he was still a bit funny-tempered, although he had calmed down a lot. When he was a young horse he was very quirky. He would often look in a bad mood in his paddock and he'd bite you if he had the chance.

However, the mellowing effect of age was allowed to get a grip of the notoriously foul-tempered Flyingbolt, who shared a retirement field with his former stable companion, the 1968 Gold Cup winner Fort Leney. He died, aged twenty-four, in 1983. Unlike Arkle, his demise barely rated a mention.

It has been the same ever since. The horse fated to remain in Arkle's shadow when they were racing is still filling the same role. Navan racecourse hosts a Grade 2 novice chase that carries Flyingbolt's name. It is run in February and serves as a trial race for, wouldn't you know it, the Arkle at Cheltenham.

Every so often, though, the subject comes up about how Flyingbolt might have done against Arkle had the two ever battled each other in earnest. Funnily enough for a horse quick enough to be placed in a Champion Hurdle, Pat Taaffe reckoned Flyingbolt might have been vulnerable to Arkle's finishing speed. Considering the triple Gold Cup winner was a handicapper over flights, and at distances beyond two miles, it may seem a questionable argument, but the great jockey reckoned it might have been the case, maybe. He wasn't sure. As he always maintained, there was little or nothing between them.

Yet the washy chestnut with the raking stride and bad attitude has become a mere footnote in the Arkle story. It seems a cruel fate for the second-best steeplechaser of all time, but rare talent doesn't always get its full recognition, at least not from the general public.

'He probably deserves better,' Jim Dreaper once reckoned. 'But we're talking years ago. When you don't have good-quality film to show people nowadays, they don't remember. What was my father's expression? He wouldn't have been much for boosting up horses. He used to say, the people who should know will know.'

That's Flyingbolt's consolation, not that he would even come close to giving a damn. But those able to recognise a great steeplechaser will always reckon on him. And that's not a bad legacy.

Sinndar

A regular criticism of top-level flat racing is that it is dominated by a small but select group of owners who happen to have the most money. Such flak often comes in a piously critical tone from those who see no contradiction in vehemently shouting for one of the Premier League's tiny cabal of football teams that wind up winning trophies. To deny the connection between money and professional sporting success is as tiresomely naive as insisting that sport and politics are somehow unconnected. Stepping into a winner's enclosure is usually as financial a gesture as it is political.

Nevertheless it is the comparatively minuscule finance required to compete that at least partly explains why it is the National Hunt scene that chiefly satisfies the Irish fascination with finding out how quick one horse might be against another. Even in the most economically depressed years, Ireland's top jumpers have managed to compete against their opponents in Britain. But in the first half of the twentieth century that competitiveness only emphasised the depressed nature of the country's flat racing in relation to the rest of Europe. Compared to Britain, France and the USA, Irish flat racing was strictly second rate.

That that situation radically turned around owes much to the training genius of Vincent O'Brien and Paddy Prendergast, but also their ability to persuade hugely wealthy international owners to keep horses in Ireland. Many of them were Irish-Americans, attracted partly by the sentimental idea of having their colours carried in the 'old country' but principally by the hard-nosed evidence that O'Brien and Prendergast were supreme masters of their trade. Nothing gets an owner more sentimental than a winner.

O'Brien in particular mined the American market for owners as effectively as he did for horses. The resultant boost to Ireland's profile as a centre for top-class flat horses to be trained in is reflected in the giant bloodstock operations that today are repre-sented on the country's racetracks alongside the omnipresent Coolmore syndicate. One family, though, can claim to have been investing in the country for longer than most. That the family should in so many aspects be so exotically different from most things Irish only emphasises the unlikely links that racing can create.

For a nation that so self-consciously repudiates the concept of monarchy, Ireland remains something of a sucker for royalty and there isn't a personality entitled to a royal monicker that is better liked than the Aga Khan. But the appeal of the head of the Ismaili followers of the Shia faith is due to much more than the mere 'His Highness' title bestowed on him by Queen Elizabeth II of England.

The current Aga Khan is the forty-ninth Imam and took over the position in 1957. His father, the dashing Aly Khan, was overlooked for the position by the old Aga Khan, Sultan Mohamed Shah. The then twenty-year-old Prince Karim became the fourth Aga, an honorific title for the Imam given by the Shah of Iran in the nineteenth century. The succession of a prince of a relatively obscure Islamic sect with millions of followers scattered around the world might not have been an obvious focus of interest around Co. Kildare. But it most certainly was because the new Aga admitted to being perplexed about this racing and breeding game and had no interest in it. And that was of major interest indeed in Kildare due to the investment made there by his family for decades before.

The third Aga Khan first purchased Sheshoon Stud in the 1920s. It became part of a bloodstock empire that came to dominate European racing. The Aga won the Epsom Derby five times, including with the Triple Crown hero Bahram. A hugely powerful stallion list included the legendary Nasrullah. The Aga's son, Aly Khan, was also passionate about racing and his star performer was the classic filly Petit Etoile. Like his father, he also had some horses in training in Ireland and even rode a bumper winner here. After Aly Khan's untimely death in 1960, the present Aga Khan inherited six studs in Ireland, a massive bloodstock investment that provoked understandable unease about what the new ruler's racing intentions, if any, might be.

Kildare got lucky. The new prince studied the intricacies of breeding and developed an appreciation of the science involved as well as a realisation of the importance of patience. The Irish studs continued to produce a stream of top-class horses for the Aga's trainers in France and England. There might not have been horses in training in Ireland but there was no doubting his commitment to the country.

After the outstanding dual Derby winner Shergar was kidnapped by the IRA from Ballymany Stud in 1983, no one could have pointed a finger at the Aga Khan if he had disassociated himself from Ireland. The outstanding racehorse and potential star stallion was kidnapped from his birthplace by the IRA and never seen again. It is now generally accepted that the horse became difficult to handle within days of the kidnapping and ended up being shot, with his carcass buried in a bog. It was a devastating blow to his owner. But instead of pulling out, the Aga made a point of investing further in his Irish bloodstock interests.

It wouldn't be the last time that such magnanimity would be required. At the height of the Celtic Tiger economic boom, the

Turf Club's desire to redesign the crumbling Curragh racecourse was facilitated by the Prince, whose purchase of a hotel behind the main stands – reportedly for a sum close on €15 million – allowed for an extensive on-site expansion. However, the proposed €100 million facelift became bogged down in the planning appeals process and by the time the green light came to build, the economic tiger had curled up its tail and slunk away.

Crucially, though, the give and take wasn't all one-way. In 1989 the Aga Khan sent horses to be trained in Ireland by John Oxx. A couple of years later the famous green colours started to make their presence felt in a major way. The fallout of Aliysa's disqualification from the 1989 Epsom Oaks due to a positive drugs test resulted in the Aga taking away his English string of about ninety horses and pledging not to return to the UK until he felt the scientific management of racing there came up to scratch. That meant a lot of blue-blooded produce needed opportunities to race and Ireland presented them.

John Oxx's ability to produce the goods for the Aga Khan was already established by the time the owner's batch of yearlings arrived at his Curragh yard in late 1998. Timarida had landed three Group 1's two years previously. Ebadiyla won the Irish Oaks and French Leger in 1997, while Edabiya had scored in that year's Moyglare.

Sinntara was never in that league. The daughter of Lashkari had run six times as a three-year-old in 1992, breaking her maiden at lowly Wexford but progressing to turn the Irish Cesarewitch at the Curragh into a nine-length procession before winding her career up with a Listed victory. Her best form was at two miles but the Aga's willingness to row against the speed-obsessed breeding tide meant Sinntara got a chance at stud. She was, however, bred to the former top miler Grand Lodge and the produce was a medium-sized bay colt with an unmistakable touch of quality about him.

'We broke Sinndar here as a yearling and he was always a beautiful colt. Very well behaved, sensible and he had a lovely action. Anyone could have picked him out of the string,' Oxx remembers. 'Very often it is easy to spot the good ones almost immediately. They have a fluency and balance that others don't. They stand out. There are exceptions, of course, horses that don't look much initially but turn out good. But there aren't many.'

Oxx's disinclination towards over-racing two-year-olds was well known and any idea that the product of a Cesarewitch winner could be forward enough to make a significant mark as a juvenile seemed fanciful. But all through the summer of 1999, Sinntara's son continued to impress with the ease with which he did his work. There was nothing flashy about him. If anything he seemed almost too laid-back. But despite that easy nature, he had no trouble stepping up through the various stages of his training. And he always looked like an athlete, a natural in what he did.

The same has always been the case for Johnny Murtagh. Even the fifteen-year-old kid who showed up at the apprentice school having never sat on anything faster than a pony looked completely at home the moment he got up on a thoroughbred. There was a polish and an innate ability to get them to run for him that no inheritance or horsey background could have guaranteed. That the school should place him in the Oxx yard for his apprenticeship only smoothed things more. The trainer's blue-blooded string might not have seemed an obvious place for a kid on the make, but Oxx was never going to miss the ability Murtagh exhibited once he started riding fast work. At nineteen he was champion apprentice. A couple of years later, in 1991, he was stable jockey. And that's when things started to get very rough indeed.

Before 1993 was out Murtagh had lost his job, plagued by an annoyingly lengthening body but also by an increasingly out-of-control fondness for alcohol. Fighting one was impossible when still in thrall to the other. But treatment allowed him to regroup and that talent never deserted him. By 1995 he was stable jockey again and when Ridgewood Pearl enjoyed a tumultuous season culminating in a Breeders' Cup success, it provided her rider with a taste for racing's top table. Some jockeys shrivel under big-race pressure. But Murtagh thrived. What he needed to make the step up to being rated on the international scene was a genuine classic star. As he rode the Sinntara colt on the gallops during the summer of '99, he suspected there might be something exceptional lurking inside the phlegmatic athlete underneath him.

He wasn't alone in thinking that. When Sinndar made his debut over a mile at the Curragh in early September he started an evens favourite despite the presence of an Aidan O'Brien-trained runner, Rainbow And Gold, and another newcomer from Dermot Weld's yard called Media Puzzle. The latter achieved fame four years later with a Melbourne Cup success and immediately signalled he had talent with a promising debut third. But it was Sinndar that really caught the eye, leading over a furlong out and beating Rainbow And Gold by a length and a half. On good to firm ground it was a hugely promising display and even the famously cautious Oxx admitted he was considering the Group 1 National Stakes a fortnight later for Sinndar's next start.

The National Stakes, then run at a mile, was sponsored by the Aga Khan Studs but the 1999 renewal was generally billed as being about one colt. Bernstein came from Ballydoyle with a huge reputation and even soft ground couldn't stop him starting a 4–11 favourite. Sinndar, in contrast, was 7–1 and looked double those odds at halfway when already scrubbed along off Bernstein's fierce pace at the front. It was Dermot Weld's second-string, the 50–1 outsider Murawwi, that best managed to keep tabs on the leader, who was still clear a furlong out. However, Bernstein folded spectacularly and suddenly Murawwi was in the lead. Murtagh had to get serious with Sinndar but the response never stopped coming and the colt overcame the testing conditions to win by a head.

'We weren't surprised he was able to win as a two-year-old. Without being spectacular he was working nicely,' Oxx recalls. 'He didn't get a great rating for winning the National Stakes. I think the handicapper had to be cautious as the second had been beaten in a Nursery (fourth at Tralee) so he only gave him 105. That was a little cautious as it turned out. At the time I remember thinking we might have a horse that might get a place in a Derby.'

After such a tough race, plans to take Sinndar to Longchamp for the Grand Criterium were understandably abandoned and he entered the winter as a promising sort but with no one falling over themselves to take 25–1 ante-post odds for the Epsom Derby.

What he did have, however, was a profile that fit perfectly into what many bloodstock experts believe is required in a top classic prospect. It might not have earned him a sparkling rating but there was no getting away from the fact that the National Stakes meant Sinndar was a Group 1 winning two-year-old with every indication he would get better as a three-year-old. Sceptics might have pointed to Murawwi as a form blemish, and that Oxx's big-race pedigree revolved almost exclusively around fillies, but Sinndar was undeniably an exciting colt.

The millennium winter, however, was dominated in classic terms by a vintage group of horses from the then emerging Ballydoyle powerhouse under Aidan O'Brien. Champion two-year-old was Fasliyev, who earned an exceptional 125 figure from the official handicappers for a spectacular success in the Prix Morny. A career-ending injury, however, meant Fasliyev would not be around in 2000. Joint-second rated among the 1999 juveniles was Giant's Causeway. He would go on to become an outstanding miler/ten-furlong horse with a streak of five Group 1s in a row as a three-year-old. Like Giant's Causeway, another O'Brien colt, Aristotle, was a Group 1 winner at two having scored in the Racing Post Trophy. But in the list of Irish juveniles alone, two dozen horses ended 1999 rated higher than Sinndar, a staggering seven - teen of them based in Ballydoyle.

Racing history is littered with the detritus of classic dreams carried into three-year careers by juveniles that looked like the second coming of Pegasus. Apalachee sent the Timeform calculators whizzing after a spectacular two-year-old career that fizzled out into nothing. Tromos managed the same a few years later. Arazi might just be the finest juvenile European racing has ever seen and the little chestnut made America's best look stationary in a Breeders' Cup success so visually impressive it still makes one shiver at the brilliance of it. But he was only a pale shadow of that at three. Storm Bird, Danzatore, even St Nicholas Abbey, the evidential list is depressingly long of how a few months during the winter can turn rankings on their head. Oxx had experienced a little of it himself. In 1993 the Aga's colt Manntari won the National Stakes by ten lengths in the style of a potential world-beater. The following summer he finished last in the Irish 2,000 Guineas. But Sinndar was a different proposition.

Most racehorses have a limited shelf-life at the peak of their ability. The precocious might sparkle at two, the immature much later. The limits of that ability can vary enormously but at least part of what distinguishes the champions from merely the very good is the capacity to keep improving. Oxx looked at the colt cantering past him on those cold winter mornings and suspected that the unflashy demeanour concealed an ability that would flower with time. The extent of it, though, was unknowable. Finding out such things at home is a sure sign of an insecure personality at the helm. Oxx has always been far too quietly sure of himself to fall into that trap. Instead he waited until the middle of April 2000.

Not one of the horses in this book can boast an unbeaten record. Usually such a distinction is boasted by those who haven't raced much or have been raced unadventurously. Not that the feat is impossible. The great Italian Ribot ended his racing career with a perfect fourteen from fourteen. Colin, the drearily named American champion of the first decade of the twentieth century, was fifteen from fifteen, although a dozen of those came as a two-year-old. But rare is the runner that can't be outrun on at least one day. Sinndar had that day on the first start of his three-year-old career in the Ballysax Stakes at Leopardstown. And even then it was only by a head that he came up short.

The distinction of being the only horse ever to beat Sinndar belongs to Grand Finale, a Sadler's Wells colt, owned by the Moyglare Stud and trained by Dermot Weld. Not that it immediately resulted in a privileged life at stud for him. Instead, after racing in America, he re-crossed the Atlantic to go hurdling in England, winning four of his eleven starts up to 2006. Only after that did Grand Finale enter a breeding shed, and only then for bargain basement fees in the bloodstock outpost of Co. Durham.

But in the Ballysax circumstances allowed him to claim a huge scalp. Not that that was obvious to most on the day. Just four lined up for the ten-furlong event and Sinndar's 7lb Group 1 penalty meant he had to concede weight all round on very soft ground. He also had to make the running and a furlong out Grand Finale had Sinndar as a perfect target. He edged ahead but Sinndar was fighting back all the way to the line and the winner looked to be only barely hanging on. It certainly wasn't an obviously flamboyant announcement of a potential classic winner – by either horse. And yet Oxx was thrilled.

'The day he got beat was actually the day we realised we had a contender. He was giving away weight on ground he didn't like and I felt, "This fella is better than we thought." And we knew he would improve,' he says now.

That became the feature of Sinndar's career. Oxx reckons he progressed by 7lb through each race of his three-year-old career. It is rare for that level of improvement to continue throughout a season, and to be so reliably consistent, but when it coincides with the spring and summer of a three-year-old campaign, it can bring spectacular results.

Not that Sinndar's speciality seemed to be the spectacular. He returned to Leopardstown's ten furlongs for the Derrinstown Derby Trial the following month, ran in another four-runner race, and this time the head verdict went his way. Again he had to concede a Group 1 penalty but he had a pacemaker to cut out a pace and slipped up his inside on the turn in. The other 7–4 joint-favourite Bach joined him a furlong out but Murtagh was ultimately not all out to keep Sinndar in front.

'That was a very good trial. I thought he ran to 117–118 that day. If he improved again I remember thinking he would have a great chance at Epsom,' Oxx recounts. 'But we had to wait and see if he would do that. As it was, the amazing thing was he improved seven pounds every time he ran. He kept doing it. I don't remember much tension about the run-up to the Derby. We knew we had a good one and he was an easy horse to deal with.'

The pre-Derby focus was definitely elsewhere. Henry Cecil supplied two fancied runners, Wellbeing and especially the highly touted Juddmonte-owned colt Beat Hollow. The son of Sadler's Wells and Wemyss Bight had won both his starts and despite obvious inexperience started a 7–2 favourite. John Dunlop's Sakhee had won both the Sandown Classic Trial and the Dante at York and it was Aristotle who emerged from the Ballydoyle battalion of classic hopefuls to fly the Coolmore flag at Epsom. Despite looking a far from straightforward type – he had been disqualified from the Prix Greffulhe for veering alarmingly left in the closing stages – Aristotle was rated a 5–1 shot ahead of Sinndar on 7-1. Godolphin had engaged the veteran American rider Chris McCarron for their hope, Best Of The Bests.

The first Derby of the new millenium didn't initially appear a particularly vintage renewal and it came on the back of a series of less than vintage winners. But time has changed the perception dramatically. Even on that wonderfully sunny day at Epsom it was a race to quicken the pulse. Sakhee and Best Of The Bests found themselves towing the field along as Kingsclere, who had bolted on the way to post, hung badly right throughout. Murtagh had Sinndar perfectly placed just behind the leaders but when Sakhee quickened in the straight, Sinndar was momentarily caught flat-footed. 'My lad just found it hard to find his feet when Sakhee quickened. But once we got out he stayed on really well. I knew a furlong out I was going to get him,' the jockey remembered. Behind the leading pair, Beat Hollow was briefly hampered but was five lengths back in third at the line. Sinndar arrived there first by a length. 'I used to dream of the Epsom Derby when I was a kid so it was some fantastic feeling to win,' Murtagh said.

Time, though, has shone an even more positive light on the race. Sakhee turned into an outstanding four-year-old, culminating in a six-length rout in the Arc. Beat Hollow landed the Grand Prix de Paris in his first start after Epsom and subsequently won three Grade 1s when switched to race in America. Two years later Best Of The Bests, fourth in the Derby, won the Group 1 Prix d'Ispahan.

'I believe the *Racing Post* rated it the best one-two in the Derby since the war,' Oxx says. 'It has to be one of the best Derby performances. For the next two years the form kept being advertised.'

The trainer's satisfaction in winning a race he describes as being 'etched in stone' was typically understated but heartfelt just the same. What completed a perfect summer was a follow-up Derby success at the Curragh. The home classic meant a lot to Sinndar's trainer. In 1962, his father John Oxx Snr saddled Arctic Storm for the inaugural Irish Sweeps Derby, only for the horse to be edged out by Tambourine. He recalled in Michael Clower's book *Kings of the Turf*:

> I have vivid memories of the 1962 Irish Derby and what the result meant in our house. Arctic Storm was an unlucky loser because he was brought to his knees at the top of the hill, and he was only beaten a short head. My father was proud of his horse but he was disappointed because Arctic Storm could have done so much better. He would have been a worthy Irish Derby winner, and he was a better horse than Tambourine who did nothing subsequently.

Thirty-eight years later Oxx felt at the top of the hill that his luck might not be in either. The previous morning Sinndar had returned from work lame with a sore heel and, although it cleared up in time, it wasn't encouraging to see Murtagh niggling the colt at halfway. By then, though, the 2,000 Guineas winner King's Best, who had had to miss out on Epsom, was pulled up with a career-ending injury. The other classic winner in the field was the Prix du Jockey Club victor Holding Court, who had made most of the running at Chantilly. He couldn't do the same at the Curragh, however. Oxx ran three others in the race including the pair of 200–1 outsiders, Raypour and Takali. They ensured a true pace and by the time the field reached the straight, Sinndar started to hit top gear.

The colt powered through the yielding ground to put nine lengths between himself and the runner-up Glyndebourne, with Ciro in third. Raypour and Takali were fourth and fifth and the latter cut out a reputation for himself afterwards with Group 2 and Group 3 victories. Those that wrote the race off as a top-class winner summarily dismissing sub-standard opposition on the back of Holding Court finishing only sixth also had to cope with the form boost later in the season of Ciro landing a Grade 1 in America. Oxx and Murtagh's satisfaction was only embellished by a million-dollar millennium bonus from the sponsors Budweiser for completing the Derby double.

Sinndar then disappeared off the big-race radar for the rest of the summer. In his place Giant's Causeway took centre stage with a series of narrow victories that earned him the sobriquet 'the Iron Horse'. He was kept to mile and a mile-and-a-quarter races so the mile-and-a-half King George appeared wide open for the previous year's three-year-old champion, Montjeu.

In the first half of 2000, the French superstar looked all but unbeatable. Winner of the French and Irish Derbys in 1999, and that year's Arc, Montjeu was at his imperious best through the Tattersalls Gold Cup and the Grand Prix de Saint-Cloud before appearing to hit another peak again in the King George. He cruised through the race à la Nijinsky but beat better opposition such as Fantastic Light while doing so. A second Arc looked his for the taking the following October. What really occupied minds that summer was the idea that Montjeu might tackle Godolphin's Dubai World Cup winner Dubai Millennium, a clash that never happened due to injury to the latter.

In terms of charisma, Montjeu and Giant's Causeway were in a different league to the apparently stolid and ultra-professional Sinndar. The depth of that Epsom success had yet to fully reveal itself and it is not the Oxx way to hype his horses. But back at the Curragh, the dual Derby winner was continuing his improvement. The aim was the Arc and a clash with Montjeu. A warm-up race was required and Oxx elected for an early trip to Longchamp for the Prix Niel rather than risk a hard race in the Irish Champion Stakes. And it was in Paris that Sinndar injected the first stirrings of doubt into the Montjeu camp.

The older horse also ran on that Arc trial day in the Prix Foy. He won, but not particularly impressively. The general consensus was that the trials were often unsatisfactory, with often no pace leading to bunch finishes. Significantly, though, there was no bunch finish to the Niel. Again led by Raypour, Sinndar cruised through the race and beat the subsequent Group 2 winner Crimson Quest by eight easy lengths. And he covered the mile and a half in almost six seconds faster than Montjeu.

'I know it was only a trial but I thought he was spectacular in the Niel. He won it very easy and it was a good time,' Oxx remembers. 'Johnny was very confident going into the Arc. He felt there was no end to the horse, no bottom to him. Sinndar had a marvellous temperament. He never turned a hair at home but once he got to the track he seemed to rise to the occasion. I could see in the trial that Montjeu had been a bit disappointing. Mick (Kinane) rode Montjeu and he would tell you himself he didn't think he was the same horse at all. But on fast ground I felt he had never put in the sort of times that Sinndar had. And our horse kept improving.'

The Irish star ran the Arc almost a second faster than the Niel. The French Oaks winner Egyptband took her chance in the race as did the Prix Vermeille heroine Volvoreta. Samum had won that year's German Derby. But the 2000 Arc was billed as a match-up between Sinndar and Montjeu, who started a 4–5 favourite. Earlier in the day Murtagh and Oxx hit the Group 1 mark in the Prix de l'Abbaye with Namid. As omens went it was hard to top.

Raypour was in again to ensure the Arc pace but he missed the break and it took a couple of furlongs for him to hit the front. Sinndar tucked into his slipstream and the pair whizzed around Longchamp in perfect synch. Montjeu travelled typically well and closed up in the false straight to be within striking distance on the turn in. When Murtagh pressed the button, though, his older rival quickly started to flounder. Instead it was Egyptband who emerged as Sinndar's main threat, but it was noticeable how much in control the colt was throughout the final hundred metres. He passed the post a length and a half ahead and looked worth more than that.

He was the first Irish-trained Arc winner for twenty-two years and the first horse ever to complete the Epsom Derby-Irish Derby-Arc treble. For Murtagh he was the centrepiece of an Arc-day treble completed by Petrushka in the Prix de l'Opera. The young jockey had yet to fully conquer his personal demons but that ambition to be a major player on the world stage was fulfilled. He wound up 2000 with a dozen Group 1 victories worldwide, including a Breeders' Cup success on Kalanisi. To Oxx, Sinndar's Arc was the perfect conclusion to a remarkable year.

'Every trainer hopes to get the top one some day and most never get the chance,' he said. 'You just feel grateful that a horse like him has come along, and when it turns out so well you get a lot of satisfaction.'

Before the decade was out, several more top ones emerged from the Oxx yard with Sea The Stars a highlight in 2009. But the Aga Khan's investment in both the trainer and Irish racing generally paid off again before that with Alamshar's Irish Derby-King George double in 2003, while Azamour secured a collection of top Group 1 prizes from a mile to a mile and a half during 2004 and 2005.

Both were outstanding horses. However, the Prince has had none better than Sinndar in recent decades. The French-based Dalakhani was a spectacular Arc winner that earned a 132 rating in the International Classifications three years after Sinndar. But that was the same as the Irish-based horse earned for his own Arc and Murtagh for one claimed that underestimated the colt. Unlike Montjeu in his pomp, or even Dalakhani who often won with his jockey showboating for the crowd, Sinndar was straightforwardly professional in his endeavours. There is a school of thought that suggests racehorses can take on the characteristics of their trainers and Sinndar reflected much of the understated good sense that characterises Oxx.

But even if that 132 is conservative, it still places Sinndar ahead of most of Ireland's other champions in recent decades. Only Hawk Wing (133) and St Jovite (135) could boast higher ratings in the 23-year period between 1985 and 2008, and Hawk Wing never came close to repeating his freakishly wide-margin victory in the 2003 Lockinge. St Jovite's reputation rests on an Irish Derby-King George double completed in one month during the summer of 1992. Ireland's senior handicapper, Garry O'Gorman, doesn't hesitate to put such figures into context.

'Ratings are really a reflection of what a horse has been asked to beat. A one-off like Hawk Wing in the Lockinge can often fare better than a horse like Giant's Causeway who can't be bothered to win by more than a neck but still wins. The name of the game is winning races — it's not a time trial,' he says.

'The International ratings began in 1977 in Europe and it is now generally accepted that in the first few years the figures were higher than since. When they started, 140 for instance was taken as being the mark of a typical champion. That's what Alleged got for his second Arc in 1978. Levels have stabilised since. And Sinndar was a really good horse. We had Sinndar at 128 for the Irish Derby and upped him to 132 in the Arc. Johnny Murtagh came out afterwards and said he knew Sinndar had improved ten pounds by the Arc but when you take into account the weight-for-age scale of six pounds, we in fact agreed with him,' O'Gorman adds.

There were plenty who felt Sinndar would have been an even better four-year-old but the Aga Khan promptly retired the colt to his Gilltown Stud in Kildare. Expectations were high for a horse that was able to win a Group 1 as a juvenile, as well as secure middle-distance championships at three. If anything those expectations deepened when Shawanda emerged from Sinndar's first crop of foals. Racing in the Aga's colours, she travelled from Alain de Royer-Dupre's Chantilly yard to turn the 2005 Irish Oaks into a procession. She followed up with an effortless victory in the Prix Vermeille.

But it quickly became obvious that Sinndar didn't tick all the fashionable speed boxes for breeders. His other Group 1 winner from that Gilltown period was Youmzain, a slow-maturing colt that won a pair of Group 1s but is best remembered for finishing runner-up in the Arc three years in a row. Late-developing middle distance was not what the top end of the market wanted.

In 2006 the stallion was switched to the Aga's French operation and found himself at the Haras de Bonneval near Le Mesnil Mauger in Normandy. Sinndar became one of the most high-profile horses in France, where the breeding industry has struggled in recent decades, especially compared to Ireland. His first French crop included the champion two-year-old filly Rosanara, who won the Prix Marcel Boussac.

But Sinndar's travels haven't ended there. In 2009 the Aga Khan agreed a leasing agreement with the Sao Paulo Breeders Association for both Sinndar and another stallion, Linngari, to shuttle to Brazil for the southern hemisphere breeding season.

'Sinndar's shuttling was only due to the generosity of the Prince Aga Khan, whose father, the late Aly Khan, had quite a few friends in Brazil,' said Eduardo Guimaraes, manager of the Belair Stud where Sinndar stood outside Sao Paolo.

Like Ireland decades before, Brazil's current economic growth has coincided with a burgeoning development in its racing industry. Hardly surprising, then, that a mixture of sentiment and finance is being turned to good effect on the other side of the world too.

Moscow Flyer

Behind all the macho bombast, Papa Hemingway could sometimes hit a nail bang on the head. The old poseur might have preferred the bulls but sauntering around Auteuil was, he reckoned, a good way to spend an afternoon too. It is remarkable how many so-called professionals can fail to really see what's happening in front of them on a racetrack yet the American writer twigged the real danger of steeplechasing instantly. In his classic short story 'My Old Man', Hemingway states it isn't the jumps you have to worry about; it's the speed you take them at. That applies to every kind of jump race over every distance. However, it is especially relevant to steeplechasing over the minimum distance of two miles. By definition everything happens faster, including the chances of disaster. Get it wrong over four miles and there can be time to recover: going flat out over fences at half that trip and even the tiniest slip-up means the difference between winning and losing, or worse.

Tony McCoy knows more about winning over jumps than any jockey who has ever peered through a set of muddy goggles. There's hardly a race worth mentioning he hasn't won: Gold Cups, Grand Nationals, the lot. Yet it is Cheltenham's Queen Mother Champion Chase that holds particular appeal. It is the race that he wanted to win more than any other and he managed it in the year 2000 on board Edredon Bleu, who won a memorable duel up the famous hill against Direct Route. That only reinforced the champion rider's view: 'Two miles jumping fences at ferocious speed. It's all got to go right, no room for mistakes. You've got to have everything. It's the supreme test for a chaser.'

That might not be a universal belief, certainly not among National Hunt purists for whom the Gold Cup remains steeplechasing's Holy Grail. However, from a jockey's point of view it is easy to see the appeal of two-mile racing. Speed is usually their narcotic of choice, the most prized substance of all. In National Hunt racing, it is two-mile chasing that represents speed in its purest form. Throw in a dozen big black obstacles that have to be negotiated accurately, with the minimum of time wasted on such fripperies as caution and self-preservation, and the challenge to nerve, eye and judgement is obvious.

It's a curious anomaly, then, that one of the modern era's supreme exponents of this high-risk, ultra-focused discipline could be a casual, unpredictable, occasionally feckless character whose overwhelming natural talent sometimes meant he ignored mundane requirements such as jumping properly. But that was Moscow Flyer, an outstanding athlete whose disposal towards 'messing' would have made him a nightmare, had it not been for his ability to produce towering performances when it really counted.

There are examples throughout sport of flamboyant talents that might engender respectful awe instead of genuine affection were it not for some all-too-recognisable flaws. Seve Ballesteros's wayward drives were familiar to club golfers the world over but they made his recovery play seem even more miraculous. In racing Henry Cecil's genius for training horses mingled with a tempestuous personal life that would have struck a 'there but for the grace of God' chord with so many, and ultimately made him hugely popular within the industry. It was an all-too-obvious vulnerability that helped Moscow Flyer become a standard-bearer for Irish jump racing in the greater public consciousness in the first half of the 'noughties'.

The Irish phrase would be messing but in many respects the American equivalent of goofing off is more appropriate to Moscow Flyer's habit of sometimes coming back down to earth with a crash. The cardinal sin for a steeplechaser is literally crashing to earth – or sending its jockey to terra firma – and for much of his career over fences there was a weird synchronicity to how the elegant bay with the big white splash on his face would fail to finish once in every four races. It got to be like clockwork, three wins followed by an exit. When he stood up, he won. But then it seemed like it got too easy. Moscow Flyer would pay attention to everything except what he was supposed to and everyone's heart would skip a beat.

Possessed of so much natural talent, he was often able to get away with doing the bare minimum which, like a bored pupil in a classroom, could lead him to goofing off. There was nothing malicious in it, nothing threatening. But at his peak he was like a precocious teenager, gifted beyond the norm, and full of the joys, but liable occasionally to take his eye off the ball.

His jockey Barry Geraghty described him as a 'nightmare ride – but a good nightmare'. Naturally quick, there wasn't a pace invented that could get him off the bridle over fences. When he concentrated, his jumping could be dead-eye accurate. But sometimes the two weren't in synch and even when they were it could lead to Moscow Flyer hitting the front very quickly. Since he was one of those horses that doesn't do much in front, that in turn could leave Geraghty sitting there feeling vulnerable. When it all came together, though, there has rarely been a more convincing two-mile champion.

Flyingbolt and Dunkirk were clearly superior to their oppo-sition when landing the Champion Chase in the 1960s. Moscow Flyer twice landed the crown, in 2003 and 2005, and only a typically careless mistake the year in-between prevented a hat-trick. The difference with most any other winner of the Cheltenham crown is that Moscow Flyer competed in a vintage era for the division. During the 2004–05 season, there was another pair of top two-milers that would have been outstanding at any other time. That Azertyuiop and Well Chief peaked at the same time as their Irish rival was one of those happy coincidences that set a benchmark for future generations. And it is a sign of the special talent possessed by Moscow Flyer that he emerged best while leaving the impression there was still enough in reserve to allow him to goof off any time he damn well wanted.

But that was just him. A horse that never grew out of dropping a shoulder occasionally and plunging his rider to the ground was always going to be just that little bit different. Most equines with a taste for the roguish drop a rider and take off into the sunset, daring everyone to catch them. Moscow Flyer dropped everyone, his trainer Jessica Harrington, the lads in the Co. Kildare yard that doted on him, even Geraghty, and would then stand still next to them, almost sniggering at having caught them out again. There were other idiosyncrasies. Normally a lover of tearing around a paddock, the champion chaser resolutely refused to leave his box for a run-around if it was raining. The stable door would be left open but he would peer dispiritedly up at the sky like a pensioner deciding it wasn't worth the wick getting the bus in such weather.

Only those whose racing experience consists solely of gambling and who have never dealt with the living, breathing creatures they are betting on cannot hope to appreciate the individuality within them. They might all look like a mass of brown quadrupeds running around a field, but think how interchangeable in our biped uniformity we must look to them. It's that individuality that helps explain how some can be so good. Not all of them. One of Vincent O'Brien's great champions, El Gran Senor, was an equine paragon, brilliantly talented and temperamentally straighter than a New Mexico highway. But many of the really top ones have a quirkiness that make a nonsense of any lazy assumption that they're somehow all the same. When Geraghty jumped off Moscow Flyer after finishing up a tumultuous 2004–05 season with an ultra-smooth success at Aintree, he told Harrington that the horse was only then becoming a nice ride. Anyone predicting at the time that Moscow would never win again would have been laughed out of Liverpool. But he didn't. It's difficult not to suspect that there might be some link between that sudden greater amenability to instruction and the subsequent diminution of his powers. However, that's to risk venturing into psychobabble. In his pomp Moscow Flyer simply liked having a say in how and where he went. And then, like all of us, he got older.

He ran just three more times the following season before being retired at twelve years old with a record of twenty-six wins from forty-four starts, and well over a million sterling earned in prize money. Timeform reckon there have been just six chasers better than him. They include Flyingbolt and Dunkirk as well as Arkle, Mill House, Kauto Star and Desert Orchid. And that's it, across the distances over fences: not bad for a goof-off.

But Moscow Flyer wasn't quite finished. A year into his retirement, some of which was spent at the Irish Horse Welfare Trust farm in Co. Wicklow, he appeared one last time at the 2007 Punchestown Festival for a charity race. Ridden by Jessica Harrington's seventeen-year-old daughter, Kate, he won easily. He returned to a tumultuous reception. Barry Geraghty applauded his old partner back into the winner's enclosure and could only laugh when a wag in the crowd enquired as to how he'd ever managed to get beaten on such a horse. If anyone knew it was Moscow Flyer, but he wasn't telling.

There's also no way of knowing what he might have achieved if he hadn't been sent over fences. It's often overlooked in the light of his subsequent steeplechase career, but Moscow Flyer was a top-class hurdler, a proven Grade 1 winner, and the sole threat, Harrington believed, to Istabraq's status as champion in 2001. More importantly, Istabraq's jockey Charlie Swan believed the same. The pair clashed three times in the winter of the 2000–01 season and there was no conclusive outcome. One of them kept falling. But that was the season ruined by a foot-and-mouth epidemic in Britain that claimed that year's Cheltenham festival. In the greater scheme of things, Istabraq's attempt on a historic fourth Champion Hurdle success getting ruled out was hardly a biggie. But by the time the following season came round, Istabraq's powers had started to fade and Moscow Flyer was being campaigned over fences.

If he'd remained hurdling, though, it is easy to argue that he could have been the logical successor to the old champ. Hors La Loi took advantage of Istabraq being pulled up to win at Cheltenham but he would hardly have got within sniffing distance of Istabraq at his best. Moscow Flyer could do, and more. Swan never conceded that he wouldn't have won but readily admitted it would have been close had the pair of them ever stood up. And what the former Irish champion jockey knew only too well was the task facing anything tackling such a horse over fences. Swan still rates Moscow Flyer the best two-mile chaser he has ever seen, no bad tribute from a man who rode Viking Flagship to win a Champion Chase.

The other imponderable is how might the great two-miler have fared if asked to stretch out to three miles. Harrington originally bought the son of Moscow Society and Meelick Lady for 17,000 guineas as a prospective staying chaser. His pedigree wasn't outstanding but what there was contained plenty of stamina. A champion at two and two and a half, Moscow Flyer was almost tested in the 2004 King George VI Chase over three miles at Kempton, only for a few weeks earlier to put up possibly the finest performance of his career in the Tingle Creek Chase at Sandown. After that it was a no-brainer to keep to shorter trips. But Harrington always wondered what might have happened at the longer distance. It's academic now, yet even the suspicion of that kind of versatility indicates the towering raw talent of the horse.

'Even when I was riding him I knew he would leave a void when he finished up, but it ended up being some void. He really was a horse in a million,' Geraghty said later.

> He was actually easier to ride on the big days. Especially in the races in England there would always be pace. Once there was pace he settled and we could concentrate on beating Azertyuiop or whoever it was. It was different in those races at home when he'd be up against small fields on heavy ground and everyone expected us to win easy. He was always taking a pull in them because it was so easy for him. He'd end up pulling and dragging, looking at fellas standing at the wings, messing around and not concentrating. That's why sometimes those races were more of a challenge. Moscow Flyer had too much time to think and that's when he'd end up forgetting to jump.

Geraghty's affection for the horse is hardly a surprise. As an unusually self-confident young rider who had just managed to win the first jockeys championship of his career, Geraghty was nevertheless acutely aware of the need to be on board a genuinely high-class animal in order to make the ascent to the true summit of his profession. Moscow Flyer took him there. In 2002 the pair won the Arkle Trophy at Cheltenham. By the following year, the star novice had graduated to senior champion. And in the process he catapulted his jockey to fame. Geraghty's four other winners at Cheltenham in 2003, along with the small matter of that year's Aintree Grand National too, placed him firmly at the top table of jump jockeys. It even led to wider recognition. He wound up 2003 as Ireland's Sports Personality of the Year, a rare excursion for racing outside its own tightly sealed parish into the country's wider sporting conscience.

Jessica Harrington explained the horse's impact on her in a book called simply *Moscow Flyer*. She wrote: 'This beast has changed my life irrevocably.' The same could be said for Brian Kearney, whose first venture into racehorse ownership seemed almost ridiculously fortunate. The Dublin engineer told Harrington and her blood-stock agent husband, Johnny, that he was prepared to spend twenty grand on a horse. He then stood back, allowed the professionals to do their job, and found himself in possession of one of the all-time-great chasers. Thousands more became enthralled by the progress of the elegant character that couldn't always be relied upon to avoid trouble but never ducked the challenge of getting out of it. That's some legacy for a horse with an unlikely background for a champion.

Moscow Society's main claim to fame was that he was by Nijinsky, trained by Henry Cecil and owned by Sheikh Mohammed. But classic aspirations didn't work out. He ran in the 1988 Queen's Vase at Royal Ascot over two miles but broke down. Instead of a multimillion-dollar stallion career for the Sheikh, he was bought as a National Hunt stallion for Ballyvolane Stud in Co. Limerick. In May 1994 the produce of Moscow Society and the unraced mare Meelick Lady came into the world, bred by the Clare man Eddie Joyce. He had never sold a horse at public auction before so got his father-in-law John Ryan to consign the horse at the Tattersalls Sales in Fairyhouse. Ryan in turn got Jim Mernagh to look after the horse at the sales and Mernagh recommended the four-year-old Moscow Society gelding to the Harringtons, who were old friends.

Jessica Harrington outlined in her book the immediate impression the unnamed and unbroken youngster made on her. It was the natural athleticism in him, that vague yet unmistakable mixture of balance and attitude that indicates a raw frame may develop into something useful. Kearney's limit was twenty thousand, and Harrington was hardly in a position to quibble since she hadn't even met her new owner. But Moscow Society was unfashionable, there wasn't a decent winner in the pedigree until quite a bit down the page and anyway, the horse was due to be sold quite late in the day. Hours spent examining hundreds of horses at a sale is a challenge that encourages many to avail themselves of the first opportunity to leave. Time would prove they missed out spectacularly.

That hardly fits with the typical caricature of the shrewd Irish horse tangler, a clichéd figure who is popularly regarded as never being far away from a large drink, a loaded syringe or a wealthy victim, sorry, customer. Dealing in National Hunt horses is a pursuit enjoyed through far more layers of Irish society, and in far more parts of the country, than its more affluent flat equivalent. Stories of unsuspecting buyers having rings run around them by twinkle-eyed farmers pulling nags out of boggy fields are unending. So if some of the 'shrewdies' were missing when Moscow Flyer went through the sales ring, it fitted perfectly that he should end up with someone who is pretty much the polar opposite of that cliché.

Jessica Harrington's family connection with Ireland goes back to the eighteenth century when King George II's personal chaplain found himself out of a job when the monarch died. He travelled across the Irish Sea in 1763 and ultimately became Archbishop of Dublin. Almost a century later the Fowler family owned about 6,000 acres of Co. Meath and were firmly part of the Anglo-Irish establishment. By the time Jessica Jane Fowler was born in London in February 1947, the estate's acreage had decreased to less than a thousand but in the economically depressed Ireland of the 1950s, there was no denying the family lived upstairs rather than downstairs.

Her father, Brigadier Fowler, experienced the horror of Passchendaele in 1917, won an Olympic silver medal for Britain in polo at the 1936 Berlin Olympics, and was a stalwart of the Meath hunting scene, riding well into his eighties. His daughter can't remember learning to ride because horses were an inherent part of her childhood. As an adult that passion for horses manifested itself in a hugely successful career in three-day eventing, competing for Ireland at World and European championship level and finishing third at the famous Badminton competition in 1983.

After the break-up of her first marriage, she remarried, to the bloodstock agent Johnny Harrington, and moved back to Commonstown Stud in the tiny village of Moone in South Co. Kildare. His business life left little time for looking after the few horses he trained under permit, so as well as maintaining a hectic schedule in the eventing world, Jessica Harrington began over-seeing the small string of racehorses. In the mid-1980s she took over the permit, quickly exchanged that for a public licence, and struck out into the then ultra-male world of training racehorses.

'There were very few women training in Ireland at the time and I felt that other trainers would be looking at me. "What's she doing here? It's about time she went home and looked after her children." You just paid no attention,' she recalled in her book *Moscow Flyer*.

> Some of the owners were funny too. A lot of them wouldn't want to speak to me. They'd want to speak to Johnny instead. They'd ring up and ask to speak to him but he wouldn't know how their horse was and he'd have to ask me. But you got over those things, and gradually it turned around. I knew I had arrived when the owners started asking for me, not for Johnny.

The tall, flaxen-haired woman cut a formidable figure anyway and there was a no-nonsense competence that fitted perfectly with the expensive accent. But what really impressed those owners was what impresses all owners – success. It quickly became obvious that the ability to get a racehorse hard fit revolved around much the same techniques that got eventers ready too. Brockley Court won ten races including a Grade 3 hurdle. Oh So Grumpy landed the Galway Hurdle in 1994. Dance Beat and Space Trucker rose through the ranks too. In 1999 the latter provided his trainer with an all-important first success at the Cheltenham Festival when winning the two-mile Grand Annual handicap. A couple of years previously Space Trucker had run third to Make A Stand in the Champion Hurdle but an attempt at the Champion Chase in 2000 yielded only a fifth to Edredon Bleu. Already in the yard, though, was a young stable companion that would do better.

One of the curios about Moscow Flyer is that he was never able to win a bumper. He had four attempts and the nearest he got was a pair of third placings. Although bred to stay, it seemed like he flattened out in the amateur flat races, which might seem to favour speed but usually reward stamina.

There is no rule of thumb but a horse capable of winning a two-mile bumper is often best suited to two and a half miles over hurdles and three over fences. More and more the trend for two-mile hurdling is to buy mile-and-a-quarter speed from the flat. But, as with most things equine, nothing is set in stone. Istabraq won over two miles on the flat, scored over almost two and three quarter miles at his first Cheltenham festival and turned into a Champion Hurdle legend. Moscow Flyer was also a relatively weak individual when he began his racing career, so that could explain how he appeared to peter out in his bumper runs. But it is also significant that when he exceeded two miles over hurdles he always got beaten. Hindsight could indicate it was an early sign about how speed would end up being his forte.

On 31 October 1999 the real Moscow Flyer story began. His first start over hurdles was at Punchestown and it came on the back of evidence that jumping would be the making of him. Schooling had gone well and he would team up for the first time with Geraghty, whose instructions were to make sure the horse enjoyed himself. The horse enjoyed himself so much he found himself in front at halfway. Anyone using the evidence of those four bumpers would have started sweating about leading so soon, but Moscow Flyer thrived on the challenge of jumping hurdles. There wasn't even a hint of weakness as Geraghty eased him home in front. Just six days later, Harrington found a winners race at Down Royal and Moscow Flyer made most of the running to win comfortably. Next on the agenda was the first Grade 1 of his career.

Just four lined up for the Royal Bond Hurdle at Fairyhouse's winter festival. Most were scared off by Dermot Weld's Stage Affair, runner-up to Daylami in a Tattersalls Gold Cup on the flat, and unbeaten in four starts over hurdles. The fancy flat-bred started a 4–11 favourite but it was a howlingly awful winter afternoon that promised trouble for anyone trading at short odds. Later in the afternoon Istabraq got turned over by Limestone Lad at odds of 1–7. Stage Affair got closer to winning but only so close as Moscow Flyer outbattled him from the last flight. Suddenly the horse that couldn't win a bumper was top class, a Grade 1 winner, a genuine Cheltenham contender. It was a helluva turnaround. But in January it was discovered he had a hairline fracture of the pelvis. Cheltenham was out. Since having a runner at the festival was Kearney's ultimate dream it was a body blow.

However, Harrington was prepared to look beyond Cheltenham. Instead she targeted a Grade 3 at Fairyhouse's Easter Festival. The long break had an impact though. Moscow Flyer was so fresh he was almost a danger to himself. 'He was like a lunatic, impossible to saddle, wouldn't walk around the parade ring, charged and stopped,' the trainer remembered. It was the same in the race. Geraghty couldn't settle him and they trailed home last. Suddenly, missing Cheltenham didn't seem so regrettable. But Harrington decided to run him one more time that season and in Punchestown's Grade 1 novice over two miles Moscow Flyer was a very different proposition. He won easily and had the Cheltenham winner Sausalito Bay back in third. Novice form didn't get better. That summer, Harrington looked at the Champion Hurdle picture for the year ahead and concluded there was only one horse to be afraid of. And she always worked off the principle that you should never be afraid of one horse, even if it is Istabraq.

Technically Moscow Flyer ended his hurdling career with a 2–1 victory tally over one of the great champions. Since one or the other failed to finish each time, the scoreline can hardly be regarded as definitive. What is beyond dispute is that the young upstart was a worthy adversary and Istabraq had precious few of those during his pomp.

Their first clash came at Leopardstown's Christmas meeting in 2000 when ground conditions were horrendous and Istabraq's last-flight fall was widely put down to exhaustion on going that was barely raceable. That in turn contributed to Moscow Flyer being written off as a slogger who got lucky. Time would prove that good ground was ideal for the supposed slogger and even underneath the pat explanations must have been a suspicion that, even in a bog, it is usually horses coming under pressure that come down.

Three weeks later in the Irish Champion Hurdle, both horses were squaring up to each other again when it was Moscow Flyer's turn to clip the top bar of the second-last and take a crashing fall. If that was annoying, it faded to nothing compared to the frustration around the 2001 Cheltenham Festival being lost to the ravages of foot-and-mouth. Nevertheless, another Irish variation on the Champion Hurdle was hosted by Leopardstown at the end of April. Nine days beforehand, Moscow Flyer had a warm-up at Gowran and got beaten. But it was a different story on the back of that.

Once again a momentous head-to-head looked assured as he and Istabraq left the back straight and turned into the straight. Even the most biased of Moscow Flyer fans would have to admit that the champ was going much better on the run to the last but, in turn, even Istabraq's colossal fan club would have to admit that jumping is the name of the game. Racing was again robbed of a conclusive decider as Istabraq fell at the last. Harrington was also robbed of a vital piece of information in her own internal debate about whether to stay hurdling the following season or go the route over fences that Moscow Flyer was bought for. He was already seven. By Cheltenham 2002 he would be eight. It would be asking a lot after that to ask a nine-year-old to go novice chasing.

'I am a firm believer in providence. Most things happen for a reason,' she said later. 'Had there been no foot-and-mouth that year, and had Moscow gone to Cheltenham, and – perish the thought – beaten Istabraq in the Champion Hurdle, we would probably have never sent him chasing. He would possibly never have scaled the heights over hurdles that he did over fences.'

The transition from hurdles to fences can be tricky with any horse. For one that was top class over the smaller obstacles, the move can be even trickier due to expectations. Even those at the coalface cannot completely block out dreams of what might happen if all that class is successfully translated into steeplechasing fluency. But fences are a different discipline and first impressions were that Moscow Flyer would find it difficult to make the move.

He schooled well enough. Geraghty was thrilled with the way he jumped fences at home and Harrington remembered him as 'much more natural over a fence than he ever was over a hurdle. He had never really been a rapid hurdler. He was fine when he was meeting one in his stride but he was never as sharp to fiddle a hurdle like Istabraq. I don't think he respected them enough. They were just finicky little things he should be able to kick out of his way.'

When Moscow made his chasing debut at Fairyhouse, however, he found out fences are anything but finicky. Full of the joys after a summer off, and brimming with confidence after a series of spectacular jumps early in the race, Geraghty afterwards said it felt like the horse thought he was Muhammad Ali. However, the fifth-last fence delivered a hammer blow. After completing a somersault it was left in the lap of the gods if Moscow Flyer would ever get up again. Such falls regularly result in broken necks. This time it didn't, but that was down to chance and nothing else. The only upside was that it might teach him something. After all, there's no point getting older unless you get a little wiser. Moscow Flyer learned his lesson.

He won a Beginners Chase at Down Royal, followed by a Grade 3 at Punchestown and then a Grade 1 at Leopardstown over Christmas, beating Youllneverwalkalone by a couple of lengths. Since that was three wins in a row, the inevitable happened: he fell in his Cheltenham warm-up back at Leopardstown.

Moscow Flyer never fell again. Instead the one-in-four sequence was brought about by a series of catastrophic blunders that sent Geraghty flying, leaving his partner to find a miraculous leg and keep himself up. It did mean, however, that on the run-up to Cheltenham's Arkle in 2002, Moscow Flyer was regarded as an iffy jumper. That in turn contributed to 11–2 odds that in hindsight look like they should have had ribbons tied around them. Seebald was the principal British hope and attracted plenty of headlines due to his owners, the England international footballers Steve McManaman and Robbie Fowler. He also had Tony McCoy on his back. Moscow Flyer had a jockey who'd never won at the festival. But all the pre-race analysis was soon redundant. The Irish hope jumped impeccably, his jockey did what he would subsequently do so many times over the years and thrived on the occasion. Seebald was fighting a losing battle from a long way out. There were four lengths between them at the line but the extent of Moscow Flyer's control exceeded that considerably.

As an exhibition of what to do around Cheltenham's two-mile circuit it was copybook stuff. All that natural pace allowed him to comfortably hold a position and those fearsome fences, even the downhill ones, were jumped with an overwhelming competence. Best of all, throughout the race, and just as much up the final climb that finds out so many, Moscow Flyer left the impression he had more to give. It wasn't surprising, then, that a return for the two-mile crown itself became the following season's target.

It opened with a routine success at Down Royal that looked to have put the horse spot-on for a clash with senior rivals for the first time in Sandown's Tingle Creek Chase. They included the reigning champ Flagship Uberalles. Confidence was sky-high among the Moscow Flyer team and everything seemed to be going to plan until the fifth fence. Geraghty had Flagship Uberalles in his sights when that horse stumbled on landing. Following behind, Moscow Flyer suddenly had nowhere to go. He cannoned into the favourite and jinked sideways, sending Geraghty the other way. It was an anticlimax but not enough to push him from the top of the betting for Cheltenham.

Back in Ireland, there were a couple of confidence-restoring victories before the Arkle winner arrived back at the festival as a 7–4 favourite and strongly fancied to win the Queen Mother Champion Chase. Flagship Uberalles was back for more, as was another former winner in Edredon Bleu. Also there was Cenkos, who had gone on to win that luckless Tingle Creek, and the star three-miler Florida Pearl dropping back in trip. The only doubt throughout was a mistake at the fourth-last, but that doubt was slight at most. Off a furious pace, the only horse taking a hold was the favourite. The race was run a full three seconds faster than the previous day's Arkle won by Azertyuiop, but again the new champion passed the post at Cheltenham with ears pricked and Geraghty gesturing to the crowd.

Moscow Flyer was on top of the world, usually a time when Geraghty needed industrial-strength adhesive to stay on his back. Sure enough, he wound up the season eating some Punchestown dirt after a desperate error when long odds-on.

That habit would come to cost him most of all the following year during his title defence at Cheltenham. By now, the sequence of failing to finish one race in every four was being widely remarked upon. That season the horse boasted a perfect three-from-three record including a defeat of Azertyuiop in the Tingle Creek. He hadn't run since Christmas but no one could quibble with his odds-on price at the festival. Moscow Flyer's claims looked cast-iron. Harrington dismissed anything sequential interfering with her horse, merely saying that the horse couldn't count. Or could he?

From the start, Moscow Flyer was always doing just that little bit too much. It was two and a half months since he had run and he gave all the signs of being extremely fresh. His big rival Azertyuiop had been reported to be below-par in the Tingle Creek three months previously and everything was brewing into a potential classic when Moscow clouted the ditch at the top of the hill, the fourth-last. Repeated viewing makes it all the more remarkable that he didn't fall. His feet seemed to end up in the ditch and he breasted the fence full-on. Momentum took him through and ended up making him almost head-butt the ground on the other side. But again he found a leg to keep himself up. Geraghty had no such luck. The jockey's first reaction was to look around for his horse. He couldn't believe Moscow hadn't fallen. It was only when he saw the riderless horse among the disappearing pack that he realised the truth.

It was bitterly disappointing. Azertyuiop went on to win but, almost like those clashes with Istabraq, there was an unsatisfactory feel to the race. Now the shoe was on the other foot. Azertyuiop fans could crow about vulnerability finding a horse out the way Moscow Flyer was. There was also little doubt the Paul Nicholls-trained winner looked the real deal. And he was. Time would prove that. But time would also prove Moscow Flyer to be his superior.

Harrington ran her star twice more that season, winning easily at Liverpool over two and a half miles, and back at Punchestown. By the law of Moscow Flyer averages, then, after an easy 2004–05 seasonal kick-off in Navan's Fortria Chase, the scene was perfectly set for another blemish in Sandown's Tingle Creek. But this was a different Moscow Flyer. At eleven, usually an age when chasers are on the down-slope of their careers, he seemed to be hitting his peak. And the absolute stick-the-flag-into-the-top-of-the-mountain pinnacle of that peak would turn out to be this Tingle Creek.

Azertyuiop's status was reflected in him starting odds-on, while his old rival was 2–1. But there was a new kid on the block who before the season was out would become part of what the *Racing Post* referred to as 'the Holy Trinity'. Well Chief was only five but had completed the Cheltenham (Arkle)-Liverpool double the previous term and came from Martin Pipe's yard, where he was suspected to be as good a prospect as had ever been through that conveyer belt of talent. That would prove correct and the first confirmation came at Sandown.

Those waiting for Moscow Flyer to exit were destined for disappointment. Chasing Cenkos down the back straight, he got close to one but was going so well Geraghty sent him to the front at the tenth. Behind him Ruby Walsh was taking a strong hold of Azertyuiop, who travelled supremely well. Going to the third-last, the Pond fence, Geraghty took a long lingering look around but didn't kick on. Then he took another peep at Azertyuiop and Well Chief, who was stealthily making progress too. Then came an exhibition of why Moscow Flyer was a supreme two-mile champion.

Any policeman measuring the speed at which all three tackled the last two fences would surely have pulled them over and booked the lot of them. It was textbook steeplechasing, formidable obstacles taken at speed by athletes at the peak of their game. At the last, both English horses were dependant on Moscow making a mistake. There wasn't a semblance of one. Geraghty powered him up the final hill to win by a length and a half from Azertyuiop, who was just a short head in front of Well Chief. It was twenty-five lengths back to Cenkos in fourth and the performance had handicappers rushing to enthuse about possibly the finest two-mile contest ever seen.

'He had won one of the highest-quality two-mile chases staged in living memory, and he had won it on merit. Nobody could think of an excuse for any runner beforehand or afterwards,' Harrington concluded.

This was Moscow Flyer at his peak. A warm-up victory at Punchestown had him spot-on for Cheltenham and another clash with his two main rivals. Azertyuiop in contrast had tried three miles in the King George and finished third. Well Chief put in a superb weight-carrying performance to win the Victor Chandler Chase and when they clashed in the Game Spirit at Newbury it was Azertyuiop who emerged best. Significantly, though, he looked to have a hard race and at Cheltenham the reigning champion never looked happy, struggling early and seeing his chance disappear with a mistake at the water jump.

Moscow Flyer, in contrast, sailed through the race, even managing to negotiate the final ditch that had scuppered his chance twelve months previously. Well Chief briefly looked a threat on the turn in but for the third time up the famous hill, Moscow once again looked as if he hadn't had to dig deep into his reserves to win. Now there was no argument: the Irish horse was the best of the best.

A quick reappearance at Liverpool yielded another ultra-smooth victory and, even at eleven years of age, suggestions that he would never win again would have been greeted scornfully. The great horse was after all on a run of nineteen straight victories in completed races. He'd never looked better. One final run in that momentous 2004–05 season looked a routine assignment. Starting at 1–4 to beat six opponents, everything looked as per normal until a slight blemish at the third-last fence. However, it was a major mistake at the next that sent Moscow Flyer's legions of fans to panic stations. Suddenly he faced an eyeball-to-eyeball struggle with an old rival in Rathgar Beau.

But if he won like a champion, then he knew how to lose like one too. From the last both horses gave it everything, exchanging the lead with each nodding stride. As they flashed past the post no one could tell for certain who'd won. For over ten minutes it seemed the judge couldn't separate them either. But he eventually came up with a verdict: Rathgar Beau by a short head. The Moscow

Flyer team took it with good grace, despite a later look at the photo-finish print revealing that maybe a dead heat would have been a fairer result. There was no mirror on the line so the print couldn't be seen from both sides.

'A dead heat would unquestionably have been the correct result. The fact it took eleven minutes for the result to be announced meant that even the judge had had a doubt,' Harrington wrote later. 'The print was inconclusive and it remains so. I don't know what the judge was thinking.'

What nobody thought on the day was that Moscow Flyer would never win again. But two runs in Ireland the following winter resulted in a pair of defeats that would have been unthinkable twelve months previously. Horses he had been kicking out of the way for years were getting their own back. The final hope was that Cheltenham would kindle one final hurrah, and in its own way it did.

Having to skip around a certain Kauto Star who exited in the early stages proved all the old agility was present and there was nothing wrong with the way he travelled down the back straight. But as the front-running Newmill accelerated down the hill to the final three fences, all of Moscow's twelve years started to show. For the first time in his life he wasn't quick enough. The pack chasing Newmill got away from him. Once they turned in for the final climb, there was a typical fightback. Newmill had flown but Moscow Flyer was hauling the others back in. He just couldn't do it quickly enough.

'I thought he was gone,' Harrington said in relation to the Kauto Star incident. 'He was lucky to survive. After that he was hard-pressed to get his position back. But his heart is still there. He kept going.'

She was speaking in the unsaddling area for unplaced horses next to the weighroom, the place known as the 'long face' enclosure, away from where the first four receive the acclaim of the crowd. It was Newmill's moment of glory, but in terms of popular appeal he couldn't compete with the fifth horse. Moscow Flyer still exerted a pull on everyone's attention even if from a media point of view it centred on retirement. Once the inevitable 'R' question was asked, Harrington turned to Brian Kearney and a minute later said in a stage whisper, 'He's not racing again.'

The overwhelming feeling was relief, not regret. The great horse was sound, well and seemingly oblivious to even the idea that he might not be the centre of the racing universe any more. Kearney said, 'He'll get the retirement he deserves. The dream is finished but it was a good dream while it lasted.'

Part of that retirement came as a 'roving ambassador' for the Irish Horse Welfare Trust, which is engaged in the rehabilitation and retraining of all types of horses. Moscow Flyer was used as an attention-getter for the project and the horse that loved attention himself was paraded at various locations including the RDS horse show in Dublin, back at Cheltenham and at various tracks around Ireland.

If it seemed a rather sedate life for a character that once epitomised steeplechase speed, then that final, final hurrah in that Punchestown charity event proved there was still plenty of life left in him. It simply didn't move quite as fast as it used to. Now approaching old-man status himself, if any horse deserves to slow down a little it is Moscow Flyer, who is assured of a place in racing history.

Not bad for a goof-off.

Alleged

illy McDonald once featured in the *Guinness Book of Records* for the record number of Rolls-Royces sold in one day. The boy brought up near Belfast pulled this feat off from a showroom in Los Angeles. But it was in Paris that the greatest deal of his life earned McDonald a little niche all of his own in thoroughbred history.

It being McDonald, of course, there is a lot more colour to the Alleged story than that. Also included is Monty Roberts, the world-renowned 'horse whisperer' who sold the yearling son of Hoist The Flag to McDonald's pal Robert Sangster, the man who could justifiably claim to be the catalyst for the transformation of the world thoroughbred industry, who in turn packed off the unprepossessing colt with wonky knees from Hollywood to Tipperary under the care of maybe the greatest combination of racing genius ever known.

Along the way came an emotional roller coaster of disappoint - ment, recrimination, multimillion-dollar gambles and exultant achievement that makes it a wonder how Alleged remains something of a 'forgotten horse' when it comes to nostalgia for the great champions.

Vincent O'Brien and Lester Piggott are forever inextricably

linked with any number of legendary names. Sir Ivor, Nijinsky, Roberto and The Minstrel all won the Derby for men whose claims to being the best trainer and jockey in the history of European racing are pretty much impossible to knock. And yet somehow the horse that Timeform rates alongside Nijinsky as the best they ever had is often ignored. Alleged was also rated the second-best Irish-trained horse of the twentieth century by the *Racing Post* historians Tony Morris and John Randall. Only Nijinsky, they reckoned, was better. But Alleged has still never tripped off the tongue in the way that say even other Ballydoyle stars of the past like El Gran Senor or Golden Fleece still do. It's a curious anomaly but it is also an injustice to a horse that emulated his great-grandsire Ribot by winning back-to-back renewals of the Prix de l'Arc de Triomphe.

The French take it for granted that their greatest race is also Europe's most prestigious. And the last few decades suggest they are right. It is certainly the most coveted all-aged contest. Maybe the Epsom Derby's history and legacy continues to give it a slight edge when it comes to most idle daydreams of what it would be like to own or ride or train a champion, but when it comes to concrete handicapping achievement, the Arc remains the pinnacle. Since its inception in 1920, just six horses have won it more than once and half of those were before World War Two. Tantieme (1950–51) and Ribot (1955–56) belonged to the world of black-and-white coverage. But Alleged remains a colourfully dazzling double Arc champion.

Maybe it's a lack of familiarity that causes Alleged to be overlooked. Despite racing for three seasons he actually ran only ten times. However, only a ride so stunningly ill-judged by Piggott that it had O'Brien reaching for a reservoir of invective rarely displayed for public perusal prevented the horse from remaining unbeaten. To British and Irish eyes there was also the fact that Alleged's greatest achievements came in France, away from first-hand examination by many. Neither was he possessed of the blinding acceleration that turned Nijinsky and Sir Ivor into

Guineas winners. But at the classic distance of a mile and a half he had the sort of middle-distance class that made him impossible to beat around Longchamp.

Yet there are still those who will argue he wasn't even the best horse of his year in Ballydoyle. It was the flashy chestnut, The Minstrel, son of the coveted Northern Dancer and closely related to Njinsky, that won the English and Irish Derbys in 1977, plus the King George. Compared to him in looks, precocity and versatility, Alleged was initially at the back of the class. But at his peak, efficient cold-eyed handicap analysis eventually had him clear. Efficiency, though, doesn't always guarantee affection.

Billy McDonald was never short of affection. If likeability was a bond, then he would have had a self-perpetuating financial source that would have made working for a living completely redundant. Possessed of a taste for the high life, but sometimes lacking the resources to generate it, McDonald found his spiritual home in California. Away from the class-conscious snobbery of Europe, a smooth-talking Irishman with a roguish twinkle in his eye and a willingness to hustle could thrive. And he did. In fact if an individual can truly be judged by their friends, then McDonald's testified to a racy flamboyance that only drew people to his easy charm even more.

There is a story of how the Irish car salesman was on a date in a fashionable LA restaurant in the 1980s at the same time as Frank Sinatra who, naturally, he was friendly with. McDonald asked Sinatra if, on his way out, he could stop by his table in order to impress the woman he was charming. Sinatra duly obliged, stopping to say hello. He was greeted with: 'Frank, not now, can't you see I'm busy!'

For a while the guy who left Belfast and worked with horses in Ireland before fetching up in the land of the transient and glib seemed to know everyone in Hollywood. And what's more, they appeared to genuinely like him for himself. Even the future James Bond, Pierce Brosnan, took a leg in a horse deal arranged by

McDonald. By then he had moved from cars to horses. Describing himself as 'the purveyor of champions to millionaires', McDonald's ability to get extremely rich people to spend money on bloodstock was only rivalled by that maddening talent that some men possess of getting beautiful women to fall in love with them purely on the strength of personality.

John Gosden was an assistant to Vincent O'Brien at the time Alleged was in Ballydoyle and when he began training himself in LA he got to know McDonald well. 'There will never be another Billy. He was one of the great characters of the game,' he said after the Irishman's death in 2009. 'He had a great eye for a horse and he lived life to the full. He was also a fast runner both into and out of trouble. He was an immensely popular man who was greatly at ease in watering holes, restaurants and racecourses around the world!'

Pointing out how McDonald had a great eye for a horse indicates that behind all the sell-ice-to-an-eskimo salesmanship was more than a little substance. Having such an eye is a rare talent. The ability to get an edge, though, is one that never goes astray in the bloodstock game. A famous McDonald anecdote recounts how an early scouting mission to Claiborne Farm promised a lot of hard work inspecting yearlings before the prestigious sales, a prospect that the visitor diluted by taking the yearling manager aside, pressing a $100 bill into his hand and saying, 'Which one do you like best?'

'Oh, I'd go for the little Bold Reason filly every time,' he replied. 'They always race over to this gate from right across the far side of the paddock, and that little filly is always yards in front when they arrive. She is a racehorse.'

The filly turned out to be Fairy Bridge, a good racer whose real value came when she foaled a Northern Dancer colt who grew up to be Europe's most successful stallion for generations, Sadler's Wells. McDonald paid $40,000 for her and she ended up part of a Coolmore syndicate that in the late 1970s took the bloodstock industry to a different level than many could even imagine. That Billy McDonald became a firm friend of Robert Sangster, the multimillionaire Englishman whose pools inheritance fortune bankrolled that transformation, would have surprised nobody who knew them.

Sangster was another who believed in living life to the fullest. The difference was that he had enormous financial means. As inheritor of the Vernons pools empire he was an incongruous amateur boxer while doing national service in Germany in the 1950s. The fact he did it, and was popular with comrades from very different backgrounds, spoke volumes for an innate charm and an easy-going nature. There was also a canniness, and a liking for a gamble, that turned an otherwise mundane meeting with another young Irishman into a seismic event.

In the early 1970s John Magnier believed there was another way to make a small fortune in bloodstock instead of starting with a big one – baby stallions. Income from stallion fees in Ireland was tax-free, a potential goldmine if one could secure the right animals. The affordable way to do that, he reckoned, was to buy them young, before they became successful on the track and hugely expensive. But that required rare judgement. Luckily Magnier was already in contact with the man who would become his father-in-law, Vincent O'Brien. The great trainer bought a half-share in Coolmore Stud from Tim Vigors, Magnier became manager and the roots of an empire were laid. What it needed to flourish was money, which was where Sangster came in. He didn't have O'Brien's flair with horses, nor Magnier's flinty business sense, but he had resources and a nose for a deal. Without the English businessman, the Irish horse miracle might still have happened, but differently, and probably not as colourfully.

Sangster, O'Brien and Magnier were the constants in the new syndicate which made its first impression at the 1975 Keeneland Sales in Kentucky. With $2 million at their disposal, the new buyers were branded the Sangster Gangsters by sceptics, but among their twelve purchases was The Minstrel. He was bought for $200,000. Another yearling at the sale barely registered with the syndicate. By the high-class dirt runner Hoist The Flag out of a Prince John mare called Princess Pout, the bay colt was not presented very well and the bidding stopped at $34,000, six grand short of his reserve. Afterwards Monty Roberts did a deal with the breeders for forty thousand dollars and took the yearling to California.

Roberts has earned global renown for his sympathetic way of dealing with horses of all kinds and his uncanny communicative skills with animals in general. Central to his theory is that coercion has no place in dealing with racehorses. Alleged's early handling was exemplary and Roberts, then a noted pinhooker, intended to sell him on as a two-year-old at a horses-in-training breeze-up sale. In the weeks before that, though, Alleged was galloped pretty seriously around Hollywood Park. Time was to prove that joint problems would be a feature of Hoist The Flag's produce and Alleged was no different. His knees couldn't stand pounding around the dirt track and he was blistered, the controversial treatment where a chemical is applied to an injured area, provoking swelling in the belief that the heat will allow the original injury to heal better. It was then that McDonald's eye came into the equation.

The bloodstock agent was already friendly with Sangster. Both men liked a good time and there was plenty of that in LA in the mid-70s. McDonald recommended Alleged to the Englishman, who bought the colt at the sale for $175,000. Sangster brought the American industrialist Robert Flour into the deal and decided Alleged's knees might prefer springy Irish turf rather than hard Californian dirt.

The unheralded colt didn't impress many of the Ballydoyle staff when he arrived in February 1976. Not surprisingly, he felt the cold compared to Hollywood and the decision to allow him time to settle in was easy. Vincent Rossiter was to get to know Alleged well over the following couple of years, riding him in most of his work. He remembers the dual Arc winner with affection.

'In the box he could be a bit nippy. If you were tacking up and he wasn't tied up, then he'd catch you. You just had to be careful around him. But once you were on him he was a lovely horse to ride, quiet, very lazy. He did a lot of his work from the front. Lazy horses will often work better in front. Instead of being stuck up the arse of something they have to concentrate and they forget how fast they're going. Even very keen horses can settle better in front,' Rossiter says. 'He wasn't ready for a race until the end of his two-year-old career but I remember we did think he was very promising.'

In the first week of November, Alleged was ready for a race and appeared on soft ground at the Curragh, winning impressively. The Minstrel was the undoubted top classic prospect for 1977, but Alleged was a prospect to savour too. However the spring of '77 was a test of character for the Sangster syndicate. The Minstrel got beaten in both the English and Irish Guineas, while Alleged only managed to scrape a victory in an ordinary race at Leopardstown. O'Brien didn't push him and it was over a month later that he reappeared in the Royal Whip Stakes at the Curragh. Valinsky, ridden by Piggott, was the Ballydoyle No. 1 and Alleged wasn't even rated No. 2 as Tommy Murphy was on board Meneval. Work rider Peadar Matthews was on Alleged, who was a 33–1 outsider. There was general shock when he cruised past Valinsky to provide a hint of his potential.

Later in the month came a smooth success in the Gallinule Stakes and Bob Flour, in whose colours Alleged ran, believed a tilt at the Epsom Derby was a realistic option. O'Brien didn't. Those knees hardly seemed ideal for speeding around Epsom's undulations, especially on quick ground, and it had already been decided The Minstrel would be Ballydoyle's representative. Flour wasn't too pleased with that call, and even less so when Alleged wasn't trained for the Irish Derby either. Instead he was given more time to develop. The benefits of that break were spectacularly obvious when the colt reappeared in York's Great Voltigeur Stakes over a mile and a half in August.

The field included Hot Grove, who had made The Minstrel pull out everything to win the Derby at Epsom, as well as the classic-placed Lucky Sovereign and Classic Example. Alleged dismissed them contemptuously, sprinting clear two furlongs out and winning by eight lengths with Piggott keeping a hard hold of his head. As big-time entrances go, it was spectacular. The Voltigeur might have been a Group 2 but it didn't require brilliant judgement to know the winner was a Group 1 horse. O'Brien was convinced Alleged's Arc entry was credible. What he needed was another run before Longchamp. The St Leger wouldn't be ideal but it was a Group 1, the opposition didn't look particularly strong and Alleged looked so progressive that he might not even have a hard race to win it. The decision was taken to go to Doncaster. It backfired in a big way.

Vincent Rossiter knew the horse better than most and his view is that Alleged simply didn't stay in the Leger. Maybe he didn't, but it hardly helped that Piggott seemed to think he was on a future Gold Cup winner. 'Lester rode an extraordinary race on him,' O'Brien said later. Starting a 4–7 favourite, Alleged's opposition included the Oaks winner Dunfermline, owned by the Queen, who had provided a perfect Silver Jubilee result at Epsom in June. A dour stayer, she had a pacemaker in the Leger to try and test out the favourite's stamina. Not unreasonably, it was expected that Dunfermline would sit off that pacemaker. Instead Piggott decided to fill that role himself and, even early in the race, Alleged was in front of the royal runner. When the pacemaker weakened, Alleged was in front with the broad expanse of the Doncaster straight in front of him. Willie Carson was characteristically busy behind him but Dunfermline ground down the leader and completed her classic double.

It seemed like she had had a pair of pacemakers in the race and O'Brien was furious. His son Charles recalled, 'This was probably the only time the Boss lost his cool on a racecourse, using some sharp language to Lester outside the weighing room – to the interest of the bystanders. Lester was totally unmoved and just shrugged his shoulders.'

Years later, in his official biography, O'Brien said, 'He looked as if he was going to win, but just inside the final furlong, the filly came on. She just outstayed him and duly she got up to beat him. What was he thinking about? I don't know.'

Rarely since Nijinsky's Arc had a ride so infuriated the trainer and now Alleged was going to Longchamp on the back of a hard race in the Leger, a similar scenario to the one that contributed to Nijinsky's Arc loss. But crucially, Alleged was going to the Arc on the back of a less strenuous season. He was also a very different beast temperamentally to Nijinsky.

If the latter lived on his nerves, Alleged could also be a handful in his box. But he was an aggressive handful rather than a nervous one. John Gosden remembered: 'He was kind but if you were silly enough to bend over in his box he'd have a go at you. He was a masculine horse, aggressive in the stable. He had a wonderful head, strong and powerful, very broad between the eyes. He was not nasty. He was straightforward. He meant business.'

Later in his stallion career there were suggestions that Alleged could almost be savage. There was never a hint of that in his racing performances. Relaxed, but blessed with a good cruising speed, his knees meant a little juice in the ground was always appreciated. When he got his conditions, that businesslike attitude made him an exceptional mile-and-a-half horse. And he got his conditions in the Arc.

By then Bob Flour had sold most of his share to Sangster, so Alleged carried Sangster's increasingly familiar blue and green silks at Longchamp. A large field of runners included his Leger conqueror Dunfermline as well as the top older runner Orange Bay, who had run The Minstrel to a nose earlier in the summer in the King George. The French Derby winner Crystal Palace, the Irish Derby winner Malacate and Crow were other high-class opposition, while the New Zealand champion Balmerino, who had been campaigned from England that year, also lined up. It was an open race and Piggott's hunch was that with everyone fancying their chances, there might not be a manic pace cut out by those looking for a brief glimpse of the limelight. He decided to stick close to the pace. There are still those who believe Alleged made all the running in the 1977 Arc. He didn't. But after tailing Yelpano in the early stages Piggott did play his hand quickly and led a full seven furlongs from home. Nothing ever came close to catching him. Balmerino came out of the pack to be second but Alleged was an utterly decisive winner.

It was a dream result for the new Coolmore syndicate. They had a pair of champions in the one season. The Minstrel had been syndicated back to America for $9 million. As if he and Alleged weren't enough, 1977 also saw high-class runners in Artaius and Godswalk. There was also the miler Be My Guest, another high-class runner who stayed in Ireland for a stallion career and became Coolmore's first champion with a first crop that included the classic winners Assert and On The House. The temptation to cash in on Alleged after that Arc and retire him to stud must have been enormous, but O'Brien felt there was more to come from the horse. And quiet and unobtrusive as he was, what O'Brien wanted, he usually got.

The trainer felt there was more to come, and the possibility of producing the first dual Arc winner since Ribot was hard to resist. Provided ground conditions weren't too fast, there would also be the opportunity to cash in on some of the summer prizes such as the King George. But the ground did turn quick in early 1978 and when Alleged ran again in the Royal Whip, he jarred his knees. He needed rest. He got that but also a bout of the virus that knocked plans back even further. The decision to keep him in training was turning costly. It was September by the time he was ready to race again and there would be time only for one warm-up before another tilt at the Arc. That meant an early return to Longchamp for the Prix du Prince d'Orange. Alleged broke the ten-furlong track record. There was less than a fortnight to the Arc but plans seemed to be back on track. The problems that niggle any top-class athlete at peak fitness, though, are many and varied. It was one of O'Brien's talents to be able to think outside the box in coping with them.

'I remember the race Alleged ran in before his second Arc,' vet Stan Cosgrove said later. 'He looked like he had quite a hard race and MV wasn't happy with him. It looked like he might not make the Arc. These days everyone does blood tests but back then it was unusual. Vincent had him tested and we found out he had a deficiency in potassium. So we loaded him up and he won the Arc.'

If it sounds easy in hindsight, it appeared almost as easy in real time. Concerns about soft going proved unfounded. Alleged wasn't ridden quite as prominently this time, but the same general tactics applied and once they hit the straight, Piggott kicked for home. The top French filly Dancing Maid tried to run him down but couldn't and it was the tough mare Trillion, subsequently the dam of Triptych, who eventually chased him home at a respectful two lengths. Alleged had become just the sixth horse to twice win the Arc – mission accomplished. Timeform summed up: 'There hasn't been a horse trained in Europe since Mill Reef who would have beaten Alleged at a mile and a half.'

Robert Sangster's instinct was always to enjoy the moment before indulging in the hard-headed financial implications of a major success. That night in Paris was no exception. The absence of pressure helped the atmosphere. There was no question but that Alleged would be retired to stud in America. He was ultimately syndicated at a value of $16 million to Walmac Farm in Kentucky. Coolmore and John Magnier's 'baby stallions' theory was still at the fledgling stage and there was no way of turning down that sort of money. What it provided was breathing space, and more resources to go to the yearling sales. Magnier used that space to learn even more about how American farms operated and how to adapt those lessons to European conditions. In many ways Alleged was one of the last superstar stallions to be syndicated on old-fashioned presumptions.

'The horse stands at $80,000 and he can cover forty mares. So he earns $3.2 million a year. And a horse is normally valued on a four-year purchase of his earnings,' Sangster explained at the time. That meant earnings after that four-year period was gravy. But what if a stallion covered more mares at the same fee? And what if the revenue from that was tax-free, as was the case in Ireland?

Magnier brought a cold-eyed calculation, as well as promotional techniques that made previous marketing efforts look stone age, to the business of bloodstock and turned it into a financial goldmine. Not that his judgement was always right. Some of the subsequent graduates from Ballydoyle to Coolmore flopped spectacularly and big-money purchases such as Hello Gorgeous were similarly unimpressive. But the flops never seemed to be as costly as they might be and when a stallion was a hit, like Danehill or Sadler's Wells, Coolmore knew how to make the most of it.

More mares covered meant more revenue coming in, as well as providing stallions with a greater chance of success, and veterinary advances quickly meant it was feasible for a potent sire to cover 150 mares in a single season. And when that was over, the pioneering move of shuttling horses to the southern hemisphere for their breeding season generated year-round revenue.

The impact on the yearling sales in the early to mid-1980s was seismic. Competition between Coolmore and the ruling Maktoum family of Dubai sent prices rocketing. The peak was reached in 1985 when a colt by Nijinsky was knocked down to Magnier & Co for $13.1 million, a sum the horse subsequently named Seattle Dancer could never hope to win on a racecourse and which appeared to be a case of hubris gone mad. Seattle Dancer turned out to be a very decent racer, a Group 2 winner and Group 1 placed. But anything other than a Derby or an Arc was always destined to be a letdown.

Alleged's stud career was anything but a letdown. The

overwhelming fashion for Northern Dancer was impossible to compete against but he became a successful match for mares with a Northern Dancer background. Although from an American background himself, Alleged was a European turf runner and his produce were overwhelmingly aimed back across the Atlantic, even if his daughter Fiesta Gal wound up winning a pair of Grade 1 prizes on dirt. Usually his stock needed grass and a minimum of a mile and a quarter to be seen at their best. They included the 1985 Irish Derby winner Law Society and Sir Harry Lewis, who won the same classic two years later. Midway Lady was hugely versatile and completed the English 1,000 Guineas-Oaks double in 1986. Miss Alleged landed a Breeders Cup and Legal Case a Champion Stakes, but their father was also a notable broodmare sire. The 1991 Arc hero Suave Dancer and the 1992 Epsom Derby winner Dr Devious both were out of Alleged mares.

Racing's last dual Arc winner was retired from breeding in 1997 and enjoyed a three-year retirement before dying, aged twenty-six, in the year 2000. Walmac Farm's owner Johnny Jones Jnr said, 'In every way Alleged was a champion. Few stallions come along that proved to be great sires and broodmare sires and continue to influence the breed for decades after their lifetime. It appears Alleged is one of those stalwarts.'

Lester Piggott paid him a glowing tribute in the *Racing Post*:

> He was one of the best horses I ever rode. Having won the Arc twice makes him one of the greats of the post-war era. He took a while to come to himself but he was terrific and won both his Arcs easily. It was just unfortunate that he couldn't run all through the summer of his four-year-old season because of the firm ground, because he would probably have won everything. He was a wonderful horse to ride. You could do anything with him in a race and he had a lovely, relaxed attitude.

The Alleged story will always involve Piggott, O'Brien, Sangster and the glorious kick-start he helped provide to the Coolmore Stud empire on those two October days in Paris in 1977 and 1978. But while they were the central players, as walk-on roles go, Billy McDonald's was wonderfully colourful. Certainly none of the others took greater pride in the horse's achievements. At one stage, the licence plate on McDonald's car proclaimed 'Alleged'.

Walmac's Johnny Jones Jnr fondly remembered: 'I bought his share of Alleged the night before he won either his first or second Arc. I can't remember which. Anyway Alleged won and the value of the share increased tremendously. But Billy didn't back out of the deal. He stayed with it, did what he said he'd do.'

McDonald continued living in California for many years. He even played the role of a bettor in the 1989 movie *Let It Ride*, which starred Richard Dreyfuss in the part of a guy on an unbelievable roll of luck gambling at the track. The film was primarily shot at Hialeah racecourse in Florida, far away at the other end of the country from the Hollywood track where McDonald's quick eye first spotted Alleged. But both were even further away, in so many senses, from where Billy McDonald had come from in the small Co. Down town of Ballynahinch.

Eventually, however, he ended up back in Northern Ireland. The high-flying LA salesman, who rumour had it was engaged seven times, finished his days living with his brother and their mother. He died in November 2009, aged sixty-five. Tributes flowed in from around the racing world, most involving one variation or another on the theme of there would never be another like him and that he would never be forgotten. That the same could be said of the great horse that he bought would have pleased him greatly.

Istabraq

It was 'Bull' Hancock, owner of the famous Claiborne stud farm in Kentucky, who observed there is a dog in the pedigree of every champion. After an eleven-race career on the flat that yielded only a pair of nondescript victories, Istabraq might not have had sticks thrown for him to chase but he was a long way from being the family's blue-eyed boy.

That role very firmly belonged to Secreto, the hero and, to some still, the villain of the 1984 Epsom Derby. Flat racing's blue riband has thrown up many credulity-stretching scenarios since it began in 1780 but rarely one to match No. 205, which revolved at least as much around El Gran Senor as it did Secreto.

The 'Senor' was a brilliant 2,000 Guineas winner, rumoured in the run-up to Epsom as being potentially the best Vincent O'Brien had ever trained. Brilliantly fast, possessed of a perfect tempera-ment and, being by Northern Dancer, bred to be a champion, El Gran Senor cruised to the lead at the two-furlong pole with Pat Eddery looking around for dangers. That he managed to find one still provokes debate today.

Secreto was also a son of Northern Dancer and also worked on the famous Ballydoyle gallops. But he was trained by Vincent O'Brien's son David, a young man of prodigious talent who had already trained a top-class horse in Assert. Secreto ran third in the Irish 2,000 Guineas to Sadler's Wells but was widely believed to be filling the numbers at Epsom. Sure enough, while Eddery peered around, Christy Roche was working feverishly on the other Irish hope. The only thing fanning Roche's competitive flames was a suspicion about El Gran Senor's stamina. It proved to be correct. When Eddery asked for maximum effort there was nothing left. The odds-on favourite hung on until inches from the finish, but at the line Roche had Secreto's nose in front.

It was a stunning result. Eddery could hardly budge for the blizzard of criticism that came his way. Vincent O'Brien was torn between parental pride and despair at being beaten. David O'Brien trained on for another four years before shocking the racing world with his decision to retire at just thirty-two. And in the midst of everything, a mare called Betty's Secret that had never raced herself was suddenly worth a fortune as the mother of a Derby winner.

Despite never making the racecourse, Betty's Secret was already racing royalty. By Secretariat, still the most impressive American Triple Crown winner of all, she was a half-sister to the French Derby winner Caracolero. Her grandam produced Majestic Prince, the 1969 Kentucky Derby winner.

After Secreto, Betty's Secret bred a succession of foals, some of whom made a lot of money in the sales ring, others who never even made it to the racecourse, and some that were just plain useless when they did. Such disappointments are not uncommon. Rare is the mare that can produce a top-class horse. Even rarer is the one that can do it again. My Charmer foaled Seattle Slew, another American Triple Crown hero, in 1974 and six years later had the subsequent English Guineas winner Lomond. Hasili, owned by Juddmonte, had a phenomenal record of producing Group 1 winners. Urban Sea was freakish, being a good enough racehorse to win the Arc and then producing Sea The Stars, Galileo and two other Group 1 winners. They are the exceptions that prove the rule.

However, when Betty's Secret's owner Eddie Taylor died, there was still enough lustre around the dam of Secreto that Sheikh Hamdan Al Maktoum of Dubai paid out a reputed $6 million for her in 1989. When she then proceeded to produce a foal to Europe's greatest sire of the twentieth century, the aforementioned Sadler's Wells, hopes for the youngster surrounded classics and a career as an income-generating stallion himself. They didn't materialise. The classically bred, rather nervous colt with the big white splodge on his forehead managed to win a couple of ordinary races before being sold off as a four-year-old by the Sheikh's Shadwell team for 38,000 guineas.

In 2009, Shadwell removed an unraced two-year-old from their team and had the excruciating experience of watching Makfi win the following year's 2,000 Guineas. That's the chance you take when your bloodstock portfolio runs into the hundreds. Makfi was a nightmare. Istabraq just looked like good business.

Sheikh Hamdan's interest is in flat racing. That his former reject subsequently morphed into a National Hunt legend, prevented from being confirmed as maybe the greatest hurdler of them all only by a freak epidemic, mattered little to him. For those whose lives are spent pondering every nick, twist and possibility in the shallow genetic pool that is the thoroughbred, Istabraq was an oddity, one of those blips sent to test the patience of bloodstock experts.

Instead of a retirement plan that involved impregnating blue-blooded broodmares on one of the Sheikh's studs, the Arab reject instead ended up spending his latter years at J.P. McManus's farm in Martinstown, Co. Limerick, alongside other National Hunt stalwarts who carried the billionaire businessman's green and gold colours to notable victories. Visitors to the luxuriously appointed Martinstown have taken in the life of Istabraq and co and pondered the value of their pension arrangements. Nothing is spared for the equine occupants. The owner makes sure of that.

McManus is a figure that provokes strong opinions. For many

within racing he is an enormously generous benefactor who has plunged millions into an extensive string that the legendary gambler characteristically underplays as being the largest collection of bad horses in Ireland. Always a figure of fascination to a media intrigued by his immense wealth, devotion to a punt and a curious amalgam of modesty mixed with occasional flashes of blingy extravagance, the man who began his working life driving a digger and became one of the wealthiest people in the country also draws flak for his tax-exile status and propensity for displaying something of an 'aw shucks' face to the world. But for someone in thrall to National Hunt racing, the thirty-eight grand he paid for Istabraq must qualify as one of racing's great bargains.

That it came to pass at all testifies to the very different test that jumping presents compared to the flat. Some horses have combined the two. Sea Pigeon was a champion over hurdles and a top handicapper when they were removed. Alderbrook could do both pretty well. Royal Gait won an Ascot Gold Cup and a Champion Hurdle. Rarely, though, has a series of hurdles had such a transformative impact on a horse as they had with Istabraq. Charlie Swan rode the champion in every one of his starts over flights and postponed his retirement specifically in order to do so. Istabraq was the jewel of an already sparkling career. And yet the first time he ever teamed up with the then untried recruit for a schooling session at the Curragh was guaranteed to stick in his mind.

'I couldn't believe how good a jumper he was. He was quite amazing, a real natural. Not once did he try to duck out or run away from a hurdle,' he later recounted. 'He always lands running and this enables him to get away from the hurdles so quickly.'

Throughout his career, the joy of jumping never wavered in Istabraq. It was hardly something he was bred for and, in the artificial environs of a racecourse, the physical act of jumping a hurdle or a fence remains a fundamentally unnatural thing to ask a thoroughbred to do. That they are asked at all is a human requirement that turns into a chore for many horses, part of the 'thrills'n'spills' appeal that is inherent to National Hunt racing. The ethics of asking dumb animals to run and jump over sometimes long distances on testing ground purely for our entertainment is starting to be questioned in other parts of the racing world and it is inevitable that, sooner or later, similar queries are likely to crop up even in the home of the steeplechase. In a world where mass agricultural production can result in horrors to make racing's casualty rate seem minute if hardly legible, the pact that allows people to acknowledge the high price jumping can exert while still extolling its virtues is hardly Faustian. But there is also the reality that some horses thrive on the challenge because the accent is firmly on courage. Few have thrived more, or exhibited such simple, uncomplicated joy at jumping an obstacle, than Istabraq.

The result was a 29-race career over hurdles that yielded twenty-three victories, a staggering fourteen of which were at Grade 1 level. They included three Champion Hurdles at Cheltenham that completed four years in a row in which Istabraq was successful at the biggest festival of all. There were four Irish Champion Hurdles too, as well as dominant displays at the Punchestown and Aintree festivals. For the last years of the twentieth century he was jump racing's greatest star. Songs were written about him in the manner of Arkle. Having McManus, Swan and trainer Aidan O'Brien as part of the story only added to its general appeal. On the eve of his third Champion Hurdle victory, a small but potentially ruinous nose bleed turned into headline news in Ireland. When he eventually cried enough and was pulled up after just two flights of the 2002 Champion Hurdle, Istabraq received a rousing reception from the massive Cheltenham crowd even while the race was being run. At a meeting where millions change hands in a feverish pursuit of finding the next winner, it stood out as a singularly sentimental gesture towards a singular champion.

As McManus, O'Brien and Swan knew better than most,

however, the man who created the basis of such a feel-good story, and the one who first identified the vital courage underneath all that flash breeding, wasn't present. John Durkan's desperately untimely death brought a bitter taste to the Istabraq story that no amount of success could eliminate. Rarely has racing seemed more trivial than when the young man who would have trained him died aged just thirty-one after a brave fight with leukaemia. And just as rare was the emotional connection made between Durkan and the horse he believed in more than any other.

Both might have been Irish born but they met in Britain. Durkan's family were steeped in racing. Bill Durkan owned and trained the top two-mile mare Anaglogs Daughter. But the Co. Mayo man who trained from stables near Stepaside in south Co. Dublin was also a major figure on the construction scene. For his son John there was never a choice between the two. Horses were going to be his life. The tragedy was that it was such a short one.

'He was an absolutely cracking kid. He was tremendous fun to be with and he managed to live life to the full without ever upsetting anybody,' remembered Ferdy Murphy, who was involved with the training of Anaglogs Daughter and who later tried to take on Istabraq with a champion of his own.

Durkan's ambitions to train had first taken him to Lambourn, where he combined being an assistant trainer with riding as an amateur jockey. It was when he joined John Gosden in Newmarket with a similar job description that his path crossed with Istabraq's. Even at the headquarters of British racing, a three-parts brother to Secreto meant the new arrival was out of the ordinary. The problem was that first indications were his talent wasn't. It wasn't until the beginning of November 1994 in his two-year-old career that Istabraq was ready for a race. He ran eighth, an OK start, but nothing exceptional. There certainly didn't appear to be a Derby of any description anywhere on his horizon.

Expectations were low for him as a three-year-old. On his fourth start, a fourteen-furlong Salisbury maiden in August, Istabraq secured the first win of his career under jockey Willie Carson, who remembered: 'He was a slow maturing type and a slow learner. He also lacked speed. On occasion I suspected his honesty. I sometimes thought he was a bit of a lad who might have needed a pair of blinkers. But I came to the conclusion that the reason he struggled was because he had no speed.' Just a few years later, Aidan O'Brien ventured the opinion that his greatest National Hunt champion was no certainty to get up the famously punishing Cheltenham hill because he had developed outstanding pace. That was a transformation that kept jump-racing fans intrigued for over half a decade. But it was John Durkan who first saw the potential for such change.

Classically bred types that are too slow for the flat are rarely successful if switched to jumps. Fundamentally if a horse is slow, then it is slow. There is always a high percentage of roguish types who are slow because they won't try rather than because they can't. However, racing over jumps is hardly an environment to encourage them to change their ways. A certain resolution and pluck is required to embrace the challenge of jumping in winter conditions. There is also the genetic inheritance of some flat-bred horses that makes them vulnerable to the different stresses and strains of tackling obstacles. Legs designed for the Rowley Mile are often not suited to landing over Becher's Brook.

In Istabraq's case there was also the mundane reality of him possessing the equine equivalent of flat feet. This contributed to other problems with cracked hooves, something that in later years would make shoeing him something of a nightmare. As if that wasn't enough, there was also a small chipped bone in his near-fore leg. This 'floating chip' remained until the end of his career and never impacted on Istabraq. But after one start as a four-year-old, Secreto's brother was hardly a collector's item at the Tattersalls July Sale of 1996.

John Durkan – or 'JD' as he was known to his circle of friends that included the then top jump jockey Jamie Osborne and future trainers, Ed Dunlop and Eddie Hales – wanted to buy Istabraq very badly indeed. On the verge of setting up as a trainer in Newmarket, he was hustling for owners and arranging premises, as well as keeping an eye on the progress of the colt he knew from John Gosden's yard. There was something about him, Durkan felt. 'He is no soft flat horse. He is the sort who does not get going until he is in a battle. He has more guts than class and that's what you need,' he told one prospective client. Another potential owner dropped out before the sales and Durkan was desperate for someone to invest in both him and the horse.

By then he was married to Carol Hyde, daughter of the renowned bloodstock buyer Timmy Hyde, who approached J.P. McManus about having a horse with his son-in-law. The champion owner agreed to pay in the region of £100,000 for Istabraq but not much more. John Durkan feared the horse would cost more and so there was widespread relief when the hammer came down at 38,000 guineas. Istabraq was sent to Hyde's Camas Park Stud in Tipperary, where any hopes of a stallion career were finally removed by a gelding operation. For some horses the impact of such an operation is negligible but Istabraq was badly affected and it took some months for him to get over it.

By now Durkan was also negotiating the purchase of a yard in Newmarket as well as continuing to work in Gosden's. However, he was also starting to feel unwell. On a trip home to Dublin, his mother Beatrice insisted he go to the doctor. Blood tests revealed he was stricken with leukaemia. It was a shattering blow for a young man on the verge of beginning a career he had dreamed of all his short life. For his wife and family, there was the exhausting struggle between grief and trying to present a positive face to their loved one. In the circumstances, where Istabraq might end up was hardly a priority, but after consulting with McManus, it was decided the horse would go to Aidan O'Brien in Ballydoyle until Durkan was fit enough to start training. It was a pledge that would have thrilled everyone involved if only it could have unfolded thus. So while his greatest supporter faced a battle for survival, Istabraq entered the most famous training establishment in the world.

It might seem ironic that the most powerful flat-race trainer in Ireland is represented here by a National Hunt star, but Aidan O'Brien's meteoric rise to the top of the racing tree was built on jumping. The son of a Co. Wexford farmer who left school at fifteen, and whose first employment was as a forklift driver at the local Co-op, emerged seemingly from nowhere in the early 1990s to turn jump racing's hierarchy on its head. Marriage to Anne-Marie Crowley, a champion trainer herself whose father enjoyed a lengthy career training, resulted in the licence switching to O'Brien. He wasn't even twenty-five years old when the Coolmore supremo John Magnier identified him as the man to rejuvenate the Ballydoyle yard after the retirement of Vincent O'Brien (no relation).

Initially O'Brien commuted between his old yard in Co. Kilkenny and Ballydoyle, juggling jumpers with the initial streams of blue-blooded classic hopefuls that were starting to emerge from the Coolmore syndicate's assembly line. McManus, as a close friend of Magnier, had his handful of jumpers stabled at Ballydoyle. Compared to the millions invested in the flat horses, the small string of National Hunt hopefuls stabled in their own yard were small beer financially, but for a young man with a colossal weight of expectation on his shoulders they also repre-sented something comfortingly familiar.

Istabraq's initial schooling was very encouraging but O'Brien also picked up quickly on the newcomer's nervous disposition. Everything was geared towards keeping him calm and relaxed and enjoying his training. At first, however, another McManus novice was regarded as being at least as good a prospect. Finnegans Hollow was bred more traditionally for the winter game and tempera-mentally didn't seem as fragile as Istabraq. But, as Durkan suspected, appearances could be deceptive. It was the flat-bred who was ready to kick off his new career in November 1996 in a competitive novice hurdle at Punchestown.

Istabraq's reputation preceded him and he started a 6–4 favourite. A last-flight mistake made the difference and Noble Thyne beat him by a head. That was to prove the winner's notable distinction. A fortnight later the pair met again in the Grade 1 Royal Bond Novice Hurdle and Istabraq, always in the first two, led from the third-last to win easily. Just two races into his new career, the flat-footed slowcoach had proven himself top-class over flights. A Christmas outing at Leopardstown produced another easy victory, but this time in front of Durkan, who had taken a short break from his treatment in New York. It was a rare sweet moment for the young man. He had pitched Istabraq as a future winner of the Sun Alliance Hurdle, the big novice event on the second day of the Cheltenham Festival. The horse was already ante-post favourite for the race and Charlie Swan was not alone in believing there was much more to come.

Rarely does a campaign go completely smoothly, though, and 1996–97 was no exception. In his Cheltenham warm-up back at Leopardstown, Istabraq, a 4–11 favourite, was hard-ridden to beat his Ballydoyle neighbour Finnegan's Hollow, who in contrast did not appear to be overly pressurised. It caused a stir of controversy at the time but it meant that McManus went to Cheltenham with major hopes in the two big novice events.

Finnegan's Hollow was a heavily backed favourite for the Supreme Novices Hurdle over two miles and was travelling noticeably well for Swan until taking a crashing fall at the third-last. As an omen it was hardly encouraging. It also heaped added expectation onto Istabraq twenty-four hours later. He was the festival's 'Irish banker' and bookmakers wary of McManus's fearsome gambling instincts also had to cope with a general public plunge on the horse. It all added to a cocktail of pressure for Swan, whose easy blond-haired charm masks a big-race temperament few if any have ever bettered around Cheltenham. Once famously instructed on another McManus hotpot to ride it with 'balls of steel', Swan exhibited tungsten-tough cojones to come out on top. But never during the course of a sparkling career was his nerve tested more than on the 1997 favourite.

As early as the parade ring, Istabraq's own notoriously fragile nerves looked to be letting him down in a big way. In front of a vast crowd and with the general festival hubbub all around him, the Irish star started to jig-jog, then sweat, and then sweat profusely. By the time they left the parade ring, Swan was convinced his chance was gone. No horse could get so upset and still have enough reserves to win. He decided to eschew the traditional canter in front of the stands and went straight to the start, securing a valuable few minutes on his own and allowing Istabraq to calm a little. It was then that Swan at least partly showed why he was a champion.

The ability to think on your feet and alter tactics is a requirement of any top jockey, but rarely has it been seen so dramatically as with Istabraq in the Sun Alliance. Usually placed prominently in a race, Swan decided a similar ploy after the horse had got so upset would be suicidal. Instead he dropped Istabraq out stone-last in a last-ditch attempt to get him to settle. As they passed the stands with a circuit to go, many thought the rider had blown it. Listening on a phone in New York, John Durkan certainly thought so. Winning is usually the only defence for a jockey who changes tack so dramatically and it requires a depth of self-confidence to do so when it really counts that Swan always possessed. Crucially in this case, Istabraq did settle at the back and started to race kindly.

Making rapid ground coming down the hill, Istabraq looked a major contender again, only for disaster to loom at the second-last. Going for a gap between rivals, he was cannoned into by Forest Ivory. He didn't fall, which he could well have done, but that bump looked to have ended his chances. It was then, however, that the courage Durkan always suspected was there came fully to the fore.

Challenged by Mighty Moss all the way up the famous hill, the flat-bred fancy-dan fought like the most grizzled old steeplechaser to hold on and win by a length when just about every circumstance had conspired against him. It was an astonishing performance and one that proved this was no ordinary horse.

One more run that season at Punchestown, when O'Brien made a point of keeping Istabraq in the parade ring for no longer than necessary, resulted in an easy victory. The future looked secure. As a Sun Alliance winner over two miles and five furlongs, Istabraq looked a natural for the Stayers Hurdle over three miles. That's what Swan believed. 'I was convinced he was a stayer, not a two-mile horse, because he stayed so well on the flat, and he was the same over hurdles,' he recounted. No Sun Alliance winner had ever won the Champion Hurdle. It looked an open-and-shut case. But O'Brien was already thinking of going back in trip rather than up.

Ever since it was set up by Vincent O'Brien in the 1950s, the primary purpose of Ballydoyle was to encourage speed. Rarely were classic horses worked beyond a mile. In a sense, stamina was left to look after itself: without speed it was useless. Aidan O'Brien has pursued his own path, but speed remains everything and working on the famous gallops appeared to be making Istabraq faster. Some of that was due to maturity but there was also the suspicion that the horse was thriving generally. There was certainly no evidence to suggest a hard race at Cheltenham had knocked him back. On the contrary, it looked to have made a man of him.

On his first start out of novice class, he made desperate ground at Tipperary look nothing at all. Then in the Hatton's Grace Hurdle at Fairyhouse, Istabraq made all over two and a half miles. If that looked a performance laden with stamina, Swan got enough from it to park his doubts about two miles to the side. What he noticed especially was that the faster the pace, the better Istabraq jumped. The Hatton's Grace was also notable because Durkan was present to see it, although his medical outlook was worse. A cancerous spot had been found on his brain. It required every bit of strength he had to go racing that day and to maintain the quiet dignity that characterised him during his entire illness. He wouldn't see Istabraq race again. The horse won easily at Leopardstown over Christmas. A few days after that, John Durkan was back in hospital in Dublin. Just three weeks later he died.

Jamie Osborne delivered a poignant tribute at his funeral, telling the packed church: 'Over the last sixteen months we all prayed that today would never be upon us. JD fought harder than we will ever know to try and prevent it. His strength and hope shone through the last months of his life, leaving us bewildered at his determination. He was a truly remarkable man and a wonderful friend. He was our standard setter.'

Sport is mostly an irrelevance in the face of grief but it isn't completely irrelevant in this case. John Durkan poured so much into racing, and invested so much of himself into Istabraq in particular, that the rest of the horse's career contained an emotional undertow which added an extra layer of resonance to an already remarkable story. It was at its most raw just the day after Durkan's burial when the horse won the Irish Champion Hurdle. Carol Hyde accepted the winner's trophy from the Taoiseach, Bertie Ahern. Only the hardest of hearts could have failed to move.

If Istabraq's performance was perfectly satisfactory, it was also without the sparkle that some reckoned should be implicit in a potential champion hurdler. What the sceptics failed to take into account were O'Brien's long-term plans to train the horse with one target in mind all season. After Leopardstown he began tightening the screw at home. The result was immediate. On the weekend before Cheltenham, Swan rode out Istabraq, who felt vastly better. The normally circumspect O'Brien added to that encouragement with the unambiguous statement: 'He will bloody destroy them!' Swan mentioned that it was the Champion Hurdle they were talking about. 'I don't care,' O'Brien insisted. 'He will destroy them.'

The parade ring again proved to be an ordeal for Istabraq's nerves. Used to the idyllic calm of Ballydoyle, Cheltenham's raucousness didn't sit right with him. But this time was different. The horse might sweat but that didn't mean his chance was dissolving into a lather. That Sun Alliance victory proved it. Even so, Swan used the sweat as a positive – 'I felt I had a ready-made excuse if I got beaten. When they sweat up, you can always blame the horse!' No one had to play the blame game this time.

At the back of Swan's mind remained a fear of being done for pace at the end. Istabraq travelled beautifully through the race and after the third-last the Irish favourites headed for home. In Michael Clower's *The Legend of Istabraq*, he said:

> I could hardly believe how well he was travelling. When he jumped the second-last he picked up again and he was really running rounding the final turn. Sixty yards after the last I looked to my right. I couldn't believe I was so far in front. But the crowds were making so much noise that I felt there had to be something coming. I looked again, this time to the left. There was nothing there.

At the line there was a dozen lengths back to his stable companion Theatreworld. It was the longest winning distance in sixty-six years. Rarely if ever has hurdling's championship been won with such total authority. Coming less than two months after John Durkan's death, there was a swirl of emotions in the winner's enclosure, awe at the ease of the victory being among the more straightforward. Aidan O'Brien had been proved right. He did destroy them. And yet McManus caught the popular mood when he said, 'I would never have been fortunate enough to own Istabraq but for John. Thinking about him makes us realise how lucky we are to be coming to Cheltenham. Winning is a bonus.'

Istabraq ran once more in that 1997–98 season, starting a 4–7 favourite for the Aintree Hurdle but getting run out of it in the closing stages by Pridwell, who benefitted from a vintage Tony McCoy ride that the British champion jockey still reckons to be among his very best. Swan blamed himself for being too close to the pace in the race, although the heavy ground was hardly ideal for a horse coming off such a barnstorming performance at Cheltenham.

Istabraq headed back for a well-deserved summer holiday at Martinstown, secure in his status as a champion. Swan's tenure as champion jockey was coming to a close. That summer he announced he was going to start training. He also would cease to ride over fences, but he would continue to ride over hurdles. The logic was obvious. No way was the nine-time champion jockey going to stop riding Istabraq, easily the greatest star of his career, while the horse was coming into his prime.

The 1998–99 season was the one that saw the new champion at his peak. Seven starts yielded seven wins. Not a cockfight was missed and never did he look remotely close to getting beaten. A warm-up success at Cork was followed by a contemptuous half-length defeat of Nomadic in the Hatton's Grace. Back for his by now expected Christmas date at Leopardstown, Istabraq started 1–10 against just two opponents and sauntered home. Less than a month later he was back at the Dublin track for the Irish Champion Hurdle and a clash with the horse billed as a pretender to the throne. French Holly had impressively won the previous year's Sun Alliance and was regarded by Ferdy Murphy as the best he had trained. The trainer who had once worked for the Durkan family just a few miles away in the Dublin mountains was by then based in Yorkshire and renowned as one of the smartest operators in the north of England. His willingness to put it up to Istabraq in his own back yard encouraged hopes of an epic pre-Cheltenham clash. The two horses clashed but it was no epic.

French Holly's intended flight to Ireland was cancelled due to fog. That resulted in a cross-country trip to the Holyhead ferry that meant the big English horse was in his horsebox for over twenty-four hours before running. It was hardly perfect preparation for taking on the best hurdler in the world and so it proved. French Holly cut out the pace but was stalked by Istabraq up the straight, with Swan glancing over at his rival more than once before settling for a cheeky length success.

By now Istabraq had become something of a poster-horse for a resurgent racing industry in Ireland that was casting off the economic austerity of the previous decade. Going to the races was becoming fashionable. Wealthy business people mixed with government ministers who appeared to be in thrall to a sport in which Ireland was able to punch far above its weight in terms of population and resources. A growing pride in the general sport centred on the reigning hurdles champion, who began to receive widespread recognition far beyond racing. McManus revealed how much a part of his life Istabraq had become and spoke of how much he felt the horse had become public property. It was easy to dismiss that as the populist schtick of a very wealthy owner, but there was also no getting away from the widespread affection this blue-blooded property of a billionaire businessman generated.

As expected for a 4–9 favourite, the shortest-priced Champion Hurdle favourite in forty-five years, Istabraq duly won at Cheltenham. It wasn't as sparkling a performance as the year before but there was complete authority in another defeat of Theatreworld with French Holly back in third. The latter had another go over the longer trip of the Aintree Hurdle but despite the distance, and the faster ground, Istabraq handed French Holly another defeat, winning hard-held by a length. The perfect campaign wound up at Punchestown as Istabraq beat Decoupage and a horse that was to make his presence felt in a big way the following season, Limestone Lad.

Istabraq's campaign to complete a Champion Hurdle hat-trick began as usual in the race sponsored by his owner, the John James

McManus Hurdle, before moving on to the Hatton's Grace again at Fairyhouse. The 1–7 favourite was obviously short of his peak in November, but no one was prepared for Limestone Lad' s front-running grind beating the champion. Istabraq got to within a couple of lengths of his rival on the run to the last but Limestone Lad wouldn't be denied. It was a first defeat in over eighteen months and Swan was criticised in some quarters for letting the winner get too far ahead.

Any suspicions that Istabraq was on the wane, however, were dismissed on the back of two more easy Leopardstown victories and a hiccup-free run-up to his fourth successive Cheltenham Festival. O'Brien's juggling act with the horse's nerves was as precise as ever, as he explained: 'Istabraq has a lot of brilliance but there is a very fine line involved and we have to ensure we keep on the right side of the balance. If he is asked to do anything different from what he normally does he doesn't like it and he is inclined to fret. He lives on the edge. If you were to shout at him in the stable he would break into a sweat.'

It was others doing the sweating the day before the Champion Hurdle, though. A trickle of blood that appeared on Istabraq's nostril at the racecourse stables in Cheltenham turned into a flood of anxiety, concern and headlines. The heavy odds-on favourite to become just the fifth hat-trick champion appeared on the verge of being pulled out of the race. A proper veterinary examination of the cause of the trickle, whether it was a burst blood vessel or just a simple bang, was impossible because the horse would need to be sedated and the medication would result in a failed dope test. The worry was that the blood was a sign of something more serious. O'Brien later admitted if it had been an ordinary race he wouldn't have run Istabraq. But this was far from ordinary.

There were no further troublesome signs overnight and the horse seemed happy in himself, so the decision was taken the following morning to run. But Swan had orders to pull up immediately if he felt something wasn't right. Istabraq, though, didn't put a foot wrong, cruising up the inner to track Blue Royal to the last and powering up the hill to join an even more exclusive club. Only Golden Miller and Arkle had previously won at four successive Cheltenham Festivals. A euphoric reception in the winner's enclosure only emphasised how exceptional the horse that had once been dismissed as a slow disappointment really was. Timeform rated Istabraq as their second-greatest Champion Hurdle winner behind Night Nurse. He'd won twice in 1976–77. No horse had ever won the championship four times. The horse that could pull that off would surely have to be considered the best ever.

For so long it looked like happening too. After a long break, Istabraq returned to action at Christmas, understandably looking a little tubby, but fully expected to win. But it was here that the first inkling of vulnerability reared its head. At the fourth-last he clipped heels with a rival and made a bad mistake. The 1–4 favourite got into a position to challenge the leader Moscow Flyer in the straight but looked held when falling for the first time in his life at the last flight. O'Brien was unconcerned and said: 'He is very laid-back when he is not fired up these days. He was also heavier than ever.'

Back at Leopardstown three weeks later for another Irish Champion Hurdle, everything looked to be back on track. This time it was Moscow Flyer who fell, at the second last, and there was a reassuring spring to the way Istabraq soared over the last. It looked all-systems-go for Cheltenham again. But then much wider concerns brought racing's tight little world grinding to a halt.

On 19 February 2001, a case of foot-and-mouth was reported on a pig farm in Britain, the start of an epidemic that cost billions and brought animal transportation almost to a halt in these islands. The impact on Irish society was considerable. Even the St Patrick's Day parades had to be cancelled. Field sports were put on hold. For racing the fallout was immense. Home meetings were cancelled but it was Cheltenham and the chances of Irish horses travelling there that was uppermost in everyone's thoughts. The government requested that Irish horses not travel to Britain. But the decision was ultimately taken out of everyone's hands because of just twenty-three sheep. Cheltenham's hopes of running the festival on schedule were destroyed when it was discovered that sheep had been grazing on the track. British government rules stated that livestock couldn't be on site twenty-eight days before a meeting. The festival was postponed to 17–19 April, but that too was cancelled due to a foot-and-mouth outbreak five miles from the track. It might have been a minor outcome in the overall scheme of things but Istabraq's chance for a unique slice of racing history had gone.

Towards the end of April Leopardstown hosted the Grade 1 Shell Champion Hurdle and that only added to the case of 'what might have been'. The champion met Moscow Flyer for the third time that season and again only one of them managed to finish. This time it was Istabraq who exited dramatically at the last. He might have looked in control of the race when he fell, but it was still a dreadful anticlimax to a race that had promised so much. It deepened many people's conviction that foot-and-mouth had robbed him. But a four-in-a-row was still possible. No new novice star had bounded over the horizon. Moscow Flyer was going chasing. Istabraq was still miles clear of his contemporaries on ratings. And he would only be ten at the time of the 2002 Champion Hurdle. Theoretically it was all sound reasoning, but there now seemed a faint vulnerability about the horse that hadn't existed previously.

O'Brien seemed to acknowledge as much when he set out plans for the upcoming season. Istabraq wouldn't be seen until Christmas. Everything would again centre around Cheltenham. But there was a growing awareness at Ballydoyle that time was not on their side. When he did return it was only to secure a scrambling victory over the demonstrably inferior Bust Out at

Leopardstown. That the horse remained a hot favourite for Cheltenham had much more to do with the legend he had already carved out than any encouraging noises from his trainer. Reports of stiffness were hardly spiked when O'Brien declared that age was starting to catch up with his champion. The run-up to Cheltenham 2002 was dominated by rumours that Istabraq was going to be scratched. But once again, the rumour-mill was wrong – at least in terms of the horse lining up.

Istabraq made it to the start, inspiring hopes of a final glorious hurrah as well as presenting punters with a quandary. At anywhere near his best, the champion looked a brilliant value bet at 2–1. The rumours weren't encouraging but his presence alone testified to the lingering hopes in Ballydoyle that Istabraq had one more trip to the big-race well still in him. They were soon dashed. Istabraq was awkward over the first flight, negotiated the second and was promptly pulled up by Swan, who explained, 'His action went after he landed over the first. I let him go on for a bit because they can sometimes come back on the bridle. But it didn't happen.'

Any groans of disappointment were quickly replaced by a spontaneous round of applause for the dethroned champ that might just be the most sporting moment seen on a racecourse for decades. Inevitably there were some suggestions that the horse shouldn't haven't run at all, but O'Brien said simply, 'We owed it to him to run. I'm happy Istabraq is happy. He obviously wasn't going and Charlie did absolutely the right thing. The horse has felt no pain. Nothing goes on forever.'

Ten days later, Istabraq's retirement was officially announced. He had picked up a hock injury at Cheltenham and, with his best days obviously behind him, McManus made the easy call to take his champion home to Martinstown. After a forty-race career that yielded twenty-five wins and seven runner-up placings, as well as over a million sterling in prize money, it was time for the horse bred to be a flat star but who became a National Hunt icon to kick back and relax.

A few years earlier, in 1999, his famous brother Secreto died in Japan after an underwhelming stallion career that resulted in one top-class offspring, the 1991 Guineas winner, Mystiko. It seemed an appropriately 'here-today-gone-tomorrow' output for a horse that raced only four times before being sold off to stud with a $40 million valuation. Istabraq's genetic legacy is nonexistent, but in terms of carving out a unique place in racing history, the kid brother eventually managed to come out on top.

It just shows what a three-and-a half-foot obstacle can do for a horse.

Sea The Stars

A lot of flowery prose was showered on Man O' War, the great American champion of the early 1920s, but nobody was as eloquent as his groom Will Harbutt, who referred to him simply as 'de mostest hoss that ever wuz'. Nearly ninety years later, and thousands of miles away, the phrasing might be grammatically more correct, and come accompanied with a different accent, but the sentiment is the same. Sea The Stars really is the mostest horse most of us will ever see. And the weird part is at least some of that is due to what we didn't see.

Michael Kinane retired at the end of 2009 convinced that after Sea The Stars no similar pinnacle was possible in an already glittering career. A couple of decades as one of the world's top riders included steering some hugely evocative names to victory, but he still places Sea The Stars on an entirely separate pedestal. Because Kinane reckons the horse only needed to show 75 per cent of his full ability to carve out a career that will resonate for as long as thoroughbreds race.

'He never even came close to the bottom of the well,' he said later. 'He was the complete racehorse in every way. All of the modern greats had frailties of some sort but not Sea The Stars. Physically, mentally, in every way, he didn't have a shortcoming.'

Kinane always brought a singularly cold-eyed determination to the business of finishing first. Never the most demonstrative of men, his natural inclination was to row along with the old American racing reporter who famously advised a young colleague that nothing he encountered on this beat would ever justify a superlative. But Sea The Stars was different. In a sport that eventually finds the boundaries of practically every horse, the bay colt uniquely blessed with the imposing size of a prospective steeplechaser and a sprinter's speed didn't have a limit. Or, if he did, no one ever came close to finding it.

If that smacks of even the faintest hint of hyperbole, then John Oxx would be the first to quibble. In the modern world of high-investment international flat racing, the trainer who masterminded Sea The Stars' unique career remains chronically allergic to hype. Possessed of the mild-spoken equanimity of a country doctor, and a natural inclination to always keep in context the business of one horse passing a red lollipop ahead of another, Oxx also has a perspective on thoroughbred history that makes his judgement uniquely respected in Irish racing. So when he describes his former champion as the culmination of hundreds of years of horse breeding, then it is not some flippant headline-grabbing remark.

Sea The Stars does appear to represent a kind of perfection. He owns the sort of blue blood that encourages those pedigree nerds to nod their heads sagely and maintain the delusion that breeding is somehow more than just a genetic crap-shoot. Physically there isn't a blemish. A depth of shoulder sweeps through to the rest of a perfectly proportioned body that was carried across the turf by four legs that never gave even the faintest twinge. With a temperament that makes Roger Federer seem combustible, Sea The Stars also has a constitution that has veterinary surgeons smiling through gritted teeth. But the only thing that really mattered was that he could run like few if any ever have.

Form books are crammed with well-bred, good-looking horses

that never took a lame step in their lives and couldn't run worth a damn. Other more moderately bred and inexpensively bought champions had achievements that surpassed every reasonable expectation. But no equine athlete has ever made the job of racing look easier.

Not in any flamboyant sense, though. Shergar won the Derby by ten lengths. Nijinksy was imperious in the Guineas. Sea Bird made winning the Arc look ridiculously easy. But no horse ever won the three great races in one season before Sea The Stars' seminal 2009 campaign. And although never winning by more than two and a half lengths, there was never less than total authority, never a hint that there wasn't more to give if any opponent ever had the temerity to really try and eyeball him. Not unnaturally, the charismatic colt couldn't see the point in busting a gut any further once he'd passed all the opposition.

So much was obvious during the rousing half-minute it took him to run that final Prix de l'Arc de Triomphe stretch that brought an unprecedented season of achievement to a tumultuous finale. Trapped on the rail and surrounded by the entire field, there was something freakish about the sang-froid that even the famously cool Kinane was able to exhibit. Dismissing Getaway's cheeky attempt to get up his inside, Sea The Stars seemed to explode into a burst of acceleration that allowed his jockey to weave a passage to the lead within little more than a hundred yards. It is as startling an exhibition of speed and class as has ever been seen at Longchamp and it happened in seconds.

But the remaining two hundred metres was notable for how the winner didn't continue to accelerate away from the opposition into the sort of wide-margin rout that sends handicapping calculators spinning like slot machines. Instead he eased up, beating the perennial Arc runner-up Youmzain by a couple of lengths. The brilliance was obvious, and so was the truth that so much more remained in the tank.

'After he won, Christophe Soumillon came alongside to

congratulate me and the horse thought he was racing again and ran away with me. It's the only time I've ever been run away with after a race,' Kinane recalls, his head shaking at the memory. 'He ended up being officially rated 136 but it would have taken an exceptional horse to bring out what he had in him. A 140 horse would have dragged it out of him. The thing is, once he hit the front he felt he'd done enough and all handicappers can go on is what they see.'

Oxx still believes he got nowhere near the bottom of the horse's well of talent and recalls: 'He was a clever devil, always knew what he was doing. I used to tell Mick to try and win further and show him off but he'd never go clear. He knew where the line was, not that he could see a red disc or anything, but he could travel on the bridle for so long that he knew he only really had to run for a furlong at the end. That's what Ballydoyle kept trying to do that season, get him off the bridle and into a fight. But they couldn't. Nothing could.'

Those free to give marks for artistic impression were never happier to be relieved of such constraints. On the BBC, commentator Jim McGrath wound up the Arc by describing the winner as 'perfection in equine form, a horse of a lifetime'. The following day's *Racing Post* headline over a picture of Sea The Stars proclaimed: 'The Greatest'. Even Mill Reef's trainer Ian Balding described him as the finest three-year-old he had ever seen.

Back at Oxx's stables on the Curragh the following day, there was an official homecoming for the colt whose name was being bandied around with Arkle in terms of equine excellence. In glorious autumnal sunshine, the hero of the hour paraded in front of the cameras, posed for photos like an old chaser with a queue of normally sceptical media types, and generally behaved as if the effort of creating indelible images and memories for generations to come less than twenty-four hours earlier had taken nothing out of him.

There was speculation about one last hurrah in Santa Anita

for the Breeders' Cup Classic. The normally insular American authorities were falling over themselves to present a case for Sea The Stars taking on the top Californian mare Zenyatta on the synthetic surface. It didn't take a mind-reader that day on the Curragh, however, to figure out Oxx felt his star had done enough. Six out of six, all of them Group 1s, and all won with complete authority. Travelling six thousand miles at the end of all that, competing on a new surface against horses raced in a culture with a less than convincing attitude to the use of drugs was never really on.

So America's 'World Championships' went ahead without the world champion, who instead travelled a few miles across Kildare to a lucrative new career as a stallion. Zenyatta duly won the Classic while Sea The Stars lined up against the handful of legendary names in that futile but endlessly fascinating competition about who the best ever might be.

Timeform slapped a figure of 140 on Sea The Stars, 4lb more than the official handicappers. That's the same mark given to Dancing Brave and Shergar. Mill Reef is a 141, Brigadier Gerard a 144, while the 1965 Arc and Derby hero Sea Bird is tops on 145. Incongruous as it may sound for such a high rating, if ever a figure justified a famous Timeform 'P', the symbol of a horse having the potential to earn a much higher mark, it must be Sea The Stars.

Mill Reef, the Brigadier and Shergar were all beaten in their pomp. Sea The Stars never looked in trouble. Brigadier Gerard never even ran in the Derby or the Arc. Shergar would have been an also-ran in a Guineas. The great Italian champion Ribot was unbeaten in fourteen starts but many of them were virtual walkovers such was his superiority at home. During a five-race three-year-old career Sea Bird too never looked to be in any danger of defeat. The great French horse used the Prix Greffulhe and the Prix Lupin as warm-ups for a stunning Epsom victory. The Grand Prix de Saint-Cloud served the same function for an even more impressive Arc success. Maybe he would have scooted up in similar fashion over a mile if he'd been tried. But he wasn't and we'll never know. With Sea The Stars we know. From a mile to a mile and a half, from one end of the season to the other, he fought every fight and hardly broke sweat: the complete racehorse.

The same was never said about Urban Sea. As a yearling, the dam of Sea The Stars was bought at the Deauville Sales for FF280,000 by trainer Jean Lesbordes for owner David Tsui. A chestnut daughter of Miswaki, she would become perhaps not the most valuable, but definitely the most valued, investment made by the Hong Kong businessman. A two-year-old winner, Urban Sea won two Listed races at three and was Group 1 placed twice. As a four-year-old she started in the 1993 Prix de l'Arc de Triomphe on the back of two wins but nevertheless was dismissed as a 37–1 no-hoper. Ridden by Eric Saint-Martin, son of the legendary jockey Yves, Urban Sea nevertheless managed to beat fourteen Group 1 winners to win Europe's greatest all-aged contest. She raced on as a five-year-old before injury ended a racing career that was to fade in comparison to what the chestnut mare achieved at stud.

Her first foal by Bering called Urban Ocean won a Gallinule Stakes and her second by Lammtara, Melikah, was a Stakes winner. But her first visit to the legendary stallion Sadler's Wells resulted in Galileo. Trained by Aidan O'Brien, he won both the English and Irish Derbys as well as the King George and remains the highest-rated runner handled by O'Brien. A return to Sadler's Wells produced another Group 1 winner, Black Sam Bellamy, whose full sister All Too Beautiful managed to be runner-up in the Oaks. A change of stallion to Giant's Causeway saw My Typhoon win a Grade 1 in America, so when the decision was taken to send Urban Sea to Cape Cross, the Sheikh Mohammed-owned stallion was getting possibly the most valuable mare in the world.

Cape Cross was picked by David Tsui's widow, Ling Tsui, and her son Christopher, who at twenty-three years of age represented the family at Epsom in 2004 where All Too Beautiful was well beaten by the Cape Cross sired Ouija Board. At 11.20 p.m. on 6 April 2006, the result of the brief union of Cape Cross and Urban Sea was foaled at the Irish National Stud. The Stud's former manager John Clarke described the new arrival.

'A big, heavy foal but beautifully put together. He was always a very nice foal, trouble free, never a sick day in his life, always an easy mover, good walker, good temperament,' he said. 'He just had this quality, a little arrogance, "I am superior to every other horse".'

What John Oxx noticed, however, when he first saw the individual that would become a future superstar, was how perfect a physical specimen he was. If the Tsui's had decided to sell him, they would have made a fortune. My Typhoon made 1.8 million guineas as a youngster. But Mrs Tsui wanted her son's interest in racing and breeding to have a new focus. It was decided to keep the strapping yearling and put him in training with Oxx.

Hugely respected within the industry, the trainer had already proved his ability to mastermind a top-class campaign with a run of success earlier in the decade. Sinndar completed the English-Irish Derby double in 2000 before landing the Arc while Alamshar landed the Irish Derby and then the King George at Ascot in 2003. Azamour was another tip-top performer owned by the Aga Khan. When Sea The Stars came to the Currabeg yard, a couple of miles from the Curragh racecourse, it was to a stables where many of the key staff had been in place for years. Liberties are not tolerated, especially with punctuality, but Oxx's is regarded as a good place to work.

The new arrival was put in box nineteen, the same one Sinndar and Alamshar had been in, and assigned to groom John Hynes, who had looked after Alamshar.

'I remember very early on after the horse arrived, Tony Shanahan, the headman, called me over and pointed to a little bone in the horse's forehead, like a little horn. He said, "You see that there. That's supposed to be the sign of a really good horse. I haven't seen one of them in a long time." I'll never forget that. That was long before he ever ran,' Hynes later recalled.

The handsome Urban Sea colt was no angel in his box. He could twist his head in an instant and nip. But there was no malice in it. It wasn't long before Hynes was sneaking an apple to him every evening as a treat. And when it came to work, the big bay youngster was always impressive. The breaking-in process is always tricky but Oxx employed the Englishman Gary Witheford and his son Craig, whose uncanny ability to get animals to co-operate with them extends to deer, llamas and even on one occasion a zebra. With thoroughbreds, Witheford is confident of having one ridden within twenty minutes. Sea The Stars took less than that.

'Everything I do is pressure release. Horses hate being pulled, yanked or pushed. With half a ton of horse, you've got to teach the animal to follow you,' he said. 'You usually have a good idea, even as yearlings, if they are going to be any good and as soon as Craig sat on Sea The Stars he thought he could be special.'

However, in the spring of 2008, there was another burgeoning talent at Currabeg that some felt was an even better prospect. The Aga Khan-owned colt Arazan, a half-brother to Azamour, was starting to show signs of being well out of the ordinary. Unusually for a trainer who views a juvenile career as very much a prelude to the real thing at three, Oxx was able to produce a two-year-old runner in May and Arazan lived up to expectations with an impressive success at Leopardstown. Mick Kinane got off him in the winner's enclosure and gave a simple nod of approval. But by then, he had also sampled the potential in Arazan's pal across the yard.

'I couldn't believe my luck,' Kinane remembered later. The veteran jockey turned up for work one morning and was presented with the imposing youngster. 'What's this?' Kinane asked, and when told it was a half-brother to Galileo, the horse he had known so well seven years previously, he turned to Oxx and laughed: 'How did you manage that?'

Even from his initial canter on the colt Kinane suspected there was something different about him. Everything felt easy. There was a flow to the stride that was impressive but even more so was the sense fizzing down the reins that there was so much more to tap into. With the good ones, it is usually clear pretty much from the start.

By Irish Oaks day on 13 July, Sea The Stars had done enough at home to justify a first racecourse start. The opening race at the Curragh that day attracted even more attention than usual due to the top-class Jim Bolger-trained pair, Teofilo and New Approach having made their own debuts in the seven-furlong event in the previous couple of years. Bolger supplied Tomas An Tsioda and not surprisingly he started favourite. Sea The Stars was a 6–1 joint-second favourite with Freemantle. Settled by Kinane on the inside, he couldn't get a clear run at a crucial stage but was running on strongly at the end to finish fourth behind Driving Snow. Black Bear Island, who the following year would win the Dante, was second, ahead of Freemantle.

Oxx was not unhappy. Being beaten first time meant getting the chance to secure valuable experience in another maiden. Defeat as a two-year-old in itself meant nothing. And it would never happen again. Like Sea Bird and Man o' War, the only time Sea The Stars would be beaten was as a juvenile. During a dreadful summer in Ireland, however, it looked for a while as if it might be his only start in 2008. Oxx and Kinane became convinced that good, quick ground was essential and yet it seemed it would never stop raining. The going at Leopardstown on 17 August was heavy but Sea The Stars ploughed through it well enough to break his duck by two and a half lengths.

One more run would be perfect, Oxx decided, and on 28 September the Curragh managed to come up with a good-to-yielding surface. In the climatic circumstances, it was a minor miracle. Sea The Stars beat his stable companion Mourayan by half a length in the Group 2 Beresford Stakes, a race previously won by both Alamshar and Azamour. A short head back in third was Masterofthehorse, who started favourite. It was a performance of some promise by a colt whose relationship to Galileo resulted in a widely held presumption that if there was a classic in him it would be a Derby. The official handicapper rated Sea The Stars on 112. Seven other juveniles were rated higher in Ireland, including the top-rated Mastercraftsman on 122.

Arazan was a 115 and after his own Group 2 triumph in the Futurity that year, there was a depth of disappointment to his National Stakes defeat that led many – and more than one were in the Oxx stable – to presume he was the yard's No. 1 classic hope.

Nothing happened during the winter and spring of 2009 to shake anybody's belief. Arazan liked a cut in the ground and looked a true miler. Sea The Stars liked quick going and seemingly was bred to go further. Oxx, however, wasn't so sure. Yes, there was stamina on the dam's side of his pedigree, but Cape Cross was mainly an influence for speed. His biggest success as a racehorse had come in the Lockinge over a mile. In many ways, his most famous daughter, Ouija Board, had been an aberration in her ability to go a mile and a half. Plus there was no escaping the raw pace Sea The Stars was starting to show.

Typically of a Currabeg horse, he was only now being asked to step up the intensity of his work. Not every horse relishes the challenge but Sea The Stars thrived on it. An iron constitution meant working in the winter rain on the Curragh was no bother to him. Each time the workload increased only seemed to make the horse happier. He was ridden in his work by Alex Da Silva, a Brazilian who was specifically teamed up with the horse by the trainer, who said, 'Alex suits him and gets on with him. He's a big, strong horse so you wouldn't put just anybody up on him.' The suspicion that they were dealing with the real thing took even greater hold among Oxx's team. Thousands of miles away in his winter stint in Dubai, Kinane's determination to be at full fitness for the season ahead was encouraged by phone calls home. Racing twice a week, riding work and running three miles a day in the desert heat, the man on the verge of his fiftieth birthday keenly looked forward to racing what he already suspected might be the best horse he had ever ridden.

But with horses nothing is straightforward. On 17 March, St Patrick's Day, just four days after the end of the Cheltenham Festival, a racing world concentrating on jumping barely registered the high temperature that threatened to derail a potentially seismic flat career. A viral infection struck down Sea The Stars to such an extent that his trainer's plans to run in May's Newmarket 2,000 Guineas looked forlorn. The classic might have been six weeks away but top-flight races are rarely won on the back of interrupted preparations. Oxx had to back off. Sea The Stars was reduced to walking for a week. In the carefully structured preparation of any Group 1 hope, such setbacks usually spell disaster. But the constitution that was to become as potent a weapon as his temperament came to Sea The Stars' rescue.

'That temperature he got would have stopped most horses, but not him,' Oxx remembers.

Far from being flattened by the virulent bug, the young three-year-old bounced back, hungry for more work. Arazan too was pleasing the trainer. It looked like he had a pair of genuine Guineas prospects. When they worked together, it was noticeable how much happier Azamour's half-brother was on the soft terrain. But Sea The Stars still more than held his own while all the time indicating there was so much more left to work on.

On 19 April, after racing at Leopardstown, both classic hopes worked over seven furlongs. Kinane rode Arazan with Fran Berry on Sea The Stars, while Niall McCullagh rode a lead horse. Arazan 'won' the gallop by a head and Oxx expressed his satisfaction with both. The ground at Leopardstown was almost good. Arazan took over in many people's minds as Oxx's principal Guineas hope, especially after Sea The Stars didn't sparkle in a gallop on soft going. However, as the weather squeezed up, another gallop, just days before Guineas weekend, revealed a much different athlete. With the ground predicted to be quick at Newmarket, the decision was taken that Sea The Stars would go to England and Arazan would wait for a softer surface in the Irish Guineas.

To many outside the Oxx camp, it smacked of a colt getting ready for the Derby. An encouraging run at Newmarket, say, a running on fourth or fifth, would be a perfect warm-up for Epsom. The more shrewd noted the trainer's past selectivity when pitching horses into top-class races. Azamour had been Oxx's only previous Guineas starter and he finished third. It might have been a rush to get Sea The Stars ready in time for Newmarket but the colt's appetite for work was remarkable. Never ones to utter bullish quotes, both Kinane and Oxx felt confident of a bold show in the Guineas. What they got surprised even them.

Training is much more about guesswork than is commonly believed. Only the stupid or the insecure try to find out the limits of a horse's capabilities at home. Sea The Stars always indicated potential but the real excitement lay in the suspicion of what remained untapped. The 95.8 seconds it took to run the Rowley Mile course was the first full glimpse of what a truly remarkable athlete he was.

Up against Sea The Stars was the champion two-year-old Mastercraftsman, whose hugely touted stable companion Rip Van Winkle was the pick of Aidan O'Brien's No. 1 jockey, Johnny Murtagh. Gan Amhras represented Jim Bolger. Oxx's runner was the outsider of the Irish quartet at 8–1, with the Craven winner Delegator 3–1 favourite. Delegator travelled supremely well through the race, but no more so than Sea The Stars. They were drawn on either side of the fifteen-strong field and both launched their challenges at the same time going into the dip. Jamie Spencer was convinced he had the race won until Kinane finally asked for everything inside the final furlong. The horse categorised as a Derby candidate managed to accelerate again and pull far enough away to win with authority and without leaving his guts all over Newmarket heath.

'You could see from a long way out he was going to make it count,' smiled Oxx, while Kinane remarked, 'We had a few hiccups and we were worried we might be chasing him here. But he worked great on a better surface and I said we had to be here.'

The irony of winning the Guineas was that suddenly any thoughts of winning the Derby too were contaminated by fears that Sea The Stars might now have too much speed for a mile and a half. In the twenty years since Nashwan completed the Newmarket-Epsom double, some Guineas winners looked to have had perfect credentials for the Derby only to find the stamina demands around that unique circuit too great. Kinane rode a heavy odds-on favourite in Entrepreneur (1997) who couldn't even make the frame. The following year, another of his Guineas winners, King Of Kings, finished last behind High-Rise. Before Nashwan it had been another nineteen years back to Nijinsky's double. Kinane, though, was happy that Sea The Stars had the exceptional gifts required.

The veteran jockey was in his element. Always a man to relish the big occasion, there had been whispers over the previous number of seasons that he was past his best, that a great career was being compromised by hanging on too long. It's remarkable how important the role of fashion is in such a self-consciously tough sport. During the first two years after his departure as No. 1 jockey to the all-conquering Coolmore team in 2003, Kinane had had Azamour to keep his name to the fore. In the three subsequent seasons, Oxx had not had a true top-flight runner. There hasn't been a jockey born who can win without the raw material underneath, but sceptics now added that lack of success to Kinane's advancing years and decided in the parlance of the game that he was 'gone'. The evidence that such a sum was badly out of whack would resonate throughout 2009.

Kinane has always insisted there is no ill feeling between himself and the Coolmore organisation, despite the breakdown in com - munication between himself and Aidan O'Brien towards the end of his tenure at Ballydoyle. But the man would be less than human if the faintest *frisson* of justification didn't accompany Sea The Stars' Group 1 romp. O'Brien possessed three genuinely top-class middle-distance colts and spent 2009 fruitlessly pitching them against their peerless compatriot.

Mastercraftsman ran fifth at Newmarket and subsequently ran away with the Irish Guineas, a race Arazan had to miss when hit with a chest infection that ruled him out for the entire season. Later, Mastercraftsman would come closer than anything else to getting the better of Ballydoyle's great rival. But on the run-up to Epsom it was Rip Van Winkle and Fame And Glory in particular that flew the Coolmore flag. Other O'Brien-trained horses mopped up the traditional trials with aplomb. Black Bear Island landed the Dante, Age Of Aquarius the Lingfield Trial and Golden Sword won the Chester Vase. Fame And Glory took the tried-and-trusted route through Leopardstown's Ballysax and Derrinstown Derby Trials. And yet Johnny Murtagh elected to again stick with Rip Van Winkle.

Half the dozen Derby runners were trained by O'Brien while Gan Amhras was also back for another crack at Sea The Stars in an unprecedented level of Irish domination at Epsom. Possibly the one factor that will have racing historians shaking their heads in future is how Sea The Stars didn't start favourite. Instead, Fame And Glory was heavily backed into 9–4 as the market indicated Murtagh had got it wrong. What punters couldn't have reckoned on was that the Ballydoyle battalion would still appear to run the race for Rip Van Winkle's benefit rather than Fame And Glory's.

There was no surprise when Golden Sword immediately went into the lead from Age Of Aquarius but what was puzzling was the sedate pace. Fame And Glory's stamina was assured but Rip's wasn't. Unfortunately from O'Brien's point of view, turning the race into a comparative sprint was going to benefit the fastest horse in the race and that was Sea The Stars. Kinane summed up the situation in seconds and, allowing the two leaders to scoot away, he had his mount in Position A alongside Kite Wood and ahead of his main rivals. The 11–4 second favourite handled the famous descent to Tattenham Corner as if he was on rails. Behind him, Gan Amhras looked as if he was on roller skates. Straightening up, the only one still on the bridle was Sea The Stars, but Kinane waited until the final furlong before finally reeling in Golden Sword. Any stamina limitations were open to question then, but at the line a quartet of Ballydoyle runners weren't gaining and ended up being firmly put in their place.

There were less than two lengths in it at the line and yet no one could have missed the control exerted by the winner throughout the race. Eight years previously his sibling Galileo had looked similarly dominant, but he was a true mile and a half horse. Sea The Stars was that and so much more besides. Amid all the furore surrounding the most famous winner's enclosure in the world, Kinane slipped the saddle off and whispered to Oxx, 'This is one of the greats.' Neither man would recount this until the end of the season but amid the relief and exultation of winning racing's blue riband there was also the new self-imposed pressure of allowing a rare talent the opportunity to be fully exploited.

'It was tense. This horse was different. We knew we had a great one and he had to leave his mark. He was capable of winning the whole shoot but anything can go wrong,' Oxx remembers. 'Probably the Arc was the most tense. We didn't want him to do a Nijinsky and fall at the last fence, so to speak.'

Initially the first port-of-call would be at home on the Curragh in the Irish Derby. Fame And Glory was set to oppose again, his supporters convinced that a true pace around a stiffer mile and a half would contribute to a turnaround. It looked set for a potentially epic clash until the weather intervened. Remarkably for Ireland in June, it rained! On the Friday evening before the classic, it rained again on ground that had already been watered. By the following morning, his head full of the memories of those relatively underwhelming gallops in the spring, the trainer confirmed that Sea The Stars wouldn't run. Instead he would wait a week for Sandown's Eclipse and a first clash with older horses. Fame And Glory duly won the Irish Derby easily, provoking some rather bullish comments from Camp Coolmore about a decider later in the season. More immediately, though, they decided to pitch Rip Van Winkle at the Eclipse as well.

By now the secret was out even among the general sporting public that here was something exceptional. Media attention descended on the Sea The Stars team with a vengeance. But as the man at the tiller, Oxx felt the full glare of the spotlight. Hardly the caricature of the modern multimedia performer, he nevertheless handled the attention with a fluently natural courtesy that only seemed to increase the feel-good factor surrounding his horse. As a child Oxx had listened while his father read books about the great champions and dreamed one day he would be in possession of such animals. The subsequent day-to-day reality of surviving in a cut-throat business had morphed into a career that included a number of true champions of his own. But Sea The Stars had it in him to be unique. The pressure to not screw up that potential must have been immense and yet from the outside it was hard to detect any stress.

It was there, however. In the Eclipse, Sea The Stars was applauded around the parade ring by the Sandown crowd. In the race itself, he led fully two furlongs out, allowing Rip Van Winkle a target which for a split second looked like being hauled in. Eyeballed by his rival, Sea The Stars quickened once more to win comfortably. Once again the horse looked in total control. In the stands, Christopher Tsui briefly fainted with the excitement of it all. The display, backed up by Oxx's declaration that the Irish Champion Stakes a couple of months later would be a major target, introduced speculation that ten furlongs was the new champion's optimum distance. His trainer disagreed and said simply, 'I don't think he has a best distance. He can do them all.'

Next up was York's Juddmonte International where Mastercraftsman was the latest Ballydoyle star to take his chance, backed up by a pair of pacemakers. It was expected to be a stroll for the 1–4 favourite but it didn't turn out like that. When Mastercraftsman launched his challenge between his two stablemates, Sea The Stars scythed his way through too. But the grey in front of him was far too tough a customer to be summarily passed. Just as Kinane took a pull, Murtagh kicked again and Mastercraftsman suddenly had his rival under pressure. Kinane's whip had to flash venomously a couple of times and it was only in the final fifty yards that Sea The Stars asserted. There was only a length in it at the line. Nothing ever got closer in 2009.

The sequence of a Group 1 every month continued into the Irish Champion Stakes, although Sea The Stars' only start in Ireland that year came perilously close to not happening. Once again, what passed for a summer was rain-soaked. Five days before the race, the going was more winter National Hunt than summer flat and bookmakers began betting on whether or not the favourite would even appear. Lying in wait was Fame And Glory in what should have been a PR opportunity that would have customers going to Leopardstown in their droves, a real head-to-head to concentrate the attention of those normally resistant to racing's charms.

Instead the run-up was focused on what surface might be acceptable to Oxx, who insisted that any mention of the word soft in the going description would rule Sea The Stars out. Forty-eight hours beforehand, it was long odds-on he wouldn't run. But Leopardstown drains famously well and a rare break in the conditions meant a surprise for the trainer when he walked the course the evening before the race. A final check the following morning and it was decided that 'good to yielding' ground would suffice. The second round of Sea The Stars versus Fame And Glory was on – except as heavyweight bouts go this was more Tyson–Spinks than Ali–Frasier.

Once again Aidan O'Brien pitched in a number of pacemakers for Fame And Glory, and even sent Mastercraftsman into battle again. Off a good pace, the contest went according to plan down the back straight. But as they began the long turn into the straight, Murtagh rushed Fame And Glory up from behind Sea The Stars and grabbed the race by the scruff of the neck. It was a remarkably similar ploy to what Murtagh did on High Chaparral in the 2002 Epsom Derby when making the most of his mount's proven stamina to edge out Kinane and Hawk Wing. Two furlongs out Fame And Glory committed everything.

If there was any chink in Sea The Stars, especially on the ground, then it would have been exposed. Kinane, though, gave every impression of not having a care in the world. A shake of the reins was enough for the 4–6 favourite to reel in the leader. Sea The Stars even condescended to pull two and a half lengths clear at the line. The response was singular enough to be remembered for some time. The majority of Irish racing fans are famously devoted to jump racing. But for those at Leopardstown that day there was an undeniable sense of having been present to witness something unique. There was a rush to the winner's enclosure that would have done credit to the Cheltenham Festival and a tumultuous reception for what both Oxx and Kinane now readily conceded was the horse of a lifetime. 'A great horse, capable of anything,' the jockey summed up. 'We have to find out what are his limits. He's going forward all the time, just a great horse,' Oxx endorsed. The only slight bum note on the entire occasion was that fewer than ten thousand people were there to savour it. Like many historic moments in Ireland, there are likely to be many more who in future will claim to have been present.

Officially the Irish Champion Stakes was the greatest per - formance Sea The Stars ever put up. But the race that catapulted him to legendary status was the Arc. Europe's greatest all-aged contest had proved a graveyard for several great horses arriving at Longchamp on the back of an extensive three-year-old campaign. Generous (1991) never even showed behind his great rival Suave Dancer. Troy (1979) could manage only third to Three Troikas. Nijinsky (1970) and Sir Ivor (1968) were runners-up. Shergar (1981) and Nashwan (1989) didn't even make it to Paris. Sea The Stars was attempting an unprecedented Guineas-Derby-Arc hat-trick as well as a sixth Group 1 of the season. Ordinarily the Arc would have been regarded as a step too far. That famous constitution, though, came to his aid. If anything the horse seemed to be thriving even more. A dry autumn provided perfect ground and all was set.

What always has to be remembered about Sea The Stars winning the Arc is how unlikely it seemed soon after the start. Fame And Glory was back for another crack, accompanied by his pacemakers, Set Sail and Grand Ducal. Sea The Stars again broke like a sprinter, forcing Kinane to try and settle him. But when the slow-starting Grand Ducal was rushed past him to fulfil his duties up front, the 4–6 favourite took it as his cue to run even faster. Fighting for his head, Sea The Stars was shuffled back through the field so that at halfway in the race he was stuck on the rails in the middle of the field. It looked disastrous. Because the pacemakers were ignored, there was hardly the sort of breakneck pace that would allow those in front to fall away. As the proven Group 1 winners Conduit, Cavalryman, Dar Re Mi, Vision D'Etat, Fame And Glory and Stacelita got into position in the false straight for the dash home, Sea The Stars was hampered and lost his footing momentarily. For a second it looked hopeless. But another second is all it seemingly took for the colt to engage top gear. In a couple of hundred metres came definitive proof that gauging this singular talent required casting aside any normal criteria.

Reaction to his Arc victory only seemed to prove that. Bookmakers caved in to demand and quoted Sea The Stars as second favourite to become Ireland's Sports Personality of 2009. In a year when Ireland's rugby team managed to win a first Grand Slam for seventy years, even the great horse couldn't hope to overhaul the rugby captain Brian O'Driscoll in that particular race.

It isn't hard to make the case, however, for Sea The Stars being the real story of Irish sporting excellence. The rugby team squeezed their way to a European title while generating a noticeable lack of fearful shivering among the real rugger power - houses of the southern hemisphere. In 2009 there was no doubt but that the horse bred and trained in Ireland and ridden by an Irishman was the best in the world. In fact he was so good, his only competition then, and his only terms of reference now, are a handful of other legendary names in racing history.

'It's interesting to debate it but nobody knows and it is futile to try and work anything out. That he is up there with them is enough for me,' Oxx declares, before adding an interesting proviso.

'He would beat the greats of the past if they raced now. The modern horse runs faster. That's the reality. The actual training might not have changed much but the changes in, say, nutrition have brought things to a different level. Horses now run that bit faster and harder. But it's not a fair comparison. It's like comparing rugby players from twenty or thirty years ago to players now who are professional.

'What I do know is that what Sea The Stars and the other greats did is the hardest thing to ask a thoroughbred to do. To be a good two-year-old, come through the spring and then come to a peak for all those races. It's the supreme test and it is what has designed the stud book. You see these top National Hunt horses that go on for years running in Gold Cups. But they might only run in two proper races in a season with big breaks in between. These horses were only three-year-olds being asked to run so often and so quickly at the top level. That's a huge ask,' he adds.

During his racing career Sea The Stars used to enter racecourse stableyards and shout out to every other horse. Anyone who has ever spent any amount of time with horses knows that noise is no indicator of talent. If it was, some of the most attention-seeking slowcoaches in racing history would have been transformed into winners. But if it is dangerous to ascribe human emotions to animals, neither is it far-fetched to believe such macho behaviour in Sea The Stars came from an instinctive desire to dominate. The difference with everything else was that he was able to back it up, no ifs, buts or maybes.

Anyone who relishes the thoroughbred as a breed will have looked at Sea The Stars and realised they were privileged to do so. So much can go wrong with racehorses. Arazan, the other great hope in John Oxx's stable, never raced again, a wonderful talent left frustratingly unfulfilled. That same can never be said of his former neighbour. What we can still wonder about, though, is how much was left untapped.

Race Records

Arkle

1961

9 December, Lough Ennel Maiden Flat Race, Mullingar, 2 miles & 1f – 3rd (5–1)
26 December, Greystones Maiden Flat Race, Leopardstown, 2 miles – 4th (5–1)

1962

20 January, Bective Novice Hurdle, Navan, 3 miles – Won (20–1)
10 March, Rathconnel Handicap Hurdle, Naas, 2 miles – Won (2–1)
14 April, Balbriggan Handicap Hurdle, Baldoyle, 2 miles – Unplaced (6–1)
24 April, New Handicap Hurdle, Fairyhouse, 2 miles – 4th (8–1)
17 October, Wee County Handicap Hurdle, Dundalk, 2 miles – Won (6–1)
24 October, Presidents Handicap Hurdle, Gowran Park, 2 miles – Won (9–2)
17 November, Honeybourne Chase, Cheltenham, 2 miles & 4f – Won (11–8)

1963

23 February, Milltown Chase, Leopardstown, 2 miles – Won (1–2)
12 March, Broadway Novices Chase, Cheltenham, 3 miles – Won (4–9)
15 April, Powers Gold Cup, Fairyhouse, 2 miles & 4f – Won (2–7)
1 May, John Jameson Gold Cup, Punchestown, 2 miles & 4f – Won (4–7)
9 October, Donoughmore Maiden, Navan, 1 mile & 6f – Won (4–6)
24 October, Careys Cottage Handicap Chase, Gowran Park, 2 miles & 4f – Won (4–7)
30 November, Hennessy Gold Cup, Newbury, 3 miles & 2f – 3rd (5–2)
26 December, Christmas Handicap Chase, Leopardstown, 3 miles – Won (4–7)

1964

30 January, Thyestes Handicap Chase, Gowran Park, 3 miles – Won (4–6)

15 February, Leopardstown Handicap Chase, Leopardstown – Won (4–7)

7 March, Gold Cup, Cheltenham, 3 miles & 2f – Won (7–4)

30 March, Irish Grand National, Fairyhouse, 3 miles & 2f – Won (1–2)

29 October, Careys Cottage Handicap Chase, Gowran Park, 2 miles & 4f – Won (1–5)

5 December, Hennessy Gold Cup, Newbury, 3 miles & 2f – Won (5–4)

12 December, Massey Ferguson Gold Cup, Cheltenham, 2 miles & 5f – 3rd (8–11)

1965

27 February, Leopardstown Handicap Chase, Leopardstown, 3 miles – Won (8–11)

11 March, Gold Cup, Cheltenham, 3 miles & 2f – Won (30–100)

24 April, Whitbread Gold Cup, Sandown, 3 miles & 5f – Won (4–9)

6 November, Gallagher Gold Cup, Sandown, 3 miles – Won (4–9)

27 November, Hennessy Gold Cup, Newbury, 3 miles & 2f – Won (1–6)

27 December, King George VI Chase, Kempton, 3 miles – Won (1–7)

1966

1 March, Leopardstown Handicap Chase, Leopardstown, 3 miles – Won (1–5)

17 March, Gold Cup, Cheltenham, 3 miles & 2f – Won (1–10)

26 November, Hennessy Gold Cup, Newbury, 3 miles & 2f – 2nd (4–6)

14 December, SGB Handicap Chase, Ascot, 3 miles – Won (1–3)

27 December, King George VI Chase, Kempton, 3 miles – 2nd (2–9)

Vintage Crop

1991

17 October, Babs Babes Welter Flat Race, Thurles, 2 miles – Won (20–1)

18 December, Thomastown Maiden Hurdle, Fairyhouse, 2 miles – Won (4–1)

27 December, Jus Royal Novice Hurdle, Leopardstown, 2 miles & 2f – Won (7–2)

1992

3 May, Mountain Ash Handicap, Gowran Park, 1 mile & 6f – Won (9–10)

9 August, Old Vic Series Handicap, Leopardstown, 1 mile & 1f – 3rd (16–1)

26 August, Carling Gold Cup, Tralee, 1 mile & 6f – Won (4–6)

19 September, Jefferson Smurfit Irish St Leger, Curragh, 1 mile & 6f – 5th (20–1)

17 October, Tote Cesarewitch, Newmarket, 2 miles & 2f – Won (5–1)

1993

16 March, Smurfit Champion Hurdle, Cheltenham, 2 miles – 6th (9–1)

14 May, Andrex Saval Beg Stakes, Leopardstown, 1 mile & 6f – 3rd (4–6)
7 June, Racal Datacomm Race, Leopardstown, 1 mile & 6f – Won (1–2)
17 June, Gold Cup, Ascot, 2 miles & 4f – 6th (9–1)
27 June, Anheuser Busch Curragh Cup, Curragh, 1 mile & 6f – Won (11–10)
21 August, Meld Stakes, Curragh, 1 mile & 2f – 2nd (12–1)
18 September, Jefferson Smurfit Irish St Leger, Curragh, 1 mile & 6f – Won (9–2)
2 November, Fosters Melbourne Cup, Flemington, 2 miles – Won (16–1)

1994

18 May, Saval Beg Stakes, Leopardstown, 1 mile & 6f – Won (7–4)
16 June, Gold Cup, Ascot, 2 miles & 4f – 2nd (11–10)
26 June, Anheuser Busch Curragh Cup, Curragh, 1 mile & 6f – 2nd (4–9)
27 August, Curragh Race, Curragh, 1 mile & 6f – Won (2–1)
17 September, Jefferson Smurfit Irish St Leger, Curragh, 1 mile & 6f – Won (7–4)
1 November, Fosters Melbourne Cup, Flemington, 2 miles – 7th (5–1)

1995

6 June, Oakley Race, Leopardstown, 1 mile & 4f – Won (2–1)
22 June, Gold Cup, Ascot, 2 miles & 4f – 4th (3–1)
2 July, Anheuser Busch Curragh Cup, Curragh, 1 mile & 6f – Won (2–1)
26 August, Ballycullen Stakes, Leopardstown, 1 mile & 6f – Won (2–5)
16 September, Jefferson Smurfit Irish St Leger, Curragh, 1 mile & 6f – 4th (11–10)
7 November, Fosters Melbourne Cup, Flemington, 2 miles – 3rd (8–1)

Monksfield

NB Starting prices were not available for many of Monksfield's early races.

1974

23 October, Elverstown Maiden Plate, Punchestown, 7 furlongs – Won (25–1)

1975

9 April, Sloppy Weather Plate, Navan, 1 mile & 2f – 3rd (6–1)
23 April, Rockbrook Stakes, Leopardstown, 7th
16 May, Royal Whip Stakes, Curragh, 1 mile & 4f – 7th
23 May, Blackrock Handicap, Dundalk, 1 mile & 4f – 9th
2 June, Louglinstown Ladies Plate, Leopardstown, 1 mile & 6f – 2nd (3–1)
7 June, Lone Bush Stakes, Curragh, 1 mile & 6f – 8th
20 September, October Handicap, Curragh, 1 mile & 4f – 11th

27 September, Harvester Handicap, Leopardstown, 1 mile & 6f – 5th

1 October, Tara Maiden Plate, Navan, 1 mile & 4f – 5th

11 October, Blessington Handicap, Naas, 1 mile & 4f – 9th

18 October, Irish Cesarewitch, Curragh, 2 miles – 3rd (33–1)

1 November, JT Rogers Gold Cup, Curragh, 2 miles – 9th

8 November, Naas November Handicap, Naas, 1 mile & 4f – 6th

22 November, Tara Maiden Hurdle, Navan, 2 miles – Won (5–1)

6 December, Ashbourne Hurdle, Fairyhouse, 2 miles – Won (7–1)

26 December, Three Year Hurdle, Leopardstown, 2 miles – 9th

1976

17 January, Proudstown Handicap Hurdle, Navan, 2 miles – 4th

24 January, Celbridge Handicap Hurdle, Naas, 2 miles & 1f – 2nd (8–1)

11 February, Tara Handicap Hurdle, Navan, 2 miles – 5th

21 February, Monaloe Handicap Hurdle, Fairyhouse, 2 miles – 2nd (9–2)

6 March, Beechmount Handicap Hurdle, Navan, 2 miles – Won (3–1)

18 March, Daily Express Triumph Hurdle, Cheltenham, 2 miles – 2nd (28–1)

10 April, Halverstown Apprentice Plate, 1 mile & 4f – Won (8–1)

21 April, Huzzar Handicap Hurdle, Fairyhouse, 2 miles – Won (4–1)

28 April, Downshire Handicap Hurdle, Punchestown, 2 miles – 3rd (7–4)

16 October, Irish Cesarewitch, Curragh, 2 miles – Unplaced

20 October, Free Handicap Hurdle, Punchestown, 2 miles – 3rd (3–1)

30 October, JT Rogers Gold Cup, Curragh, 2 miles – 8th

6 November, Naas November Handicap, Naas, 1 mile & 4f – Unplaced

20 November, Dunsany Handicap Hurdle, Navan, 2 miles – 3rd (9–2)

27 November, Naas Handicap Hurdle, Naas, 2 miles & 3f – 10th

4 December, Benson & Hedges Handicap Hurdle, Fairyhouse, 2 miles – Won (7–1)

28 December, Sweeps Handicap Hurdle, Leopardstown, 2 miles – 4th (9–1)

1977

22 January, Celbridge Handicap Hurdle, Naas, 2 miles & 3f – 4th (8–1)

24 January, Proudstown Handicap Hurdle, Navan, 2 miles – Won (8–1)

12 February, Monaloe Handicap Hurdle, Fairyhouse, 2 miles & 2f – 5th

19 February, Erin Foods Champion Hurdle, Leopardstown, 2 miles – 3rd (8–1)

5 March, Beechmount Handicap Hurdle, Navan, 2 miles – 3rd (5–1)

16 March, Waterford Crystal Champion Hurdle, Cheltenham, 2 miles –
    2nd (15–1)

2 April, Sun Templegate Hurdle, Liverpool, 2 miles & 5f – Dead heat (7–2)

16 April, Halverstown Apprentice Plate, Naas, 1 mile & 4f – Won (5–2)

27 April, Downshire Handicap Hurdle, Punchestown, 2 miles – 4th (7–1)

15 October, Irish Cesarewitch, Curragh, 2 miles – Unplaced

19 October, Free Handicap Hurdle, Punchestown, 2 miles – 6th
29 October, JT Rogers Gold Cup, Curragh, 2 miles – 3rd (14–1)
31 October, Squash Ireland Handicap Hurdle, Leopardstown, 2 miles – 3rd (6–1)
5 November, Name Of The Game Trial Hurdle, Down Royal, 2 miles – 3rd (1–3)
12 November, Leopardstown November Handicap, Leopardstown, 2 miles – 9th

1978

21 January, Proudstown Handicap Hurdle, Navan, 2 miles – 6th
18 February, Erin Foods Champion Hurdle, Leopardstown, 2 miles – 3rd (11–1)
15 March, Waterford Crystal Champion Hurdle, Cheltenham, 2 miles –
   Won (11–2)
1 April, Sun Templegate Hurdle, Liverpool, 2 mile & 5f – Won (9–4)
15 April, Halverstown Apprentice Plate, Naas, 1 mile & 4f – Won (8–11)
19 April, Saval Beg Stakes, Leopardstown, 2 miles – Won (3–1)
1 May, Royal Doulton Handicap Hurdle, Haydock, 2 miles – 2nd (100–30)
7 October, Irish Cesarewitch, Curragh, 2 miles – Unplaced
28 October, JT Rogers Gold Cup, Curragh, 2 miles – Unplaced
4 November, AR Soudavor Trial Hurdle, Down Royal, 2 miles – Won (evens)
25 November, Naas Handicap Hurdle, Naas, 2 miles & 3f – 2nd (9–2)
2 December, Benson & Hedges Handicap Hurdle, Fairyhouse, 2 miles – 2nd (11–2)
27 December, Sweeps Handicap Hurdle, Leopardstown, 2 miles – 3rd (4–1)

1979

24 February, Erin Foods Champion Hurdle, Leopardstown, 2 miles – 6th
14 March, Waterford Crystal Champion Hurdle, Cheltenham, 2 miles –
   Won (9–4)
31 March, Colt Sigma Hurdle, Liverpool, 2 miles & 5f – Won (5–4)
16 April, Welsh Champion Hurdle, Chepstow, 2 miles – Won (2–7)
7 May, Royal Doulton Handicap Hurdle, Haydock, 2 miles – 2nd (6–4)
3 November, JT Rogers Gold Cup, Curragh, 2 miles – 15th (25–1)
10 November, AR Soudavar Trial Hurdle, Down Royal, 2 miles – 3rd (1–2)
8 December, Benson & Hedges Handicap Hurdle, Fairyhouse, 2 miles – 13th (9–1)
22 December Lismullen Amateur Hurdle, Navan, 2 miles & 5f – 8th (8–11)

1980

23 February, Erin Foods Champion Hurdle, Leopardstown, 2 miles – 2nd (10–1)
11 March, Waterford Crystal Champion Hurdle, Cheltenham, 2 miles – 2nd (6–5)
29 March, Sun Templegate Hurdle, Liverpool, 2 miles & 5f – 2nd (1–2)
26 April, BMW Amateur Hurdle, Down Royal, 2 miles – Won (4–7)
5 May, Royal Doulton Handicap Hurdle, Haydock, 2 miles – 8th (3–1)

Nijinsky

1969

12 July, Erne Stakes, Curragh, 6f – Won (4–11)

16 August, Railway Stakes, Curragh, 6f – Won (4–9)

30 August, Anglesey Stakes, Curragh, 6f – Won (4–9)

27 September, Beresford Stakes, Curragh, 1 mile – Won (2–7)

12 October, Dewhurst Stakes, Newmarket, 7f – Won (1–3)

1970

4 April, Gladness Stakes, Curragh, 7f – Won (4–6)

29 April, 2,000 Guineas, Newmarket, 1 mile – Won (4–7)

3 June, Derby, Epsom, 1 mile & 4f – Won (11–8)

27 June, Irish Sweeps Derby, Curragh, 1 mile & 4f – Won (4–11)

25 July, King George VI & Queen Elizabeth II Stakes, Ascot, 1 mile & 4f – Won (40–85)

12 September, St Leger, Doncaster, 1 mile & 6f – Won (2–7)

1 October, Prix de l'Arc de Triomphe, Longchamp, 1 mile & 4f – 2nd (SP unavailable)

17 October, Champion Stakes, Newmarket, 1 mile & 2f – 2nd (4–11)

Dawn Run

1982

27 May, Corinthian Fillies Flat Race, Clonmel, 2 miles – 8th (16–1)

17 June, Devils Bit Flat Race, Thurles, 2 miles – 4th (16–1)

23 June, Castlemaine Flat Race, Tralee, 2 miles – Won (5–1)

31 July, Tonroe Flat Race, Galway, 2 miles – Won (10–11)

2 September, Sean Graham Havasnack Race, Tralee, 2 miles – Won (8–1)

13 November, Leopardstown November Handicap, Leopardstown, 2 miles – 16th (8–1)

27 November, Kilwarden Maiden Hurdle, Naas, 2 miles – 4th (5–1)

20 December, Blackhills Maiden Mares Hurdle, Navan, 2 miles – Won (4–6)

28 December, Findus Beefburger Hurdle, Leopardstown, 2 miles & 2f – Won (12–1)

1983

29 January, Delgany Hurdle, Leopardstown, 2 miles – 6th (2–1)

5 February, Forenaughts Hurdle, Punchestown, 2 miles & 4f – Won (3–1)

19 February, Monaloe Handicap Hurdle, Fairyhouse, 2 miles & 2f – 3rd (7–4)

16 March, Sun Alliance Novices Hurdle, Cheltenham, 2 miles & 5f – 2nd (11–1)

8 April, Page Three Novice Handicap Hurdle, Liverpool, 2 miles & 5f – Won
(7–2)

9 April, Sun Templegate Hurdle, Liverpool, 2 miles & 5f – 2nd (12–1)

26 April, BMW Champion Novices Hurdle, Punchestown, 2 miles – Won (5–2)

22 October, Giolla Mear Flat Race, Curragh, 2 miles – 4th (8–1)

5 November, AR Soudavor Hurdle, Down Royal, 2 mile – Won (2–5)

18 November, Vat Watkins Hurdle, Ascot, 2 miles & 4f – Won (1–3)

7 December, Racehorse Trainers Hurdle, Naas, 2 miles – 2nd (5–4)

26 December, Ladbroke Christmas Hurdle, Kempton, 2 miles – Won (9–4)

1984

18 February, Wessel Cable Champion Hurdle, Leopardstown, 2 miles – Won
(4–5)

13 March, Waterford Crystal Champion Hurdle, Cheltenham, 2 miles –
Won (4–5)

31 March, Sandeman Aintree Hurdle, Liverpool, 2 miles & 5f – Won (4–6)

28 May, Prix La Barka, Auteuil, 2 miles & 3f – Won (SP unavailable)

22 June, Grande Course De Haies d'Auteuil, Auteuil, 3 miles & 1f, Won (SP
unavailable)

1 November, Nobber Chase, Navan, 2 miles – Won (4–5)

30 December, Sean Graham Chase, Leopardstown, 2 miles & 2f – Won (4–9)

1985

14 December, Durkan Bros International Punchestown Chase, Punchestown,
2 miles & 4f – Won (5–4)

1986

25 January, Holsten Distributors Chase, Cheltenham, 3 miles & 1f – 4th (4–9)

13 March, Gold Cup, Cheltenham, 3 miles & 2f – Won (15–8)

3 April, Whitbread Gold Label Cup Chase, Liverpool, 3 miles & 1f – Fell (8–11)

23 April, 'A Match', Punchestown, 2 miles – Won (4–6)

2 June, Prix La Barka, Auteuil, 2 miles & 4f – 2nd (SP unavailable)

27 June, Grande Course De Haies d'Auteuil, Auteuil, 3 miles & 1f – Fell
(SP unavailable)

Orby

1906

25 August, Londonderry Plate, Leopardstown, 5f – 3rd (1–3)

6 September, Railway Stakes, Curragh, 6f – 3rd (6–4)

1907

20 May, Baldoyle Plate, Baldoyle, 1 mile & 4f – Won (8–13)
5 June, Derby Stakes, Epsom, 1 mile & 4f – Won (100–9)
26 June, Irish Derby, Curragh, 1 mile & 4f – Won (1–10)
26 July, Atlantic Stakes, Liverpool, 1 miles & 1f – 4th (4–7)

Flyingbolt

1963

13 May, Passing Cloud Maiden Plate, Leopardstown, 1 mile & 4f –
    5th (20–1)
9 October, Mellifont Plate, Navan, 2 miles – Won (8–11)
23 November, Cabinteely Plate, Leopardstown, 1 mile & 4f – Won (9–4)
28 December, Stand Maiden Hurdle, Leopardstown, 2 miles – Won (8–11)

1964

8 February, Killester Hurdle, Baldoyle, 2 miles – Won (4–9)
15 February, Scalp Hurdle, Leopardstown, 2 miles – Won (3–1)
5 March, Gloucestershire Hurdle, Cheltenham, 2 miles – Won (4–9)
21 November, Sandymount Novice Chase, Leopardstown, 2 miles & 1f –
    Won (4–11)
26 December, Carrickmines Chase, Leopardstown, 2 miles – Won (2–7)

1965

27 February, Milltown Chase, Leopardstown, 2 miles – Won (1–2)
10 March, Cotswold Chase, Cheltenham, 2 miles – Won (4–9)
20 April, Easter Chase, Fairyhouse, 2 miles & 1f – Won (1–2)
2 October, Peard Cup, Phoenix Park, 2 miles – 4th (evens)
28 October, Careys Cottage Handicap Chase, Gowran Park, 2 miles & 4f –
    Won (4–5)
20 November, Black & White Gold Cup Novice Chase, Ascot, 2 miles –
    Won (8–15)
18 December, Massey Ferguson Gold Cup, Cheltenham, 2 miles & 4f –
    Won (5–2)

1966

27 January, Thyestes Handicap Chase, Gowran Park, 3 miles – Won (2–5)
15 March, Champion Chase, Cheltenham, 2 miles – Won (1–5)
16 March, Champion Hurdle, Cheltenham, 2 miles – 3rd (15–8)
11 April, Irish Grand National, Fairyhouse, 3 miles & 2f – Won (8–11)

1967

11 October, Double Diamond Chase, Punchestown, 2 miles & 4f – 3rd (7–4)

29 October, National Hunt Centenary Chase, Cheltenham, 2 miles & 4f –
3rd (2–7)

4 November, Mackeson Gold Cup, Cheltenham, 2 miles & 4f – 8th (9–4)

1968

9 November, Northumbria Handicap Chase, Newcastle, 2 miles – 5th (7–2)

1969

3 January, Gamekeepers Handicap Chase, 2miles – Won (2–1)

6 December, Massy Ferguson Gold Cup, 2 miles & 4f – 6th (25–1)

20 December, SGB Handicap Chase, Ascot, 2 miles – 3rd (5–2)

26 December, King George VI Chase, Kempton, 3 miles – 2nd (4–1)

1970

19 February, Whitbread Trial Chase, Ascot, 3 miles – 4th (11–2)

26 February, Castle Chase, Warwick, 2 miles & 4f – 3rd (10–11)

1971

29 January, Easter Hero Handicap Chase, Kempton, 2 miles – 3rd (7–2)

26 February, Emblem Handicap Chase, Kempton, 2 miles & 4f – 2nd (7–2)

18 March, Cathcart Cup, Cheltenham, 2 miles – 3rd (4–1)

1 April, Topham Trophy, Aintree, 2 miles & 5f – Fell (8–1)

Sinndar

1999

5 September, Dance Design Maiden, Curragh, 1 mile – Won (evens)

19 September, Aga Khan Stables National Stakes, Curragh, 1 mile – Won (7–1)

2000

16 April, Ballysax Stakes, Leopardstown, 1 mile & 2f – 2nd (5–2)

14 May, Derrinstown Stud Derby Trial, Leopardstown, 1 mile & 2f – Won (7–4)

10 June, Vodafone Derby, Epsom, 1 mile & 4f – Won (7–1)

2 July, Budweiser Irish Derby, Curragh, 1 mile & 4f – Won (11–10)

10 September, Prix Niel – Casino D'Enghein, Longchamp, 1 mile & 4f –
Won (30–100)

1 October, Prix de l'Arc de Triomphe Lucien Barriere, Longchamp, 1 mile &
4f – Won (6–4)

Moscow Flyer

1999

30 January, Clonee Flat Race, Fairyhouse, 2 miles – 6th (9–1)

20 February, Red Mills Copper Flat Race, Gowran Park, 2 miles & 1f – 3rd (7–4)

5 April, Kelly Timber Merchants Flat Race, Fairyhouse, 2 miles – 4th (8–1)

24 April, Navan Driving Flat Race, Navan, 2 miles & 2f – 3rd (3–1)

31 October, Shamrock Classic Maiden Hurdle Punchestown, 2 miles – Won (13–2)

6 November, Tattersalls Hurdle, Down Royal, 2 miles – Won (5–2)

28 November, Pembroke Electrical Royal Bond Novice Hurdle, Fairyhouse,
   2 miles – Won (7–2)

2000

23 April, O'Dea Festival Novice Hurdle, Fairyhouse, 2 miles & 4f – 8th (6–1)

2 May, Evening Herald Champion Novice Hurdle, Punchestown, 2 miles – Won
   (10–1)

21 October, J.J. McManus Hurdle, Cork, 2 miles – 3rd (9–2)

18 November, Morgiana Hurdle, Punchestown, 2 miles – Won (2–5)

3 December, Ballymore Properties Hatton's Grace Hurdle, Fairyhouse, 2 miles &
   4f – 2nd (6–4)

31 December, AIB December Festival Hurdle, Leopardstown, 2 miles – Won (5–1)

2001

21 January, AIG Europe Champion Hurdle, Leopardstown, 2 miles – Fell (7–1)

18 April, Mount Leinster Hurdle, Gowran Park, 2 miles & 2f – 2nd (4–5)

27 April, Shell Champion Hurdle, Leopardstown, 2 miles – Won (6–1)

24 October, EBF Beginners Chase, Fairyhouse, 2 miles & 2f – Fell (4–9)

9 November, Seacat Beginners Chase, Down Royal, 2 miles – Won (2–5)

17 November, Craddockstown Novice Chase, Punchestown, 2 miles – Won (4–6)

26 December, Denny Gold Medal Novice Chase, Leopardstown, 2 miles &
   1f – Won (5–4)

2002

27 January, Baileys Arkle Trophy Chase, Leopardstown, 2 miles & 1f – Fell (4–6)

12 March, Irish Independent Arkle Trophy, Cheltenham, 2 miles – Won (11–2)

25 April, Swordlestown Cup Chase, Punchestown, 2 miles – Won (2–5)

9 November, Killultagh Properties Chase, Down Royal, 2 miles & 2f – Won (4–11)

7 December, William Hill Tingle Creek Chase, Sandown, 2 miles – Unseated rider
   (2–1)

29 December, Paddy Power Dial-A-Bet Chase, Leopardstown, 2 miles & 1f – Won
   (4–9)

2003

2 February, Byrne Group Tied Cottage Chase, Punchestown, 2 miles – Won (2–7)

12 March, Queen Mother Champion Chase, Cheltenham, 2 miles – Won (7–4)

29 April, BMW Chase, Punchestown, 2 miles – Unseated rider (4–11)

9 November, Ballymore Homes Fortria Chase, Navan, 2 miles – Won (30–100)

6 December, William Hill Tingle Creek Chase, Sandown, 2 miles – Won (6–4)

27 December, Paddy Power Dial-A-Bet Chase, Leopardstown, 2 miles & 1f – Won (2–7)

2004

17 March, Queen Mother Champion Chase, Cheltenham, 2 miles – Unseated rider (5–6)

2 April, Martell Cognac Melling Chase, Liverpool, 2 miles & 4f – Won (evens)

27 April, Betdaq Champion Chase, Punchestown, 2 miles – Won (4–11)

7 November, Ballymore Properties Fortria Chase, Navan, 2 miles – Won (30–100)

4 December, William Hill Tingle Creek Chase, Sandown, 2 miles – Won (2–1)

2005

30 January, Byrne Group Tied Cottage Chase, Punchestown, 2 miles – Won (2–11)

16 March, Queen Mother Champion Chase, Cheltenham, 2 miles – Won (6–4)

8 April, John Smiths Melling Chase, Liverpool, 2 miles & 4f – Won (4–9)

26 April, Kerrygold Champion Chase, Punchestown, 2 miles – 2nd (1–4)

13 November, Fortria Chase, Navan, 2 miles – 2nd (4–11)

27 December, Paddy Power Dial-A-Bet Chase, Leopardstown – 4th (8–11)

2006

15 March, Queen Mother Champion Chase, Cheltenham, 2 miles 5th (5–1)

Alleged

1976

1 November, Donnellys Hollow Stakes, Curragh, 7f – Won (7–4)

1977

20 April, Ballydoyle Stakes, Leopardstown, 1 mile & 2f – Won (1–3)

14 May, Royal Whip Stakes, Curragh, 1 mile & 4f – Won (33–1)

28 May, Gallinule Stakes, Curragh, 1 mile & 4f – Won (11–10)

17 August, Great Voltigeur Stakes, York, 1 mile & 4f – Won (5–2)

10 September, St Leger Stakes, Doncaster, 1 mile & 6f – 2nd (4–7)

2 October, Prix de l'Arc de Triomphe, Longchamp, 1 mile & 4f – Won (SP unavailable)

1978

12 May, Royal Whip Stakes, Curragh, 1 mile & 4f – Won (1–7)

17 September, Prix du Prince D'Orange, Longchamp, 1 mile & 4f – Won
(SP unavailable)

1 October, Prix de l'Arc de Triomphe, 1 mile & 4f – Won (SP unavailable)

Istabraq

1994

4 November, Flanders Maiden Stakes, Doncaster, 7f – 8th (8–1)

1995

26 April, Labarnum Maiden Stakes, Kempton, 1 mile & 2f – 12th (10–1)

9 May, Christleton Maiden Stakes, Chester, 1 mile & 2f – 8th (11–1)

29 July, Jif Lemon Handicap, Newmarket, 1 mile & 4f – 2nd (4–1)

17 August, Odstock Maiden Stakes, Salisbury, 1 mile & 6f – Won (5–6)

30 August, Batleys Cash & Carry Handicap, York, 1m 6f – 2nd (15–2)

14 September, Rock Steady Handicap, Ayr, 1m & 7f – Won (6–4)

23 September, Gordon Carter Handicap, Ascot, 2 miles – 11th (5–2)

19 October, Vodafone Group Handicap, Newbury, 2 miles – 2nd (4–1)

4 November Coalite Dragon Handicap, Doncaster, 2 miles & 1f – 10th (9–2)

1996

8 June, Penny Lane Handicap, Haydock, 1m & 6f – 2nd (9–2)

16 November, Locks Restaurant Novice Hurdle, Punchestown, 2 miles – 2nd
(6–4)

1 December, Avonmore Royal Bond Novice Hurdle, Fairyhouse, 2 miles – Won
(11–8)

27 December, First Choice Novice Hurdle, Leopardstown, 2 miles & 2f – Won
(30–100)

1997

2 February, Deloitte & Touche Novice Hurdle, Leopardstown, 2 miles & 2f – Won
(4–11)

12 March, Royal & Sun Alliance Novice Hurdle, Cheltenham 2 miles & 5f – Won
(6–5)

23 April, Stanley Cooker Champion Novice Hurdle, Punchestown, 2 miles & 4f –
Won (4–11)

16 October, J.J. McManus Hurdle, Tipperary, 2 miles – Won (6–4)

30 November, Avonmore Waterford Hatton's Grace Hurdle, Fairyhouse,
2 miles & 4f – Won (1–3)

29 December, AIB December Festival Hurdle, Leopardstown, 2 miles – Won (1–6)

1998

25 January, AIG Europe Champion Hurdle, Leopardstown, 2 miles – Won (4–11)

17 March, Smurfit Champion Hurdle, Cheltenham, 2 miles – Won (3–1)

4 April, Martell Aintree Hurdle, Liverpool, 2 miles & 5f – 2nd (4–7)

3 November, J.J. McManus Hurdle, Cork, 2 miles – Won (2–7)

29 November, Avonmore Waterford Foods Hatton's Grace Hurdle, Fairyhouse, 2 miles & 4f – Won (1-5)

29 December, AIB December Festival Hurdle, Leopardstown, 2 miles – Won (1–10)

1999

24 January, AIG Europe Champion Hurdle, Leopardstown, 2 miles – Won (8–15)

16 March, Smurfit Champion Hurdle, Cheltenham, 2 miles – Won (4–9)

10 April, Martell Aintree Hurdle, Liverpool, 2 miles & 5f – Won (1–2)

30 April, Shell Champion Hurdle, Punchestown, 2 miles – Won (1–4)

23 October, J.J. McManus Hurdle, Tipperary, 2 miles – Won (2–7)

28 November, Duggan Brothers Hatton's Grace Hurdle, Fairyhouse, 2 miles & 4f – 2nd (1–7)

29 December, AIB December Festival Hurdle, Leopardstown, 2 miles – Won (1–8)

2000

23 January, AIG Europe Champion Hurdle, Leopardstown, 2 miles – Won (2–9)

14 March, Smurfit Champion Hurdle, Cheltenham, 2 miles – Won (8–15)

31 December, AIB December Festival Hurdle, Leopardstown, 2 miles – Fell (2–7)

2001

21 January, AIG Europe Champion Hurdle, Leopardtown, 2 miles – Won (4–11)

27 April, Shell Champion Hurdle, Leopardstown, 2 miles – Fell (2–7)

29 December, Tote December Festival Hurdle, Leopardstown, 2 miles – Won (4–11)

2002

12 March, Smurfit Champion Hurdle, Cheltenham, 2 miles – Pulled up (2–1)

Sea The Stars

2008

13 July, Jebel Ali Stables Maiden, Curragh, 7f – 4th (6–1)

17 August, KRA Maiden, Leopardstown, 7f – Won (2–1)

28 September, Juddmonte Beresford Stakes, 1 mile – Won (7–4)

2009

2 May, Stan James 2,000 Guineas, Newmarket, 1 mile – Won (8–1)

6 June, Investec Derby, Epsom, 1 mile & 4f – Won (11–4)

4 July, Coral Eclipse Stakes, Sandown, 1 mile & 2f – Won (4–7)

18 August, Juddmonte International, York, 1 mile & 2f – Won (1–4)

5 September, Tattersalls Millions Irish Champion Stakes, Leopardstown, 1 mile & 2f – Won (4–6)

4 October, Qatar Prix de l'Arc de Triomphe, Longchamp, 1 mile & 4f – Won (4–6)

Index